DATE DUE

First Available Cell

First Available Cell

Desegregation of the Texas Prison System

CHAD R. TRULSON AND JAMES W. MARQUART
FOREWORD BY BEN M. CROUCH

University of Texas Press ⌄⌄ *Austin*

The research contained in this document was coordinated in part by the Texas Department of Criminal Justice under Research Agreements #016-R99 and #480-R05. The contents of this publication reflect the views of the authors and do not necessarily reflect the views or policies of the Texas Department of Criminal Justice.

Library of Congress Cataloging-in-Publication Data
Trulson, Chad R.
  First available cell : desegregation of the Texas prison system / Chad R. Trulson, James W. Marquart ; foreword by Ben M. Crouch. — 1st ed.
    p.   cm.
  Includes bibliographical references and index.
  ISBN 978-0-292-71983-5 (cloth : alk. paper)
  1. Prisons—Texas—History. 2. Prison administration—Texas—History. 3. Prisoners—Legal status, laws, etc.—Texas—History. 4. Segregation—Texas—History. I. Marquart, James W. (James Walter), 1954– II. Title.
    HV9475.T4T78 2009
    363'.9764089—dc22
                                   2008053783

This book is dedicated to Dr. George J. Beto,
Ein wahrer menschenkenner und mentor

The prison is not an autonomous system of power; rather, it is an instrument of the State, shaped by its social environment, and we must keep this simple truth in mind if we are to understand the prison.

GRESHAM M. SYKES

THE SOCIETY OF CAPTIVES: A STUDY OF A MAXIMUM SECURITY PRISON (1958)

Contents

    Photo section follows page 162.

Foreword

Institutionalized sanctions of serious criminal offenders mirror the society in which they are applied. Punishment rationales and practices reflect prevailing values. In turn, citizens whose behavior and lifestyles least reflect those values are invariably those most often subject to criminal sanctions. And, as society changes, so too do institutions of punishment.

The history of prisons well illustrates these connections between punishment systems and social order. Though lockups have been around for centuries, only in early-nineteenth-century America did prisons emerge as places where offenders were incarcerated as punishment rather than as places for offenders to await punishment of some other type. In a religious society where both individual freedom and personal responsibility were core values and where crime (and the possibility of redemption) was thought to hinge on the will of the offender, prisons became institutions in which extended confinement itself constituted the punishment. Incarcerated offenders were expected to become penitent and to see the error of their ways.

Prisons, then as now, were populated primarily by marginalized people whose values and behaviors fall outside society's socio-legal mainstream. Prisoners typically represent the lowest rungs of society's life-chance ladder. In the United States, they are overwhelmingly poor, uneducated, and occupationally (as well as criminally) unskilled men. Moreover, racial and ethnic minorities, especially African Americans, are disproportionately represented in U.S. prisons. In Texas prisons, for example, African American inmates constitute well over 40 percent of the population, three times their proportion in the state overall. A similar disparity exists in prisons across the country.

Though activists in the last century sought to eliminate the discrimination in law and practice that disadvantaged minorities in particular, they made only limited progress until the mid-twentieth century. By the 1940s the tide began to turn as the justification for automatic discrimination and routine segregation by race came increasingly under federal scrutiny. In 1948, President Harry Truman ordered the integration of the military in part to recognize the contributions of African American soldiers in World War II, but also due to the increasing social and legal pressures for racial equality in the country. That same year Gunnar Myrdal published his influential *American Dilemma,* which underscored the long-standing contradiction between the American ideal of individual opportunity and equality before the law on the one hand and the reality of systematic discrimination against minority populations on the other. Then, in 1954, the Supreme Court ruled in *Brown v. Board of Education* that "separate but equal" policies, which had held sway since the nineteenth century, were unconstitutional. These decisions targeted discriminatory practices in every institution in the country. And prisons also began to change.

Whether separated from society by the high stone walls of urban prisons or the remoteness of southern prison farms, these institutions have historically been places apart. When citizens think about them (seldom), they are viewed as arcane, dangerous worlds best left to the discretion of the wardens and jailers who manage them. Law-abiding citizens have tended to believe that if a felon is convicted, then he deserves whatever happens to him in prison. This attitude was shared by federal and state judges. Through the mid-twentieth century, courts routinely subscribed to a "hands-off" policy of nonintervention, allowing wardens the final say on conditions under which prisoners lived and worked. Consequently, when prisoners, especially minority prisoners, felt they were abused or treated unfairly, they could grieve only to their keepers with no appeal beyond the prison walls.

By the late 1960s, however, the civil rights movement and court rulings on behalf of citizens generally gave impetus to a prisoners' rights movement. Judges began to consider prisoner appeals, and over the next twenty years interventions by the judiciary led to often dramatic changes in prison operations. For example, in 1980 a federal district judge in Texas concluded after years of litigation that operations in the state's institutional correctional system were broadly unconstitutional and must undergo wholesale reform.

Prisons are conservative institutions marked by traditional, informal structures often deemed indispensable by officials and by many inmates who may benefit from these structures. For this reason, judicially mandated changes in how state prisons housed, fed, treated, and controlled prisoners were often met with some resistance. The resistance came not just from a desire to maintain the status quo, but also from concerns that change would undermine prison security and order. And it often did. In Texas, prisons experienced disruption and considerable violence in the wake of the federal court order for constitutional operation.

Thus, in response to a lawsuit and broader societal pressures toward eliminating barriers to segregation, Texas prison officials adopted a policy of integrating its cell blocks, of putting two men of different racial and ethnic backgrounds in the same forty-five-square-foot living space. But feelings against integration were at least as strong inside the prison as in the larger society, and many officials and state observers expected an explosion if this policy was implemented. Though Texas prison dormitories were already integrated, many believed that integrating the more intimate cells would be violently rejected by inmates with serious consequences for prison order. After all, across the country considerable racial and ethnic segregation in housing units and neighborhoods was still typical, with mixed co-habitation relatively rare.

What happened when Texas prison officials instituted a policy of racial and ethnic integration in its cell blocks is the subject of Chad Trulson and James Marquart's fine-grained account. Their analysis is instructive on every level.

Ben M. Crouch
Texas A&M University
April 2008

Acknowledgments

No undertaking of this magnitude can be accomplished without assistance and support from numerous individuals.

We would first like to thank those Texas Department of Corrections (TDC) officials who opened the door for us when we first began this project. For nearly a decade, TDC administrators, officers, and staff have been extremely open and inviting to us, despite our constant pestering. Sherman Bell took the time to meet with us and supported our project from the beginning. Ron Steffa and Wendy Ingram helped us to navigate initial barriers to our research. Amy Clute was invaluable to the research in the beginning stages and served as the link to many other TDC administrators, officers, and staff that benefited this research. Dimitria Pope and Marty Martin were extremely helpful to us when we approached TDC for a second time in 2005. Karen Hall, Brenda Riley, and Riley Tilley, of TDC Executive Services, assisted in the final aspects of this research. Jim Willett, director of the Texas Prison Museum and retired TDC officer and former warden, helped us track down many of the illustrations for this book. Without the support of these and many other present and former TDC personnel, this book would not have been possible.

Thanks also to Dr. Bruce Jackson, SUNY Buffalo, for allowing us to use photographs from his collection on Texas prisons. We also gratefully acknowledge the assistance of Jene Robbins, Digital Imaging Specialist, TDCJ Media Services, for her assistance with various photographs. We also thank Gerald Birnberg, attorney for Allen Lamar, who provided insight to the background and legal issues of the *Lamar* suit.

Thanks to the many TDC offenders who provided valuable perspective to this research over the years. Without their insight, this book would have presented only one side of the story. A special thanks goes to Jorge Antonio Renaud, whose insight on prisoner desegregation was invaluable.

Thanks also to the staff members at the Center for American History, University of Texas at Austin, for helping us retrieve records for this research.

In addition, we also appreciate the efforts of Scott Belshaw, who helped to track down legal documents and various other hard-to-access resources. Darin Haerle and Bree Kimball assisted with many of the mundane aspects of this project and their help is much appreciated. We would also like to recognize the unyielding support given by our colleagues at the University of North Texas and the University of Texas at Dallas during the course of this research.

A special thanks goes to Allison Faust and the staff at the University of Texas Press for making sure this book became a reality. We also thank the reviewers of this book for helpful comments and suggestions on previous drafts.

Finally, we thank our families for the tremendous support we received during the course of this writing: Lori and Gracie, and Cecelia, John, and Jessica. Celebrating the completion of this book is much more enjoyable with them at our side.

Introduction

It was Sunday, April 23, 1939, and it was a day of rest for the men clad in white in Otey, Texas. This was not going to be like any other Sunday at the Ramsey State Prison Farm, however. On this day a visitor drove up to the prison and had special clearance to talk to the black men. He also had permission to listen to and record the convicts sing their work songs. The visitor's name was John Lomax—the "ballad hunter"—and he set about recording the songs used by the black Texas convicts in the fields about hoeing and flat weeding, felling timber with double-bladed axes, picking and chopping cotton, their dreams of freedom and far-off places, their hated bosses and tracker dogs, their girlfriends and wives, and their mothers. He recorded various songs sung by James "Iron Head" Baker ("My Pore Mother Keeps A-prayin for Me"), Wade "Monkey" Bolden, Mose "Clear Rock" Platt, W. S. "Jaybird" Harrison, Wallace "Big Stavin' Chain" Chains, and Lightnin' Washington.

Lomax, who was raised near Meridian, Texas, right where the 98th parallel passes through and divides Texas into two distinct geographical and cultural traditions, toured other southern prison farms in search of the "perfect ballad" or song untouched by the outside world. Yet the Texas prison farms of the 1930s, or any other decade, were not isolated completely from the outside world. The inmate world he encountered was shaped by what the felons brought with them into the farms and reworked to be useful in the tanks and hoe squads and turn rows. John Lomax was, among other things, a trailblazer, and he opened the Texas prison system to successive generations of researchers and outsiders in search of their own "perfect ballads."

Bruce Jackson, Harvard-educated folklorist, picked up where Lomax left off. He recorded numerous African American convict work songs (some at the Ramsey State Prison Farm) in the 1960s and took many photographs of the convicts' world as it teetered on the brink of the sea change examined in this book. Ben Crouch, a professor of sociology at Texas A & M University, donned the gray uniform and worked as a prison guard or "boss" in the 1970s. His "perfect ballad" was to uncover or shed light on the world of the guard and how the custodians managed to keep order in a world of hostile, bitter, and violent men. Sheldon Ekland-Olson, a professor of sociology at the University of Texas at Austin, conducted surveys of prisoners in the 1980s to ascertain their thoughts and opinions about the consequences of impending change as a result of judicial intervention behind the walls.

Each of these researchers or curiosity seekers was allowed extraordinary access to Texas prisons. Most important, these researchers were on hand at a time when the penal system was on the brink of monumental change. Outside influences, often uncontrollable, were set in motion that forever altered the isolated prison farms, and these individuals saw history unfold before them.

In this book, we bring historical records and observations, prison data, court records, social survey data, guard and inmate observations, and personal observations of Texas prisons that span three decades to examine the consequences of an obscure court ruling in Texas that ordered the custodians to desegregate prison cells. This book, then, is our "perfect ballad" and extends the work of those who preceded us—those who broke down the boundary between the free world and the prison world. We trace our lineage and our inspiration to those who came before us, and we surely stand on the shoulders of giants. Like them, we seek to understand the role of the outside world as it affected the inside world.

From Segregation to Desegregation in Texas Prisons: A Timeline

1849   An "Act to Establish a State Penitentiary" is passed by the Texas legislature. The Huntsville "Walls" Unit, though not yet fully constructed, accepts its first inmate on October 1.

Prior to 1865 and the end of the Civil War, only the most serious white criminals were sent to the penitentiary. Blacks remained on slave plantations.

1865   Civil War ends. Thirteenth Amendment is ratified, prohibiting slavery and involuntary servitude except as a form of punishment. (Texas ratifies the amendment on February 18, 1870, prior to its readmission to the Union.)

Texas prison population is roughly 165 inmates.

1866   Board of Public Labor is created by the Eleventh Texas Legislature with responsibility to retain contracts for the use of inmate labor. The private-lease system is created.

Texas prisoners under the lease are sent to racially segregated camps to work on railroads, public utilities, and plantations. Serious criminals, most of whom are white, remain in Huntsville Walls Unit in cells.

1883–1919   Lease system ends, and contract-lease system ensues. Agricultural prison farms expand.

East Texas Penitentiary in Rusk, Texas, is constructed to help relieve overcrowding in Huntsville Walls Unit.

Texas begins to purchase large tracts of land in southeastern part of the state. State prison farms become operational: Wynne in 1883; Harlem I and II in 1885; Clemens in 1893; Ramsey I and II and Imperial and Blue Ridge in 1908; Central in 1909; Darrington and Eastham in 1917; and Retrieve in 1919.

Most white inmates are incarcerated in Huntsville and Rusk, Texas. Able-bodied black inmates are sent to farms near the river bottoms and to sugarcane plantations. Remaining white and Hispanic inmates are placed on other farms. Farms and their camps are completely segregated by race.

1927 Despite years of penitentiary rules and regulations that kept prisoners separated by race, the Fortieth Texas Legislature specifically authorizes the general manager of the Texas prison system, with the consent of the Texas Prison Board, to make provision for the separation and classification of prisoners according to "color."

1928– 1965 Texas prison system continues to be segregated by race, with separate prison farms for white, black, and Hispanic inmates.

Allen L. Lamar is committed to the State School for Boys in Gatesville, Texas, in 1952. He is released in 1953.

Lamar is incarcerated by the California Youth Authority in 1954. He is released in 1956 and returns to Texas.

Lamar is convicted and incarcerated in the Federal Bureau of Prisons (BOP) in October 1958. He is released in 1961 on parole.

Lamar is committed to the Texas Department of Corrections (TDC) for the first time in 1962.

Prison farms become "units" by 1965. George J. Beto desegregates individual prisons, allowing black, white, and Hispanic inmates to live at the same prison unit. Units remain segregated in all other areas including work squads, dormitories, cells, and cell blocks, according to the 1927 Texas law that authorizes the director of the Texas prison system to separate and classify inmates by "color."

1965 Lamar is discharged from TDC. He is held on detainer by the U.S. Marshal's Office and transported to a federal correctional institution in Texarkana, Texas, for violation of federal mandatory parole release guidelines from a previous federal conviction.

1966 Lamar is discharged from federal custody in April.

Lamar is convicted in July of armed robbery and receives a twenty-five-year sentence in TDC, which begins on July 6, 1967.

1972 *Allen L. Lamar et al. v. H. H. Coffield et al.* is filed in the U.S. Federal District Court for the Southern District of Texas. Lamar alleges systematic racial segregation and discrimination in TDC.

Ruiz v. Estelle is filed in the U.S. District Court for the Eastern District of Texas.

1973 The U.S. Department of Justice Civil Rights Division (DOJ) intervenes on the plaintiffs' behalf in *Lamar*.

A class of "Spanish-speaking" inmates becomes involved as plaintiff-intervenors. Among these inmates is David Ruiz of the *Ruiz v. Estelle* litigation.

A group of white, black, and Hispanic prisoners joins TDC defendants in an effort to maintain segregated housing for prisoners for fear of racial violence. Trial preparation begins.

1974   Two additional cases with complaints of racial segregation and discrimination in TDC are consolidated with *Lamar*. The case is certified as a class action, leading to scrutiny of the entire Texas penal system. Inmate plaintiffs and the DOJ allege numerous forms of racial segregation and discrimination in TDC.

The Joint Committee on Prison Reform issues its final report in December after two years of investigating the Texas prison system. Concerning racial segregation and discrimination, the Committee finds that "discrimination, prejudice, and segregation do exist in the Department of Corrections to a significant degree. Despite the fact that many Department officials voice opposition to such practices and deny they exist, the evidence is overwhelming."

1975   The Sixty-fourth Texas Legislature changes the 1927 "color" law and prohibits discrimination by race, color, creed, or national origin by prison administrators. This change in legislation is prompted by the Joint Committee's investigation of TDC.

Texas prisoners remain almost completely segregated by race in all housing areas including dormitories, cell blocks, and cells.

TDC continues preparation for *Lamar* litigation. DOJ and TDC engage in voluminous discoveries, depositions, interrogatories, and other routine court procedures in preparation for trial.

1976   Lamar files lawsuit against Len Arthur Steele, an Ellis Unit Building Major, alleging harassment due to his writ-writing activities. Lamar wins the lawsuit after offering proof that Steele burned his legal documents, asked one inmate to assault him and another to kill him, invited Lamar to pick up and attempt to use a small knife while Steele held a large hunting knife in his hand out of view, and promised to send Lamar home in a "pine box." Afterward, Lamar continues to allege harassment and attempts on his life.

1977   A consent decree and agreed judgment in *Lamar* is signed on April 14, in which the Texas prison system agrees to develop and submit an Affirmative Action Plan (AAP) to end unequal treatment and discrimination by race in housing and numerous other areas.

TDC submits Affirmative Action Plan on November 16. Director W. J. Estelle remarks: "The Texas Department of Corrections shall, in completely good faith, implement the Plan to the satisfaction of the Court and in a manner equal to the high standards of performance for which the Department is noted in the field of corrections."

1978 TDC makes progress with the consent decree. Court retains jurisdiction and requires TDC to continue to submit reports of progress with the consent decree to the court. Cell desegregation emerges as a contentious issue.

Ruiz v. Estelle trial begins on October 2. It eventually becomes the longest civil rights prison trial in American history, concluding after 159 days of hearings.

1979 Texas prison administrators argue substantial compliance with the *Lamar* decree. TDC lawyers file a brief to the court in support of termination. The court requires continued oversight of the prison system.

1980 Lamar is transferred to Ft. Leavenworth Federal Penitentiary for protection in October.

In February, DOJ releases results of a survey of TDC inmates on progress toward the consent decree, in specific cell desegregation. Responses by inmates reveal that few efforts toward desegregation are occurring, that cell desegregation is used in some cases as harassment, and that some TDC officers have actively organized inmates to file grievances against racial desegregation.

1980– DOJ and TDC are heavily involved in the *Ruiz v. Estelle* (1980)
1983 litigation, and the *Lamar* decree process is set aside.

In April 1983, *Lamar* resumes. TDC moves for termination of court's jurisdiction in case. At a status conference, Judge Robert O'Conor, rather than terminating the case, requires TDC to continue reporting to the court on compliance with the decree and agreed judgment.

Lamar is released from his second TDC incarceration in late 1983.

1984 Lamar is convicted of murder and receives a life sentence in TDC.

1985 Lamar is received by TDC for his third incarceration on February 8. Lamar is transferred to the Federal Bureau of Prisons in May.

TDC submits a proposed cell desegregation plan ten months late. DOJ files a contempt motion with the court in July.

TDC is given twenty additional days to file a plan for cell desegregation. In August, TDC files the plan. On September 9, DOJ objects to the plan, calling the "three-page document" vague and noncompulsory. The TDC plan proposed that inmates be desegregated within cells on a choice basis.

1986 U.S. District Judge Lynn Hughes takes over the *Lamar* case in March. Judge Hughes grows tired of TDC non-compliance concerning cell desegregation and other outstanding issues and finds the prison system in contempt of the *Lamar* decree on May 5.

Contempt sanctions against TDC are delayed to allow TDC and DOJ to come to an agreement on cell desegregation and other areas of the decree. The court orders the decree to be complied with "to the fastest extent possible."

TDC studies inmate attitudes toward racial desegregation and the racial dynamics of non-fatal stabbings in TDC. Results from these studies reveal that most inmates do not object to cell desegregation and that most non-fatal stabbings are between members of the same race.

On October 7, DOJ files contempt motion and asks Judge Hughes to fine TDC $1,000 per day for failing to adhere to the court's order. DOJ accuses TDC of a "blatant disregard of even the most straight-forward of court orders." Counsel for TDC disputes DOJ's contempt claims.

1987 On December 29, the court approves a stipulation concerning all outstanding issues of the *Lamar* decree, with the exception of cell desegregation. TDC and DOJ continue working toward an agreement on cell desegregation.

1988 Texas prison administrators submit a draft desegregation plan to the court and DOJ. The plan calls for the random assignment of inmates to two-person cells, without regard to race or ethnicity. The plan applies to minimum custody inmates only, excluding the general population double-celled custodies of medium and close custody.

DOJ provides major revisions to the plan and does not agree to stipulate to the desegregation of only minimum custody inmates. DOJ presses for the desegregation of all general population custodies.

TDC representatives and their counsel from the Texas attorney general's office travel to Washington, D.C., to discuss a potential cell desegregation stipulation. DOJ asks TDC to document non-anecdotally that desegregating inmates in medium and close custody would be inappropriate because of the potential for racial violence.

By October, TDC and DOJ appear close to a settlement on the outstanding issue of cell desegregation. On October 13, DOJ sends TDC revisions of the cell desegregation plan. TDC considers these revisions "minor changes."

1989 On May 3, DOJ cites major revisions to TDC's plan and requires TDC to randomly desegregate inmates in minimum, medium, and close custodies. TDC resists the DOJ's revisions, noting in a letter to DOJ lawyers that "we cannot agree to any plan that includes the medium custody, close custody, and safekeeping classifications."

TDC attempts to provide statistical proof that desegregating medium and close custody inmates would lead to greater violence. Evidence is gathered through a pilot test of the Incident Data Form (IDF). Despite finding higher rates of violence in medium and close custodies, DOJ dismisses the report, citing errors in analysis and methodology.

1990 DOJ lawyers and their expert visit numerous TDC units on March 26 and are allowed informal discovery concerning cell desegregation. TDC is still segregating inmates by race in all custodies concerning cell assignments. At the conclusion of the tour, DOJ requests that TDC clarify their policy as to cell desegregation.

In June, TDC and their counsel notify DOJ that a revised cell desegregation plan will be sent in the coming months following review by members of the Texas Board of Corrections. In July, after the Texas Board of Corrections review, TDC and their lawyers submit the plan to DOJ. The plan stipulates to the cell desegregation of inmates in minimum, medium, and close custodies, as requested by the DOJ.

From July until September, TDC and DOJ revise the cell desegregation plan. On October 5, DOJ lawyers contact the Texas attorney general's office and indicate that DOJ is contemplating contempt sanctions against TDC.

1991 On January 25, DOJ asks the court to apply contempt sanctions against TDC for non-compliance with the May 1986 court order. DOJ requests that the state of Texas be fined in excess of $5,000 per day for each non-desegregated cell unless TDC desegregates at least 20 percent of their double cells by 1993. At this time TDC had desegregated less than 5 percent of their two-person cells. TDC argues they have proceeded in good faith with cell desegregation.

On June 14, TDC submits a cell desegregation plan to the court that calls for the random assignment of inmates to double cells, without regard to race, in minimum, medium, and close custodies.

Without a court order accepting the cell desegregation plan, or DOJ approval, TDC moves to implement cell desegregation by August 1. On June 2, TDC begins massive statewide training on the desegregation of cells.

On June 22, Assistant General Counsel for TDC Leonard Peck remarks that TDC is "committed to making this thing [desegregation] work." In a message to inmates, Peck explains: "We don't care how you feel about it, we're going to do it. So go write your mothers about how miserable you are. But it is going to happen. And inmates who try to sabotage this are going to have to pay. We have lots of ways of dealing with insubordination—loss of good time, loss of classification status, and miserable work assignments."

On June 26, TDC director James "Andy" Collins issues a statewide notice to all TDC inmates on cell desegregation. Two days later, seven inmates escape from the Coffield Unit.

On July 23, the two remaining escaped inmates from the Coffield Unit are caught. In an interview with the *Palestine Herald*, they claim that racial desegregation was the reason for their escape. One inmate proclaims that he would integrate as "soon as William Wayne Justice brings a black to live with him in his house."

TDC begins cell desegregation in August 1991 without a court-approved order.

On September 4, DOJ and the court accept the provisions of TDC's plan for cell desegregation. An order is entered with the court. The court continues DOJ's January 1991 petition for imposition of contempt sanctions, and holds that if desegregation is not fully complied with by a court conference set for February 16, 1993, "coercive sanctions will be imposed on the officers and the prison system of the State of Texas."

1992–
1996 TDC advances cell desegregation without major incident or non-compliance.

Several TDC inmates write Judge Hughes to request contempt citations against TDC and injunctions to stop cell desegregation, and to demand that Judge Hughes recuse himself from the case.

On November 29, 1994, Judge Hughes orders the Texas attorney general's office to investigate compliance with the *Lamar* decree at the Darrington Unit.

On January 16, 1996, Judge Hughes issues a post-judgment opinion in the *Lamar* case in which he remarks that in "recent years, the correspondence from individual prisoners has shifted from complaints about segregation to complaints about integration, which is progress of a fashion." Although the court's jurisdiction is not terminated, the court ceases requirements that TDC report compliance to the court. Judge Hughes also remarks that inmates will not be allowed to intervene in the case. In closing, he notes: "The court is wary of being seen to test the resolve of inmates who announce that their hate will make them violently disposed to other races if they are locked together. No amount of violence, large or small, to prove one's eligibility for a single-race cell will be rewarded by the state or by this court. An inmate who proves that he is both a bigot and violent will face consequences much worse than an undesirable cellmate." The legal history of *Lamar* is over.

1998   Lamar dies in federal custody in Beaumont, Texas, of unknown causes.

1998–   The Texas prison system has remained in compliance with *Lamar*
2007   since the court order accepting the plan for in-cell desegregation in September 1991.

Currently, the Texas prison system averages over 60 percent desegregation of double cells, with some prison units over 80 percent. Overall, racial violence among desegregated cell partners is no more likely than violence among same-race cell partners in Texas prisons, a finding that has remained for more than a decade after the start of racial desegregation.

First Available Cell

PART I

THE OUTSIDE

CHAPTER I

Broken Barriers

Looking up into the ultra-blue sky, members of the crowd strained their eyes to locate the small plane. A large fireball then appeared and the object shot vertical and continued its climb for nearly three minutes. Then the show was over. But something dramatic, history-making, had just occurred and only a few people were privy to the event. The date was September 7, 1956. On this day, famed test pilot Iven Kincheloe flew his X-2 to an altitude of 126,000 feet—to the edge of outer space. He was the first person to reach that altitude and he returned to Earth as a national hero.[1] In the same month, another test pilot was the first to fly at three times the speed of sound, but his test plane veered out of control and he died in the crash. The year 1956 was one of major historical significance and involved individuals smashing barriers and crossing lines that had never before been breached. These test flights and a host of other technological breakthroughs shattered important boundaries that kept humans tethered to this planet and helped fuel the space race that would result in some of humankind's greatest achievements.

For most people, the idea of breaking a barrier or smashing through a boundary involves important scientific breakthroughs. Not every barrier, though, requires advanced technology to foster a breakthrough. Some barriers are created as a result of human ingenuity, and sometimes all it takes is one ordinary person to take a chance, to make a move at the right time and in the right place to forever alter a barrier. While most Americans in 1956 were captivated by dueling test pilots, there was a barrier of a different sort that was also being brought down. On June 5, 1956, Elvis Presley sang "Hound Dog" on the Milton Berle television show and wowed the audience with gyrating hip movements that caused a scandal. Beyond his hips, Presley also crossed over the racial divide that existed in America at the time—a barrier maintained by rigid segregationist laws and customs in most southern states—a crossing that transfused the white music of the day with black music. Presley was an innovator who opened the doors for a multitude of musicians.[2] His melding of white and black music not only defied the staunch segregationist attitudes of the day but led to mixed race audiences and an erosion of the color barrier, particularly among southern youth.[3]

Elvis Presley crossed the color line without fear and without penalty. His crossing, like most test pilots of the day, made him a legend, a hero, a teen idol, a movie star, and an icon for the ages. The same cannot be said for African Americans in Texas (or in any other southern state in 1956) who sought to break through the color line, especially in the area of public schools. These trailblazers sought neither fortune nor fame but rather an education for their children in appropriately outfitted classrooms. The battleground over the color line in Texas regarding school desegregation was located in Mansfield, a small farming hamlet on the southern edge of Fort Worth. Here is a description of the Mansfield school situation for African Americans in the early 1950s:

> The Mansfield Colored School consisted of two long shabby barracks-style buildings placed lengthwise, side by side, on a plot of land off West Broad Street. There was no electricity, running water, or plumbing. Only one teacher was hired for grades one through eight. Water was hauled in milk cans from Ben Lewis' well one-quarter of a mile north of the school by the teacher with the help of students. Two outhouses sat several feet north of the buildings. There was very little equipment, no flagpole, no fence around the playground, and no school bus. . . . Black children in the ninth through twelfth grades had no school.[4]

African American citizens in Mansfield worked throughout the 1950s to put an end to segregated schools and the color barrier, but to no avail. The U.S. Supreme Court ruling in *Brown v. Board of Education* in 1954 was not enough for white citizens to end segregation. In fact, white community members and members of the school board in Mansfield steadfastly resisted any efforts to comply with *Brown.* To move the cause of school desegregation forward, Texas NAACP members asked L. Clifford Davis, an African American attorney from Fort Worth, to represent African American students in a legal action against the Mansfield School District. Davis filed a class-action lawsuit in the U.S. Federal District Court in Forth Worth on October 7, 1955, and the case was styled *Nathaniel Jackson, a minor et al. v. O. C. Rawdon, et al.*[5] In modern parlance, the act of filing this case meant it was "game on" in Mansfield, across a wide variety of fronts. The color line, at least in Texas public schools, was now under assault.

The defendants resorted to a number of ploys to circumvent desegregation. Ultimately, the case ended up in the Fifth Circuit Court of Appeals, where on August 25, 1956, the court ruled:

> It is ADJUDGED and DECREED that the minor plaintiffs Nathaniel Jackson, Charles Moody, and Floyd Stevenson, and all other negro minors of the same class as the named minor plaintiffs, have the right to admissions to, and to attend the Mansfield High School on the same basis as members of the white race, and that refusal of the defendant [Mansfield High School] to admit plaintiffs thereto on account of their race or color is unlawful.[6]

The social climate in Mansfield throughout the legal maneuvering in the *Jackson* case was tense. Whites resented the "outside" interference of the NAACP and other "communist sympathizers" and "rabble rousers" seeking to end a comfortable life in the country. African Americans in Mansfield feared reprisals for their efforts. Their fears were not unwarranted. On the nights of August 22 and 23, 1956 (prior to the new school year), cross burnings occurred in the African American sections of Mansfield. On August 28, 1956, a straw man (with a head painted black) hung from a wire in downtown Mansfield.[7] A sign on the body read, "THIS NEGRO TRIED TO ENTER A WHITE SCHOOL." On August 30, 1956, a crowd formed outside Mansfield High School, where some were carrying signs:

NIGGER STAY OUT

WE DON'T WANT NIGGERS

THIS IS A WHITE SCHOOL

COON EARS A $1.00 A DOZEN

On September 25, 1956, lawyers for the defendants appealed directly to the U.S. Supreme Court and on December 3, 1956, the Court refused to hear their appeal. Over the ensuing months and years, the Texas Rangers were called upon by Governor Allan Shivers to maintain order and quell any possibility of violence. In addition, new laws aimed at maintaining racial segregation were passed by the Texas State Legislature, including laws supporting general elections in local school districts that could accept or reject desegregation.[8] It is worth noting that not until September 1965 were African American students finally allowed to attend classes at Mansfield High School. These actions and a host of others taken by legislators thwarted desegregation efforts for many years in Texas. Yet the actions of the lawmakers could not stop the momentum of change set in motion by the boundary "breakers" or innovators in Mansfield.

Listed below are some of the major Texas school desegregation events from the post–Civil War era until the close of the twentieth century.

1866: First Freedmen's Bureau schools open in Texas

1950: *Sweatt v. Painter,* which leads to desegregation of the University of Texas Law School

1952: Huston-Tillotson College is formed by merger of Samuel Huston College and Tillotson College

1955: African American students in Austin are allowed to attend previously all-white schools

1956: Mansfield school desegregation incident

1960: *Borders v. Rippy:* a federal ruling that begins the desegregation of Dallas public schools

1963: The University of Texas desegregates all aspects of campus life except student housing

1967: Schools in Hawkins and Big Sandy are completely desegregated

1970: *U.S. v. Texas:* a U.S. District Court orders the Texas Education Agency to assume responsibility for desegregating Texas public schools

1971: Austin's Anderson High School closes under a court-ordered busing plan

1996: *Hopwood v. Texas* ends affirmative action programs in Texas higher education

The Color Line in the "Burnin' Hell," 1956

The 1950s color line in Texas, and in America in general, was under assault. In some places, however, the color line held fast, so fast that an outsider, even another southerner, would have concluded the year was 1926, or even 1886. One such place was the Texas prison system, a place familiarly known to convicts as "the burnin' hell" or "one lost valley," where time seemingly stood still and cultural change was nonexistent. In the burnin' hell, no innovators were on hand in the 1950s to challenge or in any way cross the color line. In fact, Texas prisoners were openly confined in prison units or farms on the basis of color—a practice that had existed since the beginnings of the system in the mid-1800s. For example, the Clemens and Ramsey I farms held African American felons, while the Eastham Farm housed whites and the Harlem Farm confined Hispanic prisoners. The groups never mixed, much as in outside society, and the three groups formed unique inmate societies.

Albert "Race" Sample, an African American inmate, was sentenced to twenty years in 1956 for robbery. To begin his sentence, the prison transfer vehicle called "Black Betty" dropped Sample off inside the back gate fence at the Retrieve Farm, an exclusively African American prison for older recidivists in Brazoria County. Sample, who was no newcomer to the Texas prison system, described the onset of cotton-picking season for prisoners at the Retrieve Farm in 1956:

> Someone over in Number 4 tank hollered, "Heah they cum," referring to Cap'n Smooth and his entourage, Lieutenant Sundown and Buzzard. Thirty seconds later Big Tom rang [work bell] and the tank doors opened. This time, instead of Cap'n Smooth waiting at the end of the hall by the back door to count us as we went streaking by, he stood underneath the inside picket.
>
> "Whenever you nigguhs git outta that back door, I want ever squad to stop by in front 'uv 'at laundry, an ever nigguh gitta sack! First nigguh I ketch 'thout a sack when we git to 'at field is gon' git sump'n dun to his goat-smellin ass," and strutted down the hall to take his position at the back door. Aiming his voice back up the corridor, "Lemme have 'em, Boss!"
>
> We hit the yard following Road Runner [inmate] to the bundles of neatly stacked cotton sacks piled on the ground in front of the laundry. Road Runner grabbed a sack from the first pile and took off. Boss Deadeye was loping his horse to keep up as we sailed through the backgate, "Go Head!"
>
> Ol' Sol [the sun] was just showing its huge, orange face over the eastern horizon by the time we crossed the main turnrow. As far as the eye could see was row after row of blossoming cotton bolls. We trotted straight down the Williamson turnrow to catch our set of rows.
>
> "Count off twenty-seven row Ol' Chinaman," Boss Deadeye hollered to the tailrow man who worked the last row, and was responsible for spotting and counting off rows. Chinaman began to step them off calling out the number of each as he went. As soon as he hollered out the number, the con who had been assigned that number got on it, and began picking. "You sonsabitches ketch 'em Gotdam rows and gitcha mawdickin asses offa this turnrow!"
>
> By the time I picked the cotton from two stalks, the rest of the squad was already twenty or thirty feet ahead of me.

"Ol' Cap Rock," [convict] Deadeye hollered, "hit this sorry bastard's row a lick up thar an hep him git th' end uv his sack off 'is Gotdam turnrow."

Then Deadeye started on me, "Nigguh, you betta go to feedin 'at bag, an movin them shit scratchers lak you aim to do sump'n! Aw, I know apickin cotton's neath yore style. I betcha a few weeks in 'at pisser [solitary confinement] jes might hep you tighten yore sorry ass up a notch."

About an hour later, "Awright, Ol' Road Runner, ya'll raisem up an head to them scales. We picked up our sacks, slung them across our shoulder, and ran behind Road Runner down several turnrows.

"He's got 230, he's got 215, he's got 220, he's got 195." Cap'n Smooth stopped and commented when the weight dropped under 200 pounds, "Nigguh, you betta take yore Gotdam ass to wek an quit draggin roun fore I do sump'n to you."[9]

The story above recalled by Sample was the reality for African American inmates in the 1950s on the farms and turnrows and in the tanks of the Texas prison system.

Twenty-five years later, it was August 1981 and the cotton was blooming and ready for picking at the Eastham Farm, a Texas prison unit for older recidivists near Lovelady, in East Texas. Eastham had a notorious history: it was the place where Clyde Barrow escaped in a hail of gunfire in the 1930s. The "Ham," as it was known to bosses and convicts alike, also had a history of brutal convict bosses, of hard days in the field, and tough violent nights in the tanks for the weak. But this was 1981, and the old days were gone.

The sun was already up when the field captain yelled out, "Lemme have 'em, boss," and the line squads were called out one by one. The men went out the door by the shower room and ambled to the back gate. Each squad was counted by a "hall boss" who manned the clipboard and the count slips for the old time field captain. Each inmate was counted as they filed past the two prison guards, and then they scampered out the back gate and jumped onto a series of wheeled carts or trailers connected to each other like a train. At the head of the trailers was a nice green tractor operated by an inmate. With a pencil on his ear, the inmate drove the trainload of field workers to the cotton patch. As the train slowly pulled away, mounted guards with side arms rode up to the train and escorted the group to the field. Few inmates wore hats. Most had to be told to tuck in their shirts and to buckle their belts, to be quiet, to quit laughing or "grab assin," to tie their shoes, and to hurry up and get on the trailers.

At Eastham the inmates were assigned to squads in three major line forces called "White line," "Black line," and "Mexican line." Despite their racial connotation, the lines at the Eastham Unit in the 1980s were now completely desegregated. The squads consisted primarily of white, African American, and Hispanic inmates, but every once in a while a Vietnamese, Jamaican, Cuban, Chinese, Puerto Rican, or Arab inmate would be counted.

In the cotton patch, most of the inmates simply dragged their sacks along the hard ground; few pulled at the cotton bolls for their lives as their predecessors did in the 1950s, and there was no weigh up either.[10] The inmates were called out by their last names; gone were the colorful nicknames like "Shithouse Shorty" or "Rabbit" or "Wes' Texas," and gone were the cussing and hollering and threats and racial slights and slurs. "Doin' sumpn to somebody's ass" was now absurd. Gone, too, was the singing; there were no more convict work songs to pace the work. The line squads even returned to the building for a hot lunch and then returned to the fields afterward, and later returned early to the building for supper. More important, the field bosses had to go home at five, and so there was no more working from "can til can't." Most of the field bosses, however, lamented the lack of work effort by the inmates (they were inmates now, not convicts, not "ol' thangs," not "sorry sonuvabitches," at least in public) and stated all too often how the Ham had gone from "sugar to shit"—but this was progress, and nobody could stop progress.[11]

When the inmates returned for the evening after work, they ran straight to the showers. The mix of naked bodies appeared to be a collage of colors, like fallen leaves on the ground in October. Once they donned clean uniforms, inmates went back to the cell blocks, or line tanks, where the races were celled separately, but they mingled freely in the dayrooms to play dominos, roll cigarettes, talk to their homeboys, or watch television and gamble quietly on sporting events. Those who had school in the evening tended to their lessons in a desegregated classroom, and some even had free-world female instructors. Church services were desegregated, as was the garment factory work force, the paint squad, the laundry workers, the hospital workers, the kitchen workers, the inside maintenance crew, and the inmate work crews who handled the dairy, the chicken house, the hog barn, and the dog kennel.

Understanding the Transformation

In the course of thirty-five years, from 1956 to 1991, there was a nearly complete transformation of the Texas prison community. Virtually all aspects of prison life yielded to the forces of racial desegregation, in terms of personnel, programs, and inmate populations. One final change, however, had yet to occur: the desegregation of prison cells. This arrived in 1991, and proved to be the most radical change of all.

To a large degree, desegregation of the Texas prison system paralleled desegregation in American society as a whole, which also saw the erosion of the color line in the same period. And yet, pockets of segregation persist in the United States today. Despite the frequent contact that exists between those of different racial and ethnic groups in many public settings, most people go home to single-race environments. In contrast, the Texas prison system may be the most racially desegregated, mixed community in our society today. This is a far cry from the scene described above at the Retrieve Farm in 1956.

The reason for this stark contrast, both between the Texas prison system then and now and between the current system and society at large, is simple: the government cannot force its citizens to desegregate their households, living rooms, or bedrooms, but it did exactly that in the Texas prison system. This was a result of a carefully crafted inmate lawsuit that forced Texas prison officials to desegregate inmate work and recreation areas, job details, broader living areas, and finally prison cells. Nevertheless, desegregation was staunchly opposed by prison administrators and staff, much like the school administrators in Mansfield, who believed that desegregation would unleash a Hobbesian race war. Resistance sprang up in the courtroom and through good old-fashioned foot dragging by the prison system, but desegregation eventually became a reality. Desegregating prison cells moved the color line one step further than any other legal remedy crafted by any federal court in the land. The Texas prison experience we describe in these pages is at the outer edges of social engineering and race-based public policy and has not been duplicated in any other social environment to date.

Some people say that prisons are artificial environments and should not be used to understand or explore race relations or court-ordered racial desegregation. We believe the exact opposite. Prisons are the perfect fishbowls through which to understand human behavior in its most dense condition. Where else in our society can we observe, over time, how white, African American, and Hispanic men, many with violent pasts and tendencies and a large percentage with racial animosities, coexist in cramped nine-by-five cells for hours on end? Considering the history of race relations in Texas, which is discussed at length in subsequent chapters, the question becomes the following: Can a policy of in-cell desegregation be safely implemented and successfully remain in place in a state with a long history of racial animosity? To answer this, we describe the process of prisoner desegregation in Texas prisons, as well as bring longitudinal data on inmate-on-inmate violence to bear on the issue of in-cell desegregation.

As a way to package our analysis and help the reader understand the process of prisoner desegregation in Texas, we have relied on the work of the old Chicago School sociologists Robert Park and Ernest Burgess, who examined the social ecology of Chicago.[12] Park and Burgess were fascinated with the transformation of the city's neighborhoods. They examined the process of how one generation of immigrants moved into neighborhoods and displaced older populations, and how the process was repeated over and over again. As a result, some neighborhoods became, in their words, "socially disorganized," where criminal values and traditions replaced conventional values and were passed on from one generation to the next. Further, they found that certain areas of the city had higher rates of crime than others. To explain this situation, they used an "ecological perspective" wherein urban areas like Chicago are said to consist of concentric zones or rings extending out from the downtown central business district to the commuter zone at the fringes of the city. Each zone has its own structure and organizations, its own cultural characteristics and unique inhabitants.[13]

Zone I at the center represented the downtown central business district and was inhabited by commercial headquarters, law offices, shops, and other retail establishments. Zone II was the zone in transition, where the city's poor, unskilled, and disadvantaged lived in slums next to factories and the stockyards. Zone III housed the working class, and Zone IV was home to the middle class, professionals, small business owners, and managers. Zone V was home to the commuters, people who lived beyond the city but commuted to work and then left, areas commonly referred to as the suburbs.[14] But how can a theory of urban growth and transition be applied to prison desegregation? We suggest that in-cell desegregation in Texas prisons was the end result of a variety of social changes that began in the wider society, far away from the prison.

Zones of Desegregation

Park and Burgess's work led to a different way of thinking about cities and urban growth and the study of crime. Most important, their work demonstrated how people were distributed spatially in the process of urban growth. Their notion of zones can be applied to our task and enables us to explain just how desegregation unfolded between 1956 and 1991 in Texas and American

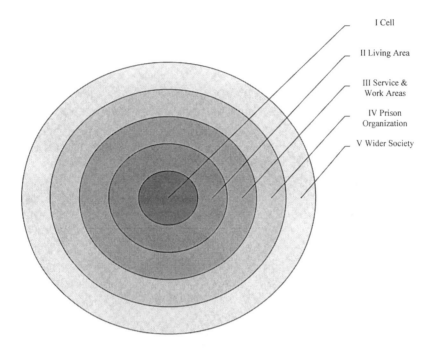

I Cell

II Living Area

III Service &
Work Areas

IV Prison
Organization

V Wider Society

Figure I.I. Zones of Desegregation

society in general, and in Texas prisons in particular. We are primarily interested in the distribution of desegregation events that occurred over time and that eventually led to in-cell desegregation in Texas prisons.

Figure 1.1 illustrates what we loosely term "Zones of Desegregation." Zone V represents the wider society where efforts to desegregate public places occurred first, mostly through legal challenges in the early 1950s. Judicial rulings in these important cases (and a multitude of others between 1950 and 1965) redefined the rules of membership or citizenship in our society. Included in these are Supreme Court rulings that eliminated the civil and social barriers put in place by *Plessy v. Ferguson* in the late nineteenth century (the doctrine of "separate but equal" and the justification for Jim Crow laws).[15] Passage of the Voting Rights Acts in 1965 and other judicial decisions in the 1960s on suffrage extended the full range of the political rights of citizenship to minorities in the United States.[16]

The combined effect of judicial rulings and federal legislation redefined the status of racial and ethnic minorities in the United States and led to their integration into the broader human community—they were extended the full complement of civil, social, and political rights of citizenship heretofore granted primarily to European Americans. We suggest that the moral worth of minorities on the "outside" had to be redefined before any shifts in the moral worth of prisoners could take place on the "inside."

Changes in the wider society ultimately filtered into the prison community. Zone IV represents the Texas prison system, a social institution enveloped within the wider society. Until 1965, Texas prisons were racially segregated (separate prisons for white, African American, and Hispanic inmates), and wholesale racial separation remained in place a full decade after the historic *Brown* decision.

In the 1960s, alert prison administrators noted the broader social changes afoot in American society and took a proactive stance, desegregating the system on a broad scale. White, African American, and Hispanic inmates were now housed together in the same prisons. No longer were inmates housed in single race/ethnic group institutions, a move that changed the prisoner community forever. Desegregation of prisoners only went so far in the 1960s, however, and inmate living areas, work areas, and a multitude of other prison areas remained strictly segregated.

Zone III represents the prison work and service areas (e.g., dining areas, barber shops, churches, and school and treatment programs), which were desegregated in the 1970s. Zone II comprises the broader prison living areas—dormitories (large open rooms with single beds) and cell blocks. In the late 1970s the cell blocks were desegregated, but in reality this meant that white cell partners, for example, were housed next to African American or Hispanic cell partners—a form of desegregation sometimes referred to as a checkerboard pattern. In other words, the cell blocks were racially mixed but the cell inhabitants remained segregated. Finally, Zone I represents actual two-man prison cells—the focus of our analysis because the cell is where the potential for violence, lethal violence, is the most apparent and the place that is perhaps the most difficult to monitor and control in the prison environment. Indeed, once the doors are rolled shut, very little can be done to stop a knife attack or an attempt by one "celly" to strangle another.

Desegregating the prisoner living areas, particularly two-person cells, drew the greatest amount of intransigence from the prison administration and custodial staff. These individuals believed that any efforts to racially mix the cells would lead to catastrophic results—a violent race war. Interestingly enough, these predictions of wholesale racial violence were almost identical to the claims made by Mansfield school officials in the 1950s and in other social arenas facing desegregation mandates. It should also be noted that when the first broad efforts to desegregate Texas prisons began in the 1960s, no one ever believed that the desegregation of cells would be the end result. Prisons are full of hard men, many who dislike themselves and many who dislike and mistrust each other. Getting a group of social miscreants like prisoners to do anything together is difficult, let alone live peaceably in a room not much bigger than a telephone booth. Nothing could have prepared Texas prison administrators for what was about to become one of the largest natural experiments in racial desegregation in American history.

Our zone theory of prison desegregation suggests that the path to prison cell desegregation was evolutionary and took decades to come to fruition, and that the seeds for this monumental event were sown by and highly dependent upon the legal and social changes in the wider society. Events in Zone V, such as school desegregation and equal access to public parks, housing, and public transportation, were the catalysts that set in motion desegregation within prison organizations that ended with in-cell desegregation in Texas.[17] Further, the deeper that desegregation efforts were pressed into the prison community, the closer the wagons were circled, as Texans say, and prison administrator and staff resistance strengthened. Nevertheless, once the forces of change were unleashed outside the prison, it was but a matter of time before the cell would become the battleground for prison attorneys seeking to prevent cell desegregation and inmate attorneys seeking mixed cells. The cell was the last barrier to be broken with regard to prisoner desegregation.

Research on prison organizations over the past two decades has clearly demonstrated that prisons are not isolated from the rest of society, nor are they insulated from the core values of the wider society. Prison walls are permeable, and changes in the wider society eventually filter into or behind prison walls.[18] It may take an extra decade or two for change to occur, but change will happen. In this case, the change that unfolded exceeded all expectations. Today, any observer of prison organizations would be amazed at the depth of desegregation in the Texas prison system. In fact, no other state in the nation enforces a strict policy of in-cell desegregation like that in Texas.[19] We imagine that if Albert "Race" Sample walked into the Retrieve prison unit today, he would be overwhelmed by the transformation. Would he consider these changes to be progress? Perhaps, but one must consider that concepts such as "progress," "successful," "better," or "improved" are heavily value-laden and depend on which side of the bars you stand. One person's progress is another's devastation.

Our goal in this book is to answer this question: Did efforts to desegregate Texas prison cells unleash a torrent of racial violence, and if not, why not? We turn now to examine the history of segregation and race relations in Texas to help frame and guide the evolution of in-cell desegregation in the Texas prison system.

CHAPTER 2

An Institutional Fault Line

When the first settlers slogged across the Sabine and Red Rivers and made their way into Texas, they felt at home among the timberlands and piney woods and river bottoms of East Texas. The great southern forests extended from the Carolinas, west of the Mississippi, and beyond Louisiana and into Texas. The land they encountered was also blessed with abundant rain. Most of the first settlers in Texas came from Louisiana, Mississippi, Alabama, the Carolinas, and other southern states. They knew, as did their ancestors, how to clear land and make it usable. Clearing land of virgin forests was back-breaking labor but it had to be done, and clearing forests took many hands and many axes. Once the trees and stumps were cleared, the land could be plowed and put to use.

As with any frontier, a number of settlers pushed onward and inland, and moved further west in the hope of finding new lands worthy of farms, towns, schools, and a good life. They too wanted to settle in the familiar forests of their parents, but these settlers discovered that the great southern timberlands did not extend forever. Just west of present-day Waco, Texas, the forests abruptly disappeared, and the land turned flat and treeless and dry. These new flat lands extended west to the Rocky Mountains, north to Canada, and south to Mexico.

This topographical nuance was noticed by the great Texas historian Walter Prescott Webb, who based his history of the Great Plains on a simple, invisible boundary—the 98th meridian. This line runs north and south around the globe but divides Texas into two distinct geographical regions, one timbered and known, one arid and dangerous. Webb also believed that the 98th meridian was more than a geographical fault; rather, the invisible boundary symbolized an institutional fault: "At this fault the ways of life and living changed."[1] West of the 98th meridian settlers had to invent new modes of life to survive. East of the 98th meridian were the great forests and river bottoms, where old modes of life took root and prospered. Most Texans in the years before the Civil War chose to remain in familiar lands.

Slavery in Texas: The Early Years

Moses Austin was a businessman who made a name for himself in the lead mining industry in Virginia and Missouri in the early 1800s. The War of 1812 and a failed banking venture in 1819 depleted his personal fortune. To escape his debt, Austin developed a plan to help settle Spanish Texas. In December 1820, he arrived in San Antonio and revealed his plan to the Spanish governor, who soon approved it. On the way home, Austin contracted pneumonia; he eventually died on June 10, 1821. His dying wish was that his son, Stephen, take over the colonization plan.[2]

Stephen learned of his father's death while in Natchitoches, Louisiana, and proceeded onward to San Antonio to carry out his father's plan. In August 1821, Stephen was granted permission to explore the area east of San Antonio to the Brazos River for the purpose of selecting land for the proposed colony. The area selected by Austin was east of the 98th meridian, an area rich with timberland and river bottoms.

Stephen carried out his father's plan and arranged to offer land to settlers — 640 acres for each head of a family, 320 acres for his wife, 160 acres for each child, and 80 acres for each slave. For his efforts, he received 12½ cents for every acre he distributed. Stephen F. Austin believed that most of the settlers immigrating to Texas would come from other slave-holding states. The "80 acres per slave" was an extra benefit to attract settlers and for the new settlers to develop a cotton culture. Austin realized that "southerners would not emigrate without their slaves, and plantations could not function without laborers."[3] A census of Austin's colony shows that the original 300 families (or 1,800 people) brought 443 slaves.[4] Slavery took root and prospered in Texas and a plantation culture quickly developed.

In the 1820s and 1830s, Austin's colony grew and the growth sparked fears among Mexican officials that the Americans were going to take over the new country. To discourage immigration and stifle any trouble between the United States, Mexican president Vicente Guerrero signed a decree to abolish slavery in Texas. However, the government eventually reneged on this decree and established legal loopholes for the Texans. Most Texans ignored the decree anyway, and immigrants continued to bring in slaves.[5] In 1836, Texas had an estimated population of 38,000 people, 5,000 of whom were slaves.

The issue of slavery continued to be a thorny one for Texans and the Mexican government until the revolution. Only after the Texas Revolution of 1835–1836 was the issue of slavery finally resolved. The Texas Constitution of 1836 "declared that all Negroes still in bondage, who had been held in slavery prior to the removal of their masters to Texas, should remain in that state."[6] These words affirmed that Texas would remain open to slavery. In 1845, Texas joined the United States, and at that time the state was home to 30,000 slaves. The census of 1850 reported 58,161 slaves out of a total population of 212,592 people, or 27 percent of the entire population (see Figure 2.1).[7]

By 1860, the plantation system or culture had taken root and prospered beyond the wildest dreams of Moses and Stephen Austin. The plantation system had even expanded to within 100 miles of the 98th meridian. Moreover, the society that took root and developed east of the 98th meridian in Texas had its own fault line as well: a color line, one white and one black, one free and one enslaved. Although fewer than one-third of Texans owned a slave, slave owners dominated the state's economy, political affairs, and social hierarchy. In fact, this "peculiar institution," as slavery was known, dominated just about every aspect of social life in Texas. Texans, prior to the Civil War, also enacted strong political and legal measures to own slaves and keep Texas open to slavery. By 1860 and on the eve of the Civil War, there were nearly 200,000 slaves in Texas, over thirty percent of the total population of the state (see Figure 2.2).[8]

Antebellum Texas was in effect little different from other states in the Old South. At the onset of the Civil War, slaves in Texas had an "economic value of $106,688,920, or twenty percent more than the assessed value of all cultivated lands."[9] So adamant were Texans about maintaining slavery that in February 1861, Texas legislators voted to secede from the United States.[10]

On April 12, 1861, the Union garrison at Fort Sumter surrendered to Confederate forces in Charleston, South Carolina. The last battle of the Civil War was fought in Texas on May 13, 1865, at Palmito Hill (in far South Texas, near Brownsville), more than a full month after Lee's surrender to Grant on April 9 at Appomattox Court House, Virginia. Among the Union forces in this battle was an African American regiment, the 62nd Infantry. Union efforts to avoid violence at Palmito Hill failed; Confederate forces, commanded by Colonel Rip Ford, attacked and killed over 200 Union soldiers. After the battle, several of Ford's troops stated that they knew the war was over and that, had white Union soldiers come forward and demanded surrender, they would have done so—but they were unwilling to "surrender to niggers."[11]

So ended the Civil War—a war that unleashed a tidal wave of social change between 1861 and 1865. The aftermath of the war also unleashed enormous changes that impacted squarely on the fault line between white and black

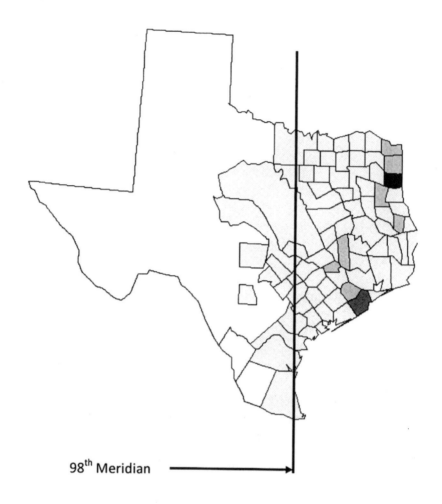

98th Meridian

☐ 1 - 1554
▨ 1554 - 3107
■ 3107 - 4660
■ 4660 - 6213
☐ Missing Data

Figure 2.1. Slave Population in Texas, 1850 Census

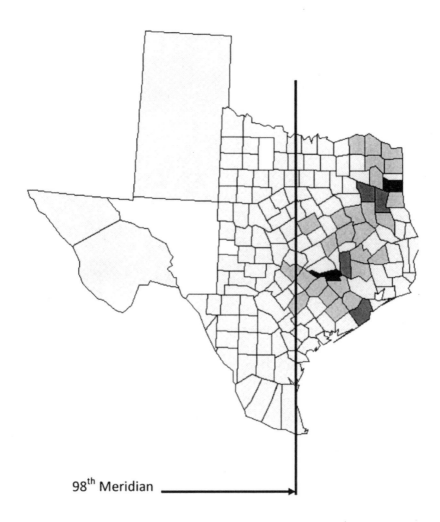

98th Meridian

	0 - 2196
	2196 - 4392
	4392 - 6588
	6588 - 8784
	Missing Data

Figure 2.2. Slave Population in Texas, 1860 Census

Texans. How would white and newly freed black Texans interact in the aftermath of the war that legally mandated equality?

A Tale of Two Societies

It was June in Texas and the weather was already hot. Corporal Martin Roof, a Union soldier aboard the steamer Sedgwick on its way from Mobile, Alabama, to Galveston, Texas, noted in his diary that the weather in mid-June was clear and hot.[12] The summer of 1865 was fast taking shape and it was indeed going to be a long, hot summer. June 1865 in Texas was a historic moment in time; it was a month that would shape the social fabric of the state for the next 100 years. June 1865 could have been the subject of Charles Dickens's memorable words: "It was the best of times, it was the worst of times, it was the age of wisdom, it was the age of foolishness, it was the epoch of belief, it was the epoch of incredulity, it was the season of Light, it was the season of Darkness, it was the spring of hope, it was the winter of despair."[13]

It was the best of times because the Civil War was over, and the national bleeding had ceased. The last day of armed combat was May 26, and on May 27 Texas soldiers began to trek home—to Houston, Brenham, Waller, and Austin. The long and bitter conflict was finally over and it was time to move on and build schools, to plant crops, tend stores, herd cattle, and settle a frontier. It was the best of times too because on June 19, Union Major General Gordon Granger read General Order #3 aloud to the people of Galveston. General Granger proclaimed that "all slaves are free" and that all freedmen in Texas had absolute equality in personal and property rights as their former masters. It was indeed the best of times as former slaves were, all at once on June 19, free citizens, free to own property, free to vote, free to establish schools, and free to live where they wanted.

Following this announcement was the issue of how white Texans, and southerners in general, would respond to the freedmen. Proclamations were one thing, actual behavior and actions another. The state's economy was in ruins, the government had collapsed, the planter class was bankrupt, and thousands of Texans, many small farmers, had died in the Civil War. Who was to blame for this state of affairs? Commenting on this combustible situation, W. E. B. Du Bois posed the question four decades later: "Then came the revolution of war and Emancipation, the bewilderment of Reconstruction,—and now, what is the Egypt of the Confederacy, and what meaning has it for the nation's weal or woe?"[14]

Many white Texans blamed the freed slaves for their and their state's misfortune and were not about to extend former slaves the freedom they had been granted by President Lincoln, now dead. The best of times quickly descended into the worst of times. The summer of 1865 became a violent hell for the newly freed men, women, and children. It did not take long after the reading of General Order #3 for violence to break out. The War Between the States was officially over, but the war over equality had just begun. General Order #3 was, in effect, a remedial decree; it was a federal order mandating racial desegregation and the dismantling of the color line.

In mid-June, when the first U.S. troops arrived in Houston, a black man named William, an enlisted cook in K Company, walked uptown in advance of the troops and was murdered in the streets by a white man named Cotton. Racial killings—white on black—soon appeared that year in such places as Washington County (northwest of Houston), Jasper County (northeast of Houston), Montgomery County (just north of Houston), and Houston County (100 miles northeast of Houston).

In 1866, racial killings spread north and west to Brazos County (100 miles northwest of Houston), Fannin County (200 miles north of Houston), Burleson County (150 miles northwest of Houston), and finally, in February 1867, racial killings reached Travis County, the home of the Texas state capital in Austin. We can only surmise by this pattern of violence that as word spread about General Order #3, violence followed. Freed men (and women and in some cases even children) were shot down, hanged, or beaten to death for such transgressions as "failing to remove their cap in the presence of a white man," "talking back," "acting sassy," "not allowing a white man to whip him," for filing affidavits or official reports in other killings, or for "no particular reason."

The ferocity and brutality of the violence prompted some white citizens to write Governor Elisha Pease and the Freedmen's Bureau seeking Union troops to restore order in an unsettled society. The following letter illustrates the chaotic state of affairs in Texas shortly after the end of the war:[15]

Jefferson, August 26, 1868
Hon. E. M. Pease
Austin

Sir:

Last Friday night about 1 O'clock, Albert Browning (a Freedman), one of the quiet inoffensive citizens of our city, was taken out from his bed and in the presence of his wife and little children, his hands tied behind him and after being robbed of his money and many articles of wearing apparel, also a gun, pistol and his horse, was led a short distance from his house and shot through the head, five balls taking effect, evidently simultaneously from different guns or pistols—as but one report was heard. From there they proceeded to the African church, tied their horses and entered the enclosure and commenced breaking down the door, whereupon some Freedmen who were there guarding their church fired upon them, and they ingloriously fled, and in their confusion they dropped the gun and pistol they had taken from Browning, and some other articles of value—also Browning's horse was left tied to a stake. Since that time our city has been in a blaze of excitement, not so much on account of the assassination as from the assemblage of Freedmen at their church every night for the purpose of protecting their property, which is certainly their right, since the civil authorities fail to do it. They go to their church, enter the enclosure, fasten their gates and remain very quiet, interrupting no one, not wishing to interfere with any one, provided they are left unmolested—

On Monday night the excitement became most intense. Mounted men well armed were riding through this city swearing vengeance against the Freedmen at the church. The citizens called a meeting and the crowd was harangued by excited orators. D. B. Culverson, I was informed by a gentleman of undoubted veracity and who was present, attacked D. Campbell, said he had organized the Loyal League here, and that such men were accountable for all this excitement and should be held accountable for anything that might happen, etc., etc., and was generally very bitter against Radicals, and all this in a public harangue to a then infuriated crowd, at a time when Campbell had been compelled to leave his house and come to town and conceal himself as best he could at night to save his life—night after night his house was surrounded by armed men, attempted to decoy him out by professions of friendship, assuming the names of his friends, forced Freedmen from their houses and ordered them to entice Campbell out and because they refused, tortured them by putting their heads under corners of fences and keeping them until life was almost extinct. I could give you many other instances of torture for similar purposes.—The civil law is a blank here, protection we must have soon or else all Union men—I mean loyal men will have to leave this country. Matters are growing worse every day—hundred of Negroes are now preparing to move to Louisiana, and I believe eventually all of them will leave this section. We need a squad of Cavalry—say 25 or 30, for the men who are committing these deeds of horror are mounted men and Infantry can never overtake them. Two mounted men dashed boldly into town yesterday and robbed a Freedman's horse and was gone in a few minutes. The civil officers started on foot to arrest them but they never—saw them—Hoping we may have protection soon. I am, Very Respectfully, Your Obedt. Servt., (sgd) W. H. Johnson.[16]

Murder is almost by definition the most serious form of violence. In reality, it was a rare event, and White Texans more frequently resorted to other acts of non-lethal violence (e.g., beatings, assaults, castrations, whippings, arson) against newly freed blacks for a wide variety of perceived "misdeeds," offenses, or personal slights:

- On the 26th of July 1865 W. S. Spencer inflicted several severe blows with the iron butt end of a heavy whip on the head of a mulatto woman named Adelaide, cutting to the bone. The said W. S. Spencer then in company with C. C. Millican then tied her hands together pulled her clothes over her hips, bucked her and gave her about two hundred lashes with a heavy leather strap, supposed to be a trace. One of the parties claimed that Adelaide had made an insulting noise when his wife passed. This case was reported by Joel Spencer an old citizen of Brazoria Co. who formerly owned Adelaide and who is the father-in-law of one of the perpetrators of this outrage.
- Jerome deBlanc planter in Liberty Co. handcuffed Stephen Bryant (col.) and wife, then brutally struck and kicked them because Stephen's two sons had left the plantation without permission. De Blanc also tied up and beat the freedman Linns because he refused to contract. Date August 1865.
- Dr. Philips of Montgomery Co. whipped the freedman Leton, threatened to kill him and put a chain on him which Leton wore to Houston. This was done because L. would not stay with him. Date September 1865.
- Stephen Patout (col.) was so severely beaten by H. Patout (white) with a club that he was confined to the house for several weeks in consequence. H. Patout claimed that Genl. Merritt had authorized him to whip his ex-slaves as usual. Date August 1865 Milan Co.
- Robert Hardy (white) beat his two female servants Emeline and Louisa over their heads with a heavy walking stick bruising them badly. Date Sept 1865 Waverly, Walker Co.
- Col. Elmore of Waverly collected a party of neighbors mounted and armed with pistols & c., took a pack of hounds used for the purpose and hunted down Slade (col.) who had left his plantation. After catching him imprisoned him for a day and two nights on a calaboose on the plantation. Date July 1865.

- Isaac freedman was chased by dogs belonging to a Mr. Addison who kept them for the purpose of chasing Negroes. During the hunt he was twice shot at by a white man named Beads, who hired the dogs of Addison. Cause. Isaac had left the plantation of Mr. Beads with whom he had been living. Date last of October 1865. Walker Co.
- John a freedman was severely beaten by a man named Porter (white) with a club. Porter also threatened to kill him, and with the assistance of Jack Roberts (white) took John into the woods, tied him to a tree and put a rope around his neck. John was saved from further violence by the interference of a neighbor who succeeded in getting him released. John was badly cut about the head. Cause. Dispute about work. Date November 1865. Robison Co.
- H. Dimlavy beat Miles a freedman severely with his heavy walking stick cutting his head and shoulders. Cause. Miles said he was too sick to pick cotton. Date October 1865. Fort Bend Co.
- Plans Stanley (col.) while quietly standing near the church just after the services were over was rushed upon and stabbed severely in the left arm by Frank Sterling (white) who said "God Damn your black soul I will learn you to stand in the way of white ladies." Date November 1865. East Liberty.
- Wm. McMahon (white) beat one of the Negro women employed on his place named Adeline brutally over the head and face with a paddle marking her up badly. Cause. Said she was lazy. Date October 1865. Harris Co.
- Jefferson a freed man was assaulted cut with a knife and robbed, on the road about a mile from Houston by two white men who succeeded in escaping. Three other freedmen were abused and robbed by the same party. Date Dec 1865.
- Dr. John Fisher of Walker Co. drew a pistol on Herod Hudson (col.) drove him from the field where he was at work, into the gin house, made a colored man beat him and place a rope around his neck. Tied his hands behind him, blindfolded him and drew him up by the rope until he had partially choked him and then let him down. Then drove him off. Cause. Said that Herod did not do enough work. Date December 1865.
- McCoy (white) assaulted and seriously injured a freedman named Ned Hernder striking him with a bar of iron. Cause. Said he was too long eating his breakfast. Date January 1866. Brazoria Co.
- Lucinda Pilot (col.) was assaulted by Capt. Johnson (white) who gave her a severe beating with a quirt over the head, face and shoulders and as she was trying to get away kicked her out of the door and threatened to kill her if she stayed. Cause. Said she spoke disrespectfully to his wife. Date June 1866. Brazoria Co.[17]

These extra-legal forms of violence were used to instill fear among blacks and to erect and maintain a stiff social barrier between the races. While slavery was legally dead, traditional social customs enforcing a segregated social order emerged. Fear, violence, and murder were used to maintain the pre-1860 caste system.

Legal means were also employed to keep the races apart. Whites were unprepared to accept blacks as equals under any circumstances. Desegregation and assimilation were not options. So intent were whites on keeping the races divided that the Texas legislature in 1866 refused to ratify the Thirteenth Amendment (abolition of slavery) and Fourteenth Amendment (which guarantees that anyone born or naturalized in the United States is a citizen and is guaranteed all the protections and due process and equal protection of the laws of the United States). The legislators also enacted a series of "black codes" (e.g., vagrancy laws, labor contracts) designed to keep the former slaves in "bondage" and "in their place" as well as to maintain, in their view, an orderly society.[18]

As a result of this egregious legislative activity in Texas and other southern states, Congress enacted the Reconstruction Acts and abolished the state governments of ten Confederate states. A new state constitution was ratified in 1869 by Texas voters, and citizens also ratified the Thirteenth, Fourteenth, and Fifteenth Amendments on February 18, 1870.[19] With this, Texas was readmitted to the Union.

The Color Line, 1870–1950

Although the plantation system was dead and the freedmen were guaranteed the rights to full citizenship under the law, including the right to vote and hold office, whites were not going to let the former slaves compete evenly with them in society. Enforcement of the Fourteenth and Fifteenth Amendments was reserved to the states; therefore the rights guaranteed under these new amendments were beyond federal jurisdiction. Texas, like other southern states, took full advantage of the amendments' nuanced language and limited African American economic, political, and social participation.

Economic segregation prevailed through the implementation of sharecropping, a form of tenantry whereby farmers worked small plots of land owned by someone else and then typically received only one-half to one-third of the land's yield.[20] Sharecroppers, most of whom were former slaves, nevertheless had to pay the landowner for seed, implements, and housing. This system of "legal slavery" kept the freedmen from joining the American money economy.[21]

Political participation was restricted through poll taxes and the white primary. Texas adopted a poll tax in 1902, which required that eligible voters
pay between $1.50 and $1.75 to register to vote—a lot of money at the time
and a big barrier to the working classes and poor, especially African Americans (and Mexican Americans in South Texas). The white primary turned the
Texas Democratic Party into a private club whose membership was restricted
to citizens of Anglo heritage. Those not in the club were disenfranchised.[22]

Educational partition was accomplished through laws and amendments
in the Texas Constitution that specified that whites and African Americans would attend separate schools, including universities. For example, in
1876, the Fifteenth Texas Legislature founded the "Alta Vista Agricultural
and Mechanical College for Colored Youth" on 1,388 acres of land in Waller
County—land that was once a plantation (later renamed Prairie View A&M
University in 1973).[23]

To restrict social interaction and further produce a divided society, much
like the 98th meridian divided the state geographically, the Texas legislature
enacted twenty-seven so-called Jim Crow laws between 1866 and 1958.

These legal and administrative provisions confirm that the intent and meaning of the Thirteenth, Fourteenth, and Fifteenth Amendments to the U.S.
Constitution were to be usurped by states' rights and that African American
citizenship existed in name only. As the legal activity in Table 2.1 illustrates,
between 1866 and 1891 Texas enacted seven laws to enforce the color line.
After 1900, however, legislators enacted twenty additional legal provisions
establishing separate educational and medical institutions, public parks, and
washroom facilities for African Americans. Why did Texas quicken the pace
of legal efforts to erect the color line after 1900? The answer to this question
can be found in the Pelican State, Louisiana.

Separate but Equal

In 1890, Louisiana enacted a "Separate Car Act" in which railroad companies
were required to provide separate but equal passenger coaches and accommodations for whites and African Americans. Homer Plessy, an African American shoemaker who was one-eighth black, purchased a train ticket on June 7,
1892, and sat in the "whites only" section of a rail car.[24] Plessy was instructed
to move but refused and he was later arrested. The case was eventually decided
by the U.S. Supreme Court in 1896.

Plessy's attorney argued that the railroad segregation law implied the inferiority of African Americans. State attorneys for Louisiana argued that
separate facilities reflected the public will. In short, segregation policies were

a state matter and not the province of the federal government. In an 8–1 decision, the Supreme Court rejected Plessy's argument of inferiority and stated that the law was intended simply to separate the races as a matter of social policy. The lone dissenter in the historic case was Justice John Harlan, who stated:

> Our Constitution is color-blind, and neither knows nor tolerates classes among citizens. In respect of civil rights, all citizens are equal before the law. . . . In my opinion, the judgment this day rendered will, in time, prove to be quite as pernicious as the decision made by this tribunal in the *Dred Scott* case. . . . The present decision, it may well be apprehended, will not only stimulate aggressions, more or less brutal and irritating, upon the admitted rights of colored citizens, but will encourage the belief that it is possible, by means of state enactments, to defeat the beneficent purposes which the people of the United States had in view when they adopted the recent amendments of the Constitution.[25]

The *Plessy* decision set the precedent that "separate" facilities for African Americans and whites were constitutional as long as they were "equal." After *Plessy,* the Texas state legislature enacted "separate but equal" statutes that covered many areas of public life, including medical facilities, public parks, libraries, restrooms, and public schools. The laws enacted to keep a boundary between whites and African Americans were also used to erect a boundary between Hispanics and white Texans. Hispanics experienced segregation in public places that ranged from barber and beauty shops to swimming pools, restrooms, water drinking fountains, public dining places and hotels, and public schools.

Ironically, the caste system that existed in antebellum Texas was fully institutionalized after the Civil War, even after thousands of Union and Confederate soldiers died on the battlefields of Shiloh, Atlanta, Chancellorsville, Cold Harbor, Gettysburg, and Antietam to maintain the Union, end slavery, and extend citizenship and the rule of law to all Americans. In Texas, the road to separate societies for whites and African Americans and Hispanics was well in place by the outbreak of World War II.

"Protecting" the Color Line

When thinking about the history of Texas, many people conjure up images of the Alamo, longhorn cattle on the free range, and trail drives. Others imagine frontier justice and hanging cattle or horse thieves from the nearest tree.

Table 2.1. Jim Crow Legislation in Texas, 1866–1958

1866: Education [Constitution]: All taxes paid by blacks to go to maintaining African American schools. The legislature is to "encourage colored schools."

1866: Railroads [Statute]: "All railroad companies shall attach one passenger car for the special accommodation of freedmen."

1876: Voting rights [Constitution]: Voters required to pay poll tax.

1879: Miscegenation [Statute]: Intermarriage law passed in 1858 is confirmed. Penalty is to apply equally to both parties.

1889: Railroads [Statute]: Railroad companies required to maintain separate coaches for white and colored passengers, equal in comfort. Penalty: Passengers refusing to sit where assigned are guilty of a misdemeanor, with fines between $5 and $20.

1891: Railroads [Statute]: Separate coach laws strengthened. Separate coaches for white and Negro passengers to be equal in all points of comfort and convenience. Designed by signage posted in a conspicuous place in each compartment. Trains allowed to carry chair cars or sleeping cars for the exclusive use of either race. Law did not apply to streetcars. Penalty: Conductors who fail to enforce law face misdemeanor charge punishable by a fine from $5 to $25. The railroad company may be fined from $100 to $1,000 for each trip. Passengers who refuse to sit in designated areas face fines from $5 to $25.

1907: Streetcars [Statute]: All streetcars required to comply with the separate coach law passed in 1889. Penalty: Streetcar companies to be fined from $100 to $1,000 for failing to enforce law. A passenger wrongfully riding in an improper coach is guilty of a misdemeanor, with fines from $5 to $25.

1909: Railroads [Statute]: Depot buildings required to provide separate waiting areas for the use of white and Negro passengers.

1914: Railroads [Statute]: Negro porters shall not sleep in sleeping car berths nor use bedding intended for white passengers.

1915: Miscegenation [State Code]: The penalty for intermarriage is imprisonment in the penitentiary from two to five years.

1919: Public accommodations [Statute]: Negroes must use separate branches of county libraries.

1922: Voting Rights [Statute]: "In no event shall a Negro be eligible to participate in a Democratic party primary election held in the State of Texas." Overturned in 1927 by U.S. Supreme Court in *Nixon v. Herndon.*

1925: Education [Statute]: Racially segregated schools required.

1925: Public accommodations [Statute]: Separate branches for Negroes to be administered by a Negro custodian in all county libraries.

1925: Miscegenation [Penal Code]: Miscegenation declared a felony. Interracial marriages nullified if parties went to another jurisdiction where such marriages were legal.

1926: Public carriers [Statute]: Public carriers to be segregated.

1935: Health Care [Statute]: State tuberculosis sanitarium for blacks established.

Table 2.1. Continued

1935: Public carriers [State Code]: Separate coaches for whites and blacks on all common carriers.

1943: Public carriers [State Code]: Separate seating on all buses.

1949: Employment [Statute]: Coal mines required to have separate washrooms.

1950: Public accommodations [Statute]: Separate facilities required for white and black citizens in state parks.

1951: Voting rights [Constitution]: Voters required to pay poll tax.

1951: Miscegenation [Statute]: A person of Caucasian blood marrying person of African blood declared unlawful. Penalty: Two to five years imprisonment.

1952: Health Care [Statute]: Establishment of TB hospitals for blacks.

1953: Public carriers [Penal Code]: Public carriers to be segregated.

1958: Education [Statute]: No child compelled to attend schools that are racially mixed. No desegregation unless approved by election. Governor may close schools where troops used on federal authority.

Source: Texas State Library and Archives Commission.

Vigilante justice in Texas was one mechanism for maintaining law and order. In antebellum Texas, mob justice circumvented formal court procedures, and "offenders" were typically whipped and/or banished from a county. Fears over slave insurrections also prompted panicked whites to form "vigilance committees" and secret societies that flogged suspected abolitionists and hanged slaves thought to be planning rebellions.[26] In those days, it was considered best to err on the side of preemption than risk a full-scale revolt.

Following the Civil War, most African Americans in the late nineteenth and early twentieth centuries lived in small towns and separate areas alongside their white counterparts. As long as blacks stayed within their own communities, the state's civil and criminal codes were not rigidly enforced. When the color line was breached, however, mob violence often erupted in Texas, and former slaves were usually the targets.[27]

Texas witnessed many lynchings, a form of lethal violence regarded by many whites at the time as a necessary form of social control. Lynchings were used primarily by whites to intimidate, degrade, and control African Americans, especially in the six decades after the Civil War. Data show that between 1882 and 1968 there were a total of 4,743 recorded lynchings (1,297 white and 3,446 black victims) in the United States. Texas's 493 recorded lynchings ranked the state third in the United States, behind Mississippi (581) and Georgia (531).[28]

Between 1885 and 1942, there were 468 lynching victims in Texas, and of these 339 were African American, 77 were white, 53 were Hispanic, and 1 was Native American. Moreover, between 1889 and 1942, charges of murder or attempted murder precipitated at least 40 percent of the mobs. Rape or attempted rape accounted for 26 percent of lynchings, and African American males were more likely than any other group to be lynched for rape.[29] The heaviest concentration of mob activity stretched along the Brazos River from Waco in the west, south to the Gulf of Mexico, and into the counties of East Texas and neighboring western Louisiana. East Texas was an area rich in plantations, sharecropping, and a strong cotton economy both before and after the Civil War. It was in East Texas where efforts were the strongest to maintain the color line.

A Saturnalia of Death: Texas Lynchings, 1890–1899

The following is a list of lynchings in Texas from 1890 to 1899, some with mention of the so-called crime that precipitated mob violence. As noted, the vast majority of lynching victims were African Americans.[30]

March 27, 1890: a Negro man was lynched in Hedsville.

April 5, 1890: a Negro named Williams was lynched in Kosse.

April 5, 1890: a Negro man was lynched in Thornton.

April 20, 1890: Simeon Garrette was lynched in San Augustine.

April 20, 1890: Stephen Jacobson was lynched in Fay.

April 24, 1890: Jerry Teel was lynched in San Augustine.

May 12, 1890: Edward Bennett, a Negro, was lynched for rape in Hearne.

June 1, 1890: Thomas Brown was lynched in Hooks Ferry.

June 20, 1890: a Negro man was lynched in Livingston.

June 28, 1890: a Negro man was lynched in Antlers.

July 3, 1890: Patrick Henry was lynched in Nechesville.

July 22, 1890: Andy Young was lynched in Red River County.

July 30, 1890: William Hawkins was lynched in Cypress.

August 4, 1890: John Brown, a Negro, was lynched in Navasota.

August 14, 1890: two Negro men were lynched in Mexia.

January 1, 1891: Charles Bealle was lynched in Lang.

February 17, 1891: Thomas Rebin, a Negro, was lynched in Douglas.

February 24, 1891: Thomas Rowland, a Negro, was lynched in Douglas.

June 28, 1891: William Hartfield and Munn Sheppard were lynched in Cass County.

July 22, 1891: William Johnson was lynched in Henderson.

October 26, 1891: Leo Green was lynched in Linden.

November 13, 1891: two Negro men were lynched in Burnet.

November 22, 1891: William Black was lynched in Moscow.

February 20, 1892: Edward Coy was burned alive in Texarkana for the rape of a white woman. The alleged victim applied the match.

April 26, 1892: a Negro man was lynched in Riesil.

June 10, 1892: Tobe Cook was hanged for murder by a lynch mob in Bastrop County.

June 28, 1892: Henry Gaines, Thomas Smith, and Prince Wood were lynched in Spurger.

September 6, 1892: William Armor, John Ransom, and John Walker were lynched in Paris.

September 19, 1892: a Negro man was lynched in Paris.

September 23, 1892: William Sullivan was lynched in Plantersville.

November 25, 1892: Rosalie Castillo, a Hispanic man, was hanged for rape by Texas.

February 1, 1893: Henry Smith was burned alive for murder in Paris.

February 17, 1893: William Butler, a Negro, was lynched for "race prejudice" in Hickory Creek.

April 28, 1893: three Negroes, Jim Burke, Zedolph Davis, and Sam Massey, were hanged for rape by Texas.

June 14, 1893: George Williams was lynched for rape in Waco.

July 28, 1893: Alexander Brown, a Negro, was lynched for murder in Bastrop.

July 28, 1893: Henry Miller, a Negro, was lynched for murder in Dallas.

August 3, 1893: a Negro man was lynched in Yarborough.

August 31, 1893: a Negro man was lynched in Yarborough.

September 2, 1893: Perry Bratcher was lynched for rape in New Boston.

September 3, 1893: a Negro man was lynched in Houston.

December 9, 1893: Alf Watson, a Negro, was lynched for murder in Cold Springs.

February 10, 1894: Jessie Dillingham, a Negro, was lynched for train wrecking in Smokeyville.

April 14, 1894: Jack Crews, a white man, was lynched for murder in Gainesville.

May 9, 1894: a Negro man was lynched in West.

May 17, 1894: Henry Scott was lynched for murder in Jefferson.

June 13, 1894: Bascom Cook and Lon Hall were lynched for murder in Sweet Home.

June 29, 1894: John Williams was lynched for murder in Sulphur Springs.

July 30, 1894: William Griffith was lynched for rape in Woodville.

October 8, 1894: Henry Gibson was lynched for attempted rape in Fairfield.

November 12, 1894: Rafael Garza was lynched in Kimble County.

December 20, 1894: James Allen was lynched for arson in Brownsville.

March 14, 1895: Isaac Manion was lynched for robbery in Athens.

April 12, 1895: Richard Burleson was lynched for murder in Groesbeck.

April 18, 1895: Nelson Calhoun was lynched for an assault on a "respectable lady" in Corsicana.

June 11, 1895: John Cherry and Alexander White were lynched in Keno.

June 11, 1895: William Johnson was lynched in Lufkin.

July 20, 1895: a Negro woman and her 2 children were lynched in Mant.

July 23, 1895: a Negro woman was lynched in Brenham.

July 29, 1895: Squire Loftin was lynched in Lexington.

August 12, 1895: a Negro man was lynched in Delta County.

August 22, 1895: a Negro man was lynched in Wharton.

August 26, 1895: Jefferson Cole was lynched in Paris.

October 28, 1895: Henry Hilliard, a Negro, was burned alive for murder in Tyler.

November 20, 1895: a Negro man was lynched in Madison County.

1896: The San Saba County lynchers, a vigilante organization, claimed some twenty-five victims over a seventeen-year period through 1896.

January 1896: Aureliano Castellon was lynched in San Antonio.

February 27, 1896: bank robbers Foster Crawford and Elmer Lewis were hanged by a lynch mob in Wichita Falls.

May 3, 1896: William Benby was lynched in Beaumont.

June 10, 1896: George Johnson and Louis Whitehead were lynched in Bryan.

August 13, 1896: Benjamin Gay was lynched in Hopkins County.

1897: The Texas legislature passed an anti-lynching law, the governor called out the Texas Volunteer Guard to help defend prisoners on numerous occasions, and local officers sometimes went to great lengths to protect their prisoners.

1897: Texas state troops were called out four times to protect prisoners from mobs; in one instance they failed to protect their charge from lynching.

January 25, 1897: Eugene Washington was lynched for rape in Bryan.

March 5, 1897: a Negro man was lynched for burglary in Elgin.

April 27, 1897: Robert Brown, Russell Wright, and Hal Wright were lynched for robbery and arson in Sunnyside.

April 30, 1897: William Gates, William Williams, Lewis Thomas, James Thomas, Benjamin Thomas, Aaron Thomas, and Fayette Rhone were lynched for murder in Sunnyside.

May 14, 1897: David Cotton, Sabe Stewart, and Henry Williams were lynched for attempted rape in Rosebud.

May 18, 1897: John and William White and a third Negro man were lynched for murder in San Augustine.

May 21, 1897: Peter Zajelach was lynched in Braun County.

May 23, 1897: William Jones was lynched for murder in Tyler.

July 3, 1897: James Thomas was lynched for "entering a woman's room."

August 6, 1897: Esseck White was lynched for rape in Nacogdoches.

August 10, 1897: Rev. Capt. Jones was lynched for elopement in Paris.

August 26, 1897: a Negro man named Bonner was lynched for rape in Bellville.

November 18, 1897: Thomas Sweat, a Negro, was lynched in Bryan.

April 5, 1898: Carlos Guilen was lynched in Brownsville.

June 3, 1898: Levi Hayden was lynched in Texarkana.

June 6, 1898: George Washington was lynched in Weimar.

August 8, 1898: Dan Ogg was lynched in Palestine.

October 28, 1898: Emanuel Morris, a Negro, was hanged for rape by Texas.

January 13, 1899: Fred Sawyer, a white man, was hanged for rape by Texas.
April 28, 1899: Tom Robinson, a Negro, was hanged for rape by Texas.
July 1, 1899: Allie Thomas was lynched in Waskom.
July 14, 1899: Abe Brown, a Negro, was lynched in Gilead.
July 14, 1899: a Negro man was lynched in Iola.
July 25, 1899: Henry Hamilton was lynched in Navasota.

With the onset of the twentieth century, the number of lynchings in Texas continued; there were twenty-three in 1908, fifteen in 1909, and thirty-two in 1915.[31] One of the most gruesome lynchings in the Lone Star State, and perhaps the nation, occurred in 1916 in Waco. The victim was seventeen-year-old Jesse Washington, an illiterate and "feeble-minded" young African American teen accused of the murder of Lucy Fryer, a white woman married to a prominent cotton farmer from the area. A hasty trial was conducted in which Washington was convicted. Shortly after the trial, a mob grabbed Washington, chained and beat him, castrated him, and then dragged the teenager to the town square and burned him alive. Some 15,000 onlookers witnessed the burning, and also watched as Washington's charred torso was dragged through the streets. Bits of the body were torn off for souvenirs, including fingers and ears, and pictures of the body were used for post cards.[32]

The 1916 Waco lynching focused national attention, once again, on the problem of lynching: a systemic, persistent, and horrifying practice that occurred throughout the South for decades. These killings were often committed with the full knowledge, and sometimes with the active assistance, of law enforcement officials. Lynchings were also treated as entertainment events, and much like the Waco incident, often attended by thousands of spectators, young and old alike.

In 1922 there were fifteen lynchings in Texas but none in 1925. One of the last lynchings occurred on July 13, 1942, in Texarkana when a mob dragged accused rapist Willie Vinson from a hospital bed and hanged him. Governor Coke Stevenson took no action for the crime and stated that "even a white man would have been lynched for this crime."[33]

Although mob action was prevalent in Texas, it must also be said that Texans made important contributions to the anti-lynching movement. Part of this was unintentional: the gruesome and widely publicized 1893 torture-burning of Henry Smith before an assembly of thousands in Paris helped galvanize the emerging anti-lynching movement into action. In a more positive vein, Jessie Daniel Ames of Georgetown, Texas, founded and served as president of the Association of Southern Women for the Prevention of Lynching, the most effective anti-lynching group in the country.[34]

Cracks in the Color Line

In 1903 a prescient W. E. B. Du Bois wrote, "Gentle Reader, for the problem of the Twentieth Century is the problem of the color line."[35] In the face of lynchings and intimidation, social and political segregation, emboldened African Americans and Hispanics began to use the courts and the rule of law to level the playing field in Texas and chip away at the color line.

During the early years of the twentieth century, poll taxes were used to keep African Americans and Hispanics from voting. Another tool to disenfranchise minorities was the "white primary." In Texas, as in most southern states after the Civil War, the Democratic Party was dominant, and any candidate who won a Democratic primary race was virtually assured of victory in the general election. Thus Democratic Party leaders adopted rules that excluded African Americans and Hispanics from participating in Democratic primaries. Furthermore, in 1922, the Texas Legislature passed a law barring African Americans from voting in Democratic primaries altogether.

In 1927, the U.S. Supreme Court, in *Nixon v. Herndon*, overturned the 1922 Texas law as a violation of the Fourteenth Amendment.[36] In response to this ruling, the Texas legislature enacted a new law in which the executive committee of each political party could decide who could vote in its primaries. In 1932, in *Nixon v. Condon*, the Supreme Court struck down this new law as well.[37] In response, the Texas Democratic state convention adopted a resolution banning African Americans from participating in the party's primary. Against the advice of the NAACP, private citizens in Houston promptly challenged the resolution in court. In *Grovey v. Townsend* (1935), the Supreme Court unanimously decided that the Democratic Party was a private organization whose state convention could determine membership qualifications.[38] Later, these same Houstonians—this time working together with the NAACP—fought back, bringing the case of Lonnie E. Smith, a Houston dentist, to the Supreme Court.

In *Smith v. Allwright* (1944), eight justices overturned the *Grovey* decision. They concluded that several state laws made the Texas primary more than just a function of a private organization, but an integral component of the electoral process.[39] As a consequence, the Court ruled, it was unconstitutional to prohibit African Americans from voting in the Democratic primary, including votes for party officials.

In 1929, the League of United Latin American Citizens (LULAC) was formed in Corpus Christi to champion the cause of Mexican Americans. The actions of this group led to the desegregation of a variety of public places in Texas. In 1930, a group of Mexican American parents, with support from

LULAC, filed a lawsuit against the Del Rio Independent School District, challenging the segregation of children of "Mexican and Spanish descent" from white students in the same grade.[40] This was the first class-action lawsuit against a segregated "Mexican school." Although the Texas Court of Civil Appeals did not find school officials guilty of willfully segregating Mexican children, the suit was a harbinger of things to come and put a crack in the color line.

At approximately 8:00 A.M. on December 7, 1941, 181 Japanese warplanes dropped their bombs and torpedoes on the vessels of the U.S. Navy anchored in Pearl Harbor, Hawaii. The Japanese attack ended around 10:00 A.M., leaving severe damage to numerous American warships and airplanes and killing 2,403 military personnel and civilians. The surprise attack quickly vaulted the United States into the Second World War.[41]

Like Reconstruction, World War II represented for minorities the best of times and the worst of times. Ironically, it was the best of times because the war allowed minorities to step up and serve their country, showcasing their patriotism and valor. Oddly enough, it was the worst of times because even in conflict, the social boundaries so well entrenched in the wider society were also institutionalized in the military.

This was reflected in the army's policy on the treatment of black soldiers: the military application of "separate but equal,"[42] which grew out of a statement of policy that the army prepared on September 27, 1940, and subsequently was approved by President Franklin Delano Roosevelt.

In December 1941, the troop strength of the army was 1.6 million soldiers, of which 99,206 (or 6.2 percent) were African Americans; by December 1945 there were 4.2 million individuals in the army, 372,369 of whom were African Americans (roughly 9 percent).[43] Altogether, more than a million African Americans participated in World War II, most serving in racially segregated units.[44] The majority of the 80,000 black Texans who saw military service in World War II were assigned to segregated units usually commanded by white officers. At the same time, it has been estimated that somewhere between 250,000 and 500,000 Hispanics served in the armed forces during the war.

The wartime experiences of African American and Mexican American soldiers from Texas and throughout the South led to a sense of rising expectations regarding their place in society. In other words, many of these nonwhite soldiers believed that if they could fight and die for their country, why couldn't they be treated as equals at home? However, despite helping to win the wars in Europe and the South Pacific, African American and Mexican American soldiers returned home to Texas to face the color line once again. But change was in the offing, and it came from an unlikely source.

In February 1946, in a state that counted 7,724 lawyers, only 23 of whom were African American, Herman Sweatt, a postal worker from Houston, applied for admission to the University of Texas Law School.[45] His application was denied, however, solely because he was African American. Sweatt retained W. J. Durham and future U.S. Supreme Court Justice Thurgood Marshall as his attorneys and brought suit against University of Texas president T. S. Painter and others, claiming that the educational opportunities of African Americans were unequal to those of whites and thus a violation of the equal protection clause of the Fourteenth Amendment.

The court hearing the case delayed it for six months. The continuance was politically motivated in order to allow the state breathing room, and in December, Sweatt's claim was finally denied as the court cited the state's plan to establish a law school for African Americans in February 1947. The Houston-based institution, to be known as the Texas State University for Negroes (later Texas Southern University), was to "serve" African American students by offering them "equal facilities" to those of their white counterparts. In reality, the Texas legislature established the university and its law school to prevent students like Herman Sweatt from attending the University of Texas Law School.[46] Undaunted, Sweatt appealed his case, and it eventually landed at the U.S. Supreme Court.

Meanwhile, on the national scene, the color line was seriously breached on April 10, 1947, when Jackie Robinson signed a contract with the Brooklyn Dodgers and became the first African American to play in white-dominated Major League Baseball.[47] Robinson even went on to garner Rookie of the Year honors and appeared on the cover of *Time* magazine.[48]

The color line in the United States was now under full assault, and the crack broadened and deepened on July 26, 1948.[49] On this day, President Harry S. Truman signed Executive Order #9981, which ended racial segregation in the U.S. Armed Forces. The policy of desegregation was put to the test during the Korean War (1950–53), where it was found that desegregated units fought better than segregated units.[50] If the army could desegregate even during a war, why could not the rest of American society?

In Texas, another event in 1948 stressed the color line, involving LULAC and their legal challenge to segregated schools in the case *Delgado v. Bastrop Independent School System*. The plaintiffs argued that segregation deprived their children of equal facilities and educational instruction. Judge Ben Rice agreed and ordered the cessation of separation by September 1950. The lawsuits challenging segregation and Truman's Executive Order #9981 laid the groundwork for the death blow to segregation in Texas and throughout the South.

In 1950, Herman Sweatt's lawsuit finally found its way to the U.S. Supreme Court.[51] Sweatt's attorneys argued that the state of Texas violated the equal protection clause of the Fourteenth Amendment. Lawyers for the state of Texas argued that Sweatt had no claim due to the doctrine of separate but equal contained in the *Plessy v. Ferguson* case of 1896.[52]

On June 5, the Court issued a unanimous decision, stating that the "Equal Protection Clause of the 14th Amendment required that Sweatt be admitted to the University of Texas Law School."[53] In the fall of that year, Sweatt, along with several other African Americans, enrolled in the UT law school, making it the first southern law school to desegregate. Others were now motivated to challenge the color line as well. Mrs. Myrtle Washington was arrested in Austin, Texas, in August 1953 for refusing to move to the rear of a bus when asked by the driver; she was defended by the Austin chapter of the NAACP. Such actions helped to lead to the demise of Jim Crow laws in Austin and elsewhere in Texas.[54]

The Color Line Collapses

Even though Sweatt never graduated from law school, his actions and persistence paved the way for other minority students challenging the color line.[55] The real deathblow to the color line occurred on May 17, 1954, as a result of a lawsuit that began in Topeka, Kansas. On this day the Supreme Court issued a unanimous decision in the historic case of *Brown v. Board of Education:*

> Segregation of white and Negro children in the public schools of a State solely on the basis of race, pursuant to state laws permitting or requiring such segregation, denies to Negro children the equal protection of the laws guaranteed by the Fourteenth Amendment—even though the physical facilities and other "tangible" factors of white and Negro schools may be equal.[56]

The justices also stated that the separate but equal doctrine as set forth in *Plessy v. Ferguson* had no place in the field of education. The real issue in *Brown* was the timeline for desegregation, and in 1955 the Court determined that desegregation should be implemented "with all deliberate speed."[57]

The legal implications of *Brown* were enormous, but segregation was still a social reality in the United States. A catalyst was needed to shake the social foundations of segregation. The change agent that facilitated a civil rights revolution in America occurred on December 1, 1955, when Rosa Parks refused to give up her seat to a white man on a bus in Montgomery, Alabama.

She was arrested and, after a thirty-minute trial, convicted of violating state law that mandated segregation on public conveyances. (The case led to the famous 381-day Montgomery bus boycott organized by Martin Luther King.) Her case subsequently went before the U.S. Supreme Court, which ruled in 1956 that Alabama's laws requiring segregation on public transportation vehicles were unconstitutional.[58]

The *Brown* decision and the events in Montgomery effectively led to the demise of segregation policies in the South. Although in Texas, public places would no longer be legally segregated, actual desegregation took decades to complete. Controversy was inevitable as well. In 1956, the Mansfield School District (near Fort Worth) was the first in the state ordered to desegregate by a federal court. White mobs then descended on Mansfield High School and prevented three African American students from attending. Governor Allan Shivers sided with the mob, sending in the Texas Rangers to uphold the segregation policies in active defiance of the federal court.[59] Although the Eisenhower administration did not intervene, the episode was a precursor to the showdown at Little Rock's Central High one year later, in which President Eisenhower called in federal troops to enforce the desegregation of the high school despite the governor's attempt to keep the school all-white.[60]

Texas Moves toward a Melting Pot Society

In the history of court-ordered social change, lasting change was achieved primarily through incrementalism, not radical upheavals; through generational transition, not immediate birthing; not after days or months or years, but after decades. In the 1960s, here and there desegregation was taking root in Texas. The racial desegregation of many public facilities in Texas began in the 1960s. For example, on August 15, 1961, a carefully orchestrated plan sent African Americans to lunch counters and businesses throughout the city of Dallas for equal service. This plan, which proceeded without incident, was the work of a biracial committee appointed by the Dallas and African American Chambers of Commerce, which devised a publicity campaign and notified business owners in advance.[61]

Perhaps the earliest examples of desegregation occurred in the realm of sports. In 1965, nearly two decades after Jackie Robinson crossed the color line in professional sports, high school sports in Texas ended racial segregation. The regulating body of Texas high school sports, the University Interscholastic League (UIL), included among its membership criteria, dating from 1919, that only "white" high schools could belong to the organization. Soon after, the Texas Interscholastic League of Colored Schools was formed at Prairie View A&M University to provide the same rules and organization for African American high school sports, and both organizations sponsored playoffs and state championships. It was in 1965, however, that the UIL dropped the color barrier, allowing the organizations to merge.[62]

Also notable on the sports front was the action of Don Haskins, head basketball coach at Texas Western University (now the University of Texas at El Paso). In 1966, Haskins elected to start an all-African American lineup in the NCAA championship game, in which his team upset an all-white Kentucky squad coached by the legendary Adolph Rupp.[63] Haskins is credited with revolutionizing collegiate basketball by opening the door to African American players as never before.[64] In the same year, John Westbrook Hill of Baylor University became the first African American to play varsity football in the Southwest Conference, in spite of horrific abuse at the hands of some of his teammates and coaches.[65]

During the same period, the federal government pursued an agenda designed to achieve racial equality, and Texas Mexican Americans and African Americans both profited from this initiative. On January 23, 1964, the Twenty-fourth Amendment was ratified, barring the poll tax in federal elections; and that same year Congress passed the Civil Rights Act, outlawing Jim Crow. In 1966, Texas repealed the poll tax as a requirement for voting in all elections by amendment to the Texas Constitution. In 1966, Barbara Jordan, a graduate of Texas Southern University, was elected to the Texas Senate, representing part of Houston; she was the first African American to serve there since 1883.[66]

While racial desegregation was slowly transforming Texas politics and athletics, many public school systems were dragging their feet in terms of fully implementing desegregation mandates. The notion of "with all deliberate speed" was mired in litigation. Court-ordered reforms sometimes sped up only after the defendants receive a serious jolt. In November 1970, for example, William Wayne Justice, chief judge of the Eastern District of Texas in Tyler, ordered the Texas Education Agency (TEA) to take over the state's responsibility for desegregating public schools.[67] The decision in *United States v. Texas* applied to the entire Texas public school system and was one of the most extensive desegregation orders in legal history.

United States v. Texas originated with investigations in the late 1960s by the U.S. Department of Health, Education, and Welfare (HEW) into alleged discriminatory practices in a number of small Texas public school districts, most in East Texas. Lacking effective enforcement power, HEW referred the matter to the Justice Department, which was then at the height of its efforts to desegregate the nation's schools. The Justice Department sought to place the state as a whole under federal court order by naming both TEA and the state itself as parties to the lawsuit.[68]

Judge Justice's order consolidated all-African American school districts with adjoining white districts and prohibited school officials from using race as a method for assigning students to schools, from discriminating in extra-curricular activities, or from using segregated bus routes.[69] The TEA was to oversee these remedies and punish violators with the loss of accreditation. Justice's ruling would impact thousands of schools and millions of Texas public school children.

Texas Today

The color line in Texas has been erased, and for all intents and purposes Texas has become a desegregated society. While some may disagree, the old caste systems no longer remain. At issue for many is the definition of a "desegregated society." Do African American, Hispanic, and white children attend public schools and state universities together? Do they compete on desegregated sports teams? Do the three groups shop together at the same malls? Do the three groups live alongside each other in the same apartment complexes across the state? Can you find members of the three groups sitting next to each other at the cinema, lunch counters, restaurants, bars, sporting events, and concerts? Are there African American, Hispanic, and white elected officials serving together in the state capitol? The answers to these questions are unabashedly "Yes."

The latter questions we posed represent objective indicators of racial de-segregation. As measured by these indicators, racial desegregation has been achieved, yet one should not equate racial desegregation with race relations or the more ambiguous concept of racial integration. Indeed, we are not suggesting that race relations in Texas have moved into a period of racial nirvana or that Texas has become the quintessential melting pot. Racial desegregation was achieved only after a bitter and protracted struggle pitting whites against African Americans and Mexican Americans. An untold number of individuals have probably died along the way to preserve a way of life as well as in the attempt to introduce a new way of life. The battle was also waged on urban streets as well as dirt roads in rural backwaters, in the capitol, in the halls of Texas schools, and in the courtroom. Memories of these battles may dim but they are not forgotten. Events such as the one that occurred in Jasper in 1998, when three white men dragged James Byrd, an African American, to his death on a country road, rekindled in the memories of many African Americans images of lynchings and hate.[70]

In the 2006 Houston Survey of African Americans, conducted by researchers at Texas Southern University, African Americans gave race relations an average grade of only forty-eight out of one hundred. Most important, only one out of three African American respondents thought race relations had improved over the last few years, and roughly two out of three believed the government puts the needs and interests of white Americans above those of minorities.[71]

These poll data clearly show the lingering effects of the not-so-distant past when minorities were treated as less than human beings. It will take generations to erase these feelings and suspicions. This much we know: the society initially established by the settlers east of the 98th meridian has been moved to the dustbin of history. Between Reconstruction and 1980, Texas moved along the path of desegregation; sometimes the path was bumpy, and sometimes efforts were launched to derail desegregation, but those efforts ultimately failed and Texas became racially desegregated.

As we suggested in Chapter 1, the first moves against racial segregation began in the wider society with discussions about the political rights of citizenship regarding minorities, especially in the post–World War II years. Such changes as equal access of minorities to public schools and minority participation in professional sports forever altered the relationship between majority and minority in the United States.

Despite the obvious progress, pockets of segregation remained well into the 1980s and 1990s, especially in one peculiar Texas institution, the state prison system. The question we seek to address is this: Based on the history of race relations and efforts to desegregate Texas, what would happen if white, African American, and Mexican American convicts were mixed together in two-person cells? To situate this question in the larger context, we first turn to an examination of desegregation in the Dallas Independent School District and also to desegregation in the one free-world social institution that perhaps most closely resembles that of the penitentiary society—the military.

CHAPTER 3

18,000 Days

In May 1954, the U.S. Supreme Court decided in *Brown v. Board of Education* to end racial discrimination in public educational facilities as well as put an end to the "separate but equal" doctrine that divided the nation into two communities, black and white. On paper, segregation was now illegal, but how in reality was the Court's order to be implemented within school hallways and classrooms? The marbled halls of the Supreme Court in Washington seemed light years away from the segregated schools in states like Texas. Indeed, the timing and implementation of *Brown* weighed heavily on the minds of the justices, especially Chief Justice Earl Warren, who believed that without guidelines for the lower courts there would be confusion and delay.[1]

On May 31, 1955, Chief Justice Warren delivered the Court's opinion in the second *Brown v. Board of Education* decision (known as *Brown II*), setting out the nation's road map to racial desegregation. *Brown II* was a seven-paragraph opinion that reaffirmed the principle that racial discrimination in public education was unconstitutional, and that all federal, state, or local laws requiring or permitting such discrimination was unlawful. *Brown II* also contained the now famous statement that desegregation of the nation's schools must be accomplished "with all deliberate speed."[2]

A Line in the Sand

Soon after the Court's opinion, 100 U.S. congressmen and senators from southern states drafted and signed the Southern Manifesto, a document that voiced opposition to the racial desegregation of public places, especially public schools. The only member of the Texas delegation in Washington who signed the Manifesto was Senator Price Daniel, who was elected in 1952.[3]

Daniel had earlier served as Texas attorney general, and it was he who had defended the University of Texas in the *Sweatt v. Painter* (1946) case, a prelude to the *Brown* litigation.

By etching a line in the sand, the Southern Manifesto foretold a rough implementation process for the desegregation of public schools in the South. The most visible example occurred in Little Rock, Arkansas, where, on September 25, 1957, federal troops from the 101st Airborne Division escorted nine African American students to Central High to begin court-ordered desegregation over the objections of Governor Orval Faubus.[4] Fifty years or some 18,250 days later, in February 2007, the Little Rock school district was finally released from federal supervision in one of the nation's longest school desegregation cases.[5] Was this what Justice Earl Warren intended when he stated that desegregation must proceed with "all deliberate speed"?

Desegregation was also adamantly opposed in the Magnolia State, where white Mississippians were totally unprepared in September 1962 to accept the federal court order issued by Justice Hugo L. Black to register James Meredith, a native African American, as a student at the University of Mississippi. On Sunday afternoon October 1, 1962, a force of 320 federal marshals entered the university campus at Oxford and ushered Meredith to a dormitory. That evening President John Kennedy addressed Mississippians over national television, appealing to their reason and patriotism: "The honor of your university and the state are in the balance." He was already too late, however: the overwhelmed federal marshals were under furious attack, first by students and then by much larger armed mobs admitted by the state troopers that Governor Ross Barnett had promised the president would be used to maintain order. This was not an attack on African Americans or demonstrators per se. Rather, it was an insurrectionary assault on officers and soldiers of the U.S. government and the most serious challenge to the Union since the Civil War.

The mob fought with stones, bricks, clubs, bottles, iron bars, gasoline bombs, and firearms. The besieged marshals, supplemented by federalized Mississippi national guardsmen and later by federal army troops, relied mainly on tear gas. The battle raged all night and by dawn, when the troops had routed the mob, 2 people had been killed and 375 injured, 166 of them marshals, 29 by gunshot wounds. The campus battlefield was littered with wrecked cars and trucks, tear-gas canisters, and other debris. Of the maximum commitment of 30,000 troops, 300 remained until July 1963.[6]

At the time of *Brown*, laws in seventeen southern and border states (Delaware, Maryland, Virginia, West Virginia, Georgia, North Carolina, South Carolina, Florida, Tennessee, Kentucky, Alabama, Mississippi, Louisiana,

Arkansas, Texas, Oklahoma, and Missouri) and the District of Columbia required that public schools be racially segregated. Four other states—Arizona, Kansas, New Mexico, and Wyoming—had laws permitting segregated schools. Although discrimination existed in the other states of the Union, it was not sanctioned by law with regard to segregated public schools.

By the end of 1957, nine of the seventeen states and the District of Columbia had begun desegregating their school systems. No two desegregation implementations were identical. The process and pace all differed. For example, in 1954 at the time of *Brown*, not one public school district in Kentucky was desegregated; however, by 1959, seventy-three districts were desegregated to some degree, and all were desegregated by 1964. A similar pattern of 100 percent compliance with *Brown* by 1964 was observed in West Virginia, Maryland, and Delaware, which, like Kentucky, were border states that had not seceded from the Union during the Civil War era. In contrast, Louisiana, Georgia, Alabama, and Mississippi reported that less than 10 percent of its school districts had been desegregated over the same time period.[7]

Central High and the University of Mississippi represent two examples of the initial impact of desegregation efforts in American educational institutions.[8] Although the "Little Rock Nine" and James Meredith were eventually allowed access to all-white educational settings, vehement opposition meant that it took decades for desegregation to be fully accomplished in accordance with federal court guidelines. Such remedies have varied from place to place, but clearly the most steadfast opposition to desegregation has occurred in the South—especially in the former rebel states that seceded from the Union during the Civil War. In these states, efforts to desegregate often involved periods of extreme violence and intimidation and years of official intransigence. Below, we more fully explore the process of desegregation that unfolded in the Dallas Independent School District (DISD) and in the U.S. Army in order to better understand how desegregation might play out in prisons, and specifically in prison cells. Our focus is on what lessons can be learned about the process of desegregating large social institutions marked by a history of racial and ethnic segregation.

Desegregation of a Free World Institution:
The Dallas Public School System

In Texas, the responses to the *Brown* decisions varied across the 98th meridian. Public schools in West Texas voluntarily desegregated, and sixty school boards decided that the 1955–56 school year would open with biracial classes.

School boards in East Texas, however, blocked efforts to desegregate schools. The lands west of the 98th meridian were open to change. The long-settled area east of this invisible fault line resisted change.

For the black community, the *Brown* decisions represented a means by which to upend the status quo. While the first desegregation battleground was the Mansfield public school system in 1955, this was a rural school system with only a small number of black children. A bigger challenge arose when the black community in Dallas set about to gain access to white schools through the courts. As a result, the Dallas Independent School District (DISD) was the scene of extensive litigation in the 1950s through the 1980s.

In 1955 Rosa and Maude Sims (ages ten and nine) applied for admission to the John Henry Brown School, just four blocks from their home. The school principal refused to admit the girls, citing a school board directive wherein "no negro children could go to school with the whites."[9] The girls were forced instead to attend school at the Charles Rice Elementary School, some eighteen blocks from their home. The school board also maintained that implementation of the *Brown* decree was impractical until an intensive study of the issue was conducted.

Lawyers for the girls filed a lawsuit, *Borders v. Rippy,* against the school district board of trustees, its presidents, and school board members to desegregate the DISD.[10] U.S. District Court Judge William S. Atwell, however, ruled against the plaintiffs. Around the same time, the NAACP brought suit against the DISD in the case of *Bell v. Rippy,* in which once again Atwell ruled against the plaintiffs, claiming that the U.S. Supreme Court had overstepped its power in the *Brown* case.[11] Specifically, Atwell criticized the Court for making law on sociological and not legal principles. In both cases, however, Atwell was overruled by the Fifth Circuit Court of Appeals. Under order of the Fifth Circuit, Dallas began desegregating its schools in the fall of 1961.

The DISD litigation stretched out over six years, twelve court hearings, and eighteen judges, including members of the U.S. Supreme Court.[12] And yet, despite the intense litigation, the DISD in 1961 was still essentially a segregated school system. It was in that year, however, that the DISD implemented the "stair step plan" under the order of the Fifth Circuit Court of Appeals to desegregate the schools. In September 1961, eighteen black students started first grade in previously all-white schools in Dallas, and in 1967 the DISD declared that all its schools had been desegregated.[13] This announcement was premature, however, and actually set the stage for a new round of litigation.[14]

In 1970, Sam Tasby filed a lawsuit that included about two dozen other

African American and Hispanic parents in federal court that charged the DISD with still maintaining a segregated school system. These parents argued that their children were bused all over Dallas to attend same-race schools, whereas the school closest to Tasby's home was an all-white school that had better resources. School officials there had turned down Tasby's request to attend the nearby school and so his son was forced to ride a city bus (at his own expense) to attend another school.[15]

The trial was heard by Federal Judge William Taylor in July 1971. Taylor ordered DISD officials to devise a new desegregation plan for the coming school year. He also ordered the DISD to cease counting Hispanics as whites. DISD officials appealed the ruling, but in the meantime 15,000 school children were bused to new schools to initiate the new desegregation plan. In 1975, the Fifth Circuit Court of Appeals rejected portions of the plan and ordered a new one. In February 1976, Judge Taylor presided over a second trial following which a new plan was devised, which again the Fifth Circuit rejected. When the case returned to his court in 1981, Judge Taylor removed himself from the proceedings.

Judge Harold Barefoot Sanders Jr., who had grown up in Dallas and graduated from North Dallas High School in 1942, took over the case. Sanders held several hearings and ordered both parties to submit new desegregation plans; he also ruled that busing would not solve the problem of segregated schools. In August 1983, the DISD ended its fight against court-ordered desegregation after the Fifth Circuit upheld Sanders's desegregation plan, which involved the discontinuation of busing, the use of local learning centers, the building of magnet schools, and new bond initiatives. Judicial oversight of the case finally ended in 2003 when DISD was declared to be desegregated.

Lessons from the Dallas Situation

The initial school desegregation litigation in Dallas began in 1955, and Dallas schools were finally declared desegregated in 2003, almost five decades or roughly 18,000 days later, or nearly three generations of school children after the first lawsuit. How can the events in the DISD situation inform us about the trajectory of desegregation in Texas prisons? On the face of it, a federal judicial order to desegregate a large prison system appears to be a fairly straightforward matter. Prison administrators could simply get on with it by mixing up the inmates. But one could have said the same thing about desegregating a school system, and yet the Dallas Independent School District example shows that such a process is anything but simple. School desegregation in Dallas required decades to be accomplished in full, given the long history of race relations in the district, the intransigence of local officials, and the ever-changing players who tried to devise a solution acceptable to all parties. Why should prison systems be any different? A prison holds the most violent and least stable individuals in American society, a place where race and racial identity is a dominant influence on behavior. Prison administrators themselves are fiercely traditional and often resist major changes to the institutional setting.

One of the primary lessons from the DISD story is that implementing any desegregation remedy is no easy task. The road is contentious and fraught with emotionalism, resistance, and intransigence. Change is never easy, whether in schools or in prison settings. Indeed, Judge William Taylor's remedies were overturned several times by the Fifth Circuit Court of Appeals, and new solutions were mandated. Achieving a desegregated Dallas public school system involved extensive litigation with numerous lawyers and plaintiffs, numerous judges and numerous plans, and numerous courts at various levels.

Another critical lesson to be learned from the DISD situation involved the issue of time. The DISD was under scrutiny for nearly five decades. Successful compliance with a federal court order was not achieved overnight; instead, the decision to end litigation or federal oversight ended only after thousands of days and many incremental steps. The financial cost of ending a successful remedial decree approaches millions of dollars.

Has desegregation in the DISD been accomplished? In the end we can emphatically say the answer is "yes." Yet numerous unintended consequences developed in the wake of desegregation. Can we say that the desegregation experience within the DISD was worth it? It depends heavily on the yardstick being applied. There are numerous angles by which to suggest an answer to this highly complex and charged question. At the legal level, for example, the DISD has been declared desegregated, and students now attend schools with diverse populations. Along the way, however, the percentage of Anglo students has shrunk considerably due to white flight to the surrounding suburbs. In 1975, Anglos composed 41 percent of the DISD, and this percentage declined to 32 percent in 1979 and to just 8 percent in 2003.[16]

Our goal here is not to thoroughly examine or cover all the complexities of desegregation and white flight or other unintended consequences of school desegregation. Answers to these issues warrant sophisticated statistical analyses beyond the scope of this book. Schools are not prisons, and though students are exposed to a "batch living" situation, their exposure to each other, and to school desegregation policies, is typically less than ten hours per day. Indeed, public high school students can leave campus for lunch, some have "late arrival," and some leave early. School populations are not forced to live with each other in cramped living conditions over a twenty-four-hour span. Yet desegregation of DISD was still a protracted affair.

We intended our limited foray into one school system's protracted experience with school desegregation to illustrate the notion of time. Federal remedies to complex social issues are not implemented immediately, nor are they typically adopted with open arms. Implementation occurs over time, in the Dallas case over decades, involving different judges and decrees, different administrators, and succeeding generations of students. Further, figures on white flight illustrate another important facet of judicial decrees—unintended consequences. Irony often surrounds most judicially mandated solutions to complex social problems, in that the original issue might be successfully remedied but other sizeable and seemingly intractable issues arise. This paradox of reform is not a new finding with regard to judicial intervention into social problems.[17]

The ideas of time, irony, and unintended consequences feature prominently in the desegregation of the Texas prison system. In the next section, we examine the efforts to desegregate another large American social institution, the U.S. military, where individuals are exposed to each other, often times in cramped quarters, seven days a week and twenty-four hours at a time. The experience of desegregation in a school system and the army will prepare us to examine and more fully understand the desegregation of the Texas prison system—including intended and unintended consequences.

Desegregation of a Free World Institution: The Military

In the years preceding World War II, African American journalists, the National Urban League, the NAACP, and the National Negro Congress lobbied hard at the local, state, and national levels to expand opportunities for African Americans. In 1938 the *Pittsburgh Courier*, the largest and one of the most influential of the nation's African American newspapers, called upon the president to open the armed services to African Americans; to help achieve this goal, the newspaper also organized the Committee for Negro Participation in the National Defense Program. These moves led to an extensive lobbying effort that in time spread to many other newspapers and local civil rights groups. Beyond insisting upon equal treatment and opportunity in the armed forces, the activists also argued that the issue was critical to American preparedness for war.[18] Momentum for change was gaining. First Lady Eleanor Roosevelt was firmly behind the burgeoning civil rights movement and used her influence to decry the "separate but equal" treatment of African American citizens at every opportunity.

Other influential voices took the opposite view, however. Secretary of War Henry L. Stimson and Army Chief of Staff George C. Marshall believed the military's segregated units should follow prevailing public attitudes against the co-mingling of the races. After all, racial segregation was the norm in most states, especially in the South, and both Stimson and Marshall respected military tradition: segregated units had been a part of the army since 1863. Also, the ominous specter of war was looming on the horizon, and many believed that this was no time to be making serious changes in military life. Even the attack on Pearl Harbor was not enough to sway top military commanders from their belief in maintaining longstanding conventions. The color line would persist.

On December 8, 1941, the day the United States officially entered World War II, army leaders met with a group of black publishers and editors. The conference concluded with a speech by Col. Eugene Householder, who offered what many considered the final word on desegregation during the war:

> The Army is made up of individual citizens of the United States who have pronounced views with respect to the Negro just as they have individual ideas with respect to other matters in their daily walk of life. Military orders, fiat, or dicta, will not change their viewpoints. The Army then cannot be made the means of engendering conflict among the mass of people because of a stand with respect to Negroes which is not compatible with the position attained by the Negro in civil life. . . . The Army is not a sociological laboratory; to be effective it must be organized and trained according to the principles which will insure success. Experiments to meet the wishes and demands of the champions of every race and creed for the solution of their problems are a danger to efficiency, discipline and morale and would result in ultimate defeat.[19]

Military leaders at the time rejected any attempt to use the armed forces as a laboratory to experiment with desegregation, or to offer the military as an institution that would right the wrongs of discrimination and incivility in the wider society. In effect, then, the army imported the mores of the South into military life, and African American soldiers were separated from white soldiers in almost all aspects of military life. The army even established racially segregated blood banks, a policy approved by the surgeon general that lasted throughout the war.[20] And even though they were segregated from white soldiers, African American servicemen were still subjected to discrimination, both in camps in the United States and in the European and Pacific theaters of operations throughout the war, which inevitably contributed to morale and discipline issues.

In 1943, steps were taken to foster racial harmony and lessen the effects of racial separation. The War Department issued orders to end the policy of racial separation in camp recreational facilities, in post exchanges, and on base transportation. In most cases, however, voluntary separation among the soldiers became the norm. The place where racial separation really held sway was in the units and outfits, the places where the closest of social interactions and encounters eventually took place—like a foxhole in a combat situation.[21]

But what did the ordinary soldier think about racial segregation, especially in wartime? Individuals enter the military from all walks of life, from every corner of American culture, and they bring with them their personal prejudices. Although military commanders did not consider the wartime army to be a laboratory for implementing social policy, it turned out to be the perfect laboratory setting for social researchers. As a result, some of the most comprehensive studies examining race relations have focused on the armed forces. From 1941 to 1946 the Research Branch of the War Department's Information and Education Division was directed by Samuel Stouffer, a prominent American sociologist at the University of Chicago and later at Harvard, who advanced survey research methods and the use of social statistics. Under Stouffer's direction, the Research Branch surveyed over 500,000 American soldiers and examined numerous complex issues, including segregation, race relations, and officer performance, leading to the publication of perhaps the greatest social science work ever produced, *Studies in Social Psychology in World War II: Volumes I–V*, in 1949.[22]

In a 1943 survey examining race relations in the military, Stouffer and colleagues surveyed a nationally representative sample of white and black soldiers from the North and South. We reexamined these data to ascertain white and African American soldiers' attitudes toward desegregation five years before the U.S. Army was officially desegregated in 1948. The results from our reanalysis of Stouffer's data provide a fascinating window at a point before desegregation of one of the largest social institutions in American society, an institution that closely parallels many aspects of life in a prison. The military experience with desegregation also provides us with a window into how incarcerated felons might contemplate or respond to forced desegregation.

The data presented in Table 3.1 illustrate white and African American soldier's attitudes toward racial separation in three areas in military life: the Post Exchange (PX) or commissary/store, the service club, and the outfit.

Table 3.1: White and African American Soldiers' Attitudes toward Segregation, 1943

	Whites (N=4,973)		African Americans (N=7,442)	
Area in military milieu	All	Texans	All	Texans
Separate PX's	79%	84%	34%	54%**
Separate service clubs	83%	93%**	41%	58%**
Separate outfits	86%	94%**	34%	47%**
At least two of the three areas above	54%	56%**	33%	51%**

Source: Author reanalysis of data in "The American Soldier in World War II: Attitudes of Negroes and Attitudes toward Negroes" (1943, March). The Roper Center for Public Opinion Research (USAMS—SO32) at http://www.ropercenter.uconn.edu/.
**p < .01.

These three areas of military life also reflect a social distance scale or zones by which we can measure social relationships. The PX and the service club represent social environments that are "distant" or anonymous and where social relations are not intense or long-term. The military outfit represents that zone where lengthy and intense face-to-face interaction occurs. In our analysis, we also split the soldier respondents into four unique groups for comparison purposes: all white soldiers, white soldiers from Texas, all African American soldiers, and African American soldiers from Texas.

The vast majority of white soldiers favored segregation in all three military milieus. Yet the same cannot be said for African American soldiers. African American soldiers from outside Texas were far more amenable to desegregation, perhaps reflecting a regional bias. African American soldiers from Texas were far more likely to support separation. However, over one-half (53 percent) of the Texas African American soldiers favored desegregated outfits. In short, in military areas where soldiers had to get along to survive, African American soldiers were far more likely to be open to desegregation.

Additional data on the attitudes of soldiers prior to desegregation of the U.S. Army comes from personal interviews of 250 "white company officers and white platoon sergeants" in the European Theater of Operations. The interviews were conducted between late May and early June 1945. The officers were asked to assess the combat performance of "Negro rifle platoons" that

Table 3.2. White Officers' Attitudes on the Combat Performance of "Negro Rifle Platoons," 1945

	Officers	Noncommissioned
Percentage who were initially skeptical about serving in a company with white and African American platoons	64%	64%
Percentage who became more favorable toward African Americans after having served in the same unit with them	77%	77%
Percentage who believed that white and African American soldiers have gotten along "fairly well" or "very well"	80%	96%

Source: Author reanalysis of data in "The American Soldier in World War II: Attitudes of Negroes and Attitudes toward Negroes" (1943, March). The Roper Center for Public Opinion Research (USAMS—SO32) at http://www.ropercenter.uconn.edu/.

were attached to their companies and fought "side by side" with white platoons through the end of the Second World War.[23] The interview data show that nearly two-thirds (64 percent) of the officers and noncommissioned officers or sergeants were "skeptical" at the idea of serving in a company that had both white platoons and African American platoons. These sentiments echo the 1943 survey data presented earlier on the attitudes of ordinary soldiers toward separation of the races.

The data in Table 3.2 underscore the overall skepticism of many white soldiers and officers toward a policy of desegregation of the armed forces. The data also suggest that after contact with African American soldiers in combat situations, feelings of skepticism subsided. Indeed, over three quarters (77 percent) of the officers were more favorable toward African American soldiers, and most believed that white and African American soldiers got along well. The same can be said for ordinary soldiers as well, as one white soldier remarked:[24]

When I heard about it [desegregation], I said I'd be damned if I'd wear the same shoulder patch as they [African American soldiers] did. After that first day when we saw how they fought, I changed my mind. They're just like any of the other boys to us.

In the aftermath of the war, civil rights activists took dead aim at the military and pressed their claim for desegregation to the highest levels of the federal government. A military historian noted:

Civil rights spokesmen had several points to make regarding the use of Negroes in the postwar armed forces. Referring to the fact that World War II began with Negroes fighting for the right to fight, they demanded that the services guarantee a fair representation of Negroes in the postwar forces. Furthermore, to avoid the frustration suffered by Negroes trained for combat and then converted into service troops, they demanded that Negroes be trained and employed in all military specialties. They particularly stressed the correlation between poor leaders and poor units. The services' command practices, they charged, had frequently led to the appointment of the wrong men, either black or white, to command black units. Their principal solution was to provide for the promotion and proper employment of a proportionate share of competent black officers and noncommissioned officers. Above all, they pointed to the humiliations black soldiers suffered in the community outside the limits of the base. One particularly telling example of such discrimination that circulated in the black press in 1945 described German prisoners of war being fed in a railroad restaurant while their black Army guards were forced to eat outside. But such discrimination toward black servicemen was hardly unique, and the civil rights advocates were quick to point to the connection between such practices and low morale and performance. For them there was but one answer to such discrimination: all men must be treated as individuals and guaranteed equal treatment and opportunity in the services. In a word, the armed forces must integrate. They pointed with pride to the success of those black soldiers who served in integrated units in the last months of the European war, and they repeatedly urged the complete abolition of segregation in the peacetime Army and Navy.[25]

Ending all doubts about desegregation, President Harry S. Truman issued *Executive Order #9981* on July 26, 1948:

EXECUTIVE ORDER 9981

Establishing the President's Committee on Equality of Treatment and Opportunity In the Armed Forces.

WHEREAS it is essential that there be maintained in the armed services of the United States the highest standards of democracy, with equality of treatment and opportunity for all those who serve in our country's defense:

NOW THEREFORE, by virtue of the authority vested in me as President of the United States, by the Constitution and the statutes of the United

States, and as Commander in Chief of the armed services, it is hereby ordered as follows:

I. It is hereby declared to be the policy of the President that there shall be equality of treatment and opportunity for all persons in the armed services without regard to race, color, religion or national origin. This policy shall be put into effect as rapidly as possible, having due regard to the time required to effectuate any necessary changes without impairing efficiency or morale.

2. There shall be created in the National Military Establishment an advisory committee to be known as the President's Committee on Equality of Treatment and Opportunity in the Armed Services, which shall be composed of seven members to be designated by the President.

3. The Committee is authorized on behalf of the President to examine into the rules, procedures and practices of the Armed Services in order to determine in what respect such rules, procedures and practices may be altered or improved with a view to carrying out the policy of this order. The Committee shall confer and advise the Secretary of Defense, the Secretary of the Army, the Secretary of the Navy, and the Secretary of the Air Force, and shall make such recommendations to the President and to said Secretaries as in the judgment of the Committee will effectuate the policy hereof.

4. All executive departments and agencies of the Federal Government are authorized and directed to cooperate with the Committee in its work, and to furnish the Committee such information or the services of such persons as the Committee may require in the performance of its duties.

5. When requested by the Committee to do so, persons in the armed services or in any of the executive departments and agencies of the Federal Government shall testify before the Committee and shall make available for use of the Committee such documents and other information as the Committee may require.

6. The Committee shall continue to exist until such time as the President shall terminate its existence by Executive order.

Nearly five decades later, sociologists Charles C. Moskos and John Sibley Butler maintained that the army had become the most successfully desegregated free world institution in America.[26] This is not to say that the army has evolved into a racial utopia or is a "colorless society" devoid of racial conflict.

Following President Truman's executive order in 1948, there were instances of racial unrest, including race riots, aboard navy ships and other military installations.[27] Over the years there have been incidents of racially motivated violence in the military, including a race-related killing in 1995 at Fort Bragg and the formation of skinhead groups and other racist organizations.[28] Moreover, several military service men and women have reported negative racial encounters in today's military, such as being drawn into racially offensive conversations based on one's race or ethnicity.[29]

Despite these negative events, racial incidents have been rare in the military overall and do not represent the majority experience. Moskos and Butler believe that certain aspects of the military are attributable to positive racial outcomes following desegregation. They maintain that interracial relations are better in combat than in the garrison, stronger on duty than off, and better on the military post than off the base—in short, the more military the environment (and the closer the living conditions), the better the interracial relations. The findings from research on military desegregation suggest that even though soldiers may prefer to be among their own race, forced desegregation did not lead to disproportionate levels of violence, negative interracial attitudes, or racially motivated attacks. These findings seem to mesh well with numerous examinations of military life couched within a discussion of race relations.[30]

The reasons for the success of desegregation in the military were examined in a 2004 research note in the *Harvard Law Review* called "Lessons in Transcendence: Forced Associations and the Military," which provides a useful example for studying the consequences of forced desegregation in a prison environment. The author notes that the military "is not only the most thoroughly but also the most successfully integrated institution in American society—once plagued by rampant racial exclusion and hostility, the military has transcended many of the conflicts, with lasting effects on individuals who pass through it."[31] The military has characteristics that promote an environment for positive interracial coexistence, including discrete groupings, rigid equality, enforced discipline structure and shared missions, experiences, responsibilities, and rewards. In short, the military environment promotes "equal status" contact, many aspects of which are not foreign to prison environments.[32]

Lessons Learned from the Military Situation

Desegregation of the U.S. military involved a massive undertaking on the part of the military establishment as well as a complete shift in military thinking, ethos, and administration. Old customs died hard, and pressure from outside forces provided the eventual impetus for change. Military leaders certainly did not want to desegregate the armed forces in the months and years prior to World War II, and urged elements seeking change to leave well enough alone. However, change was in the offing, and the culmination of pressure from forces outside and inside the armed forces eventually led to desegregation.

From our brief review of the military's experience with desegregation, several themes have emerged that will guide our examination of desegregation within the Texas prison system. First, pressure from the outside was exerted on military leaders to end separation. Second, military leaders resisted any effort to change longstanding polices about segregation and strove to maintain the status quo. Third, the pattern of desegregation within the military paralleled the "zones of desegregation" outlined in Chapter 1—from the broad to the specific. The War Department instructed camp commanders to end long-standing policies of separation within recreational facilities, general transportation arrangements, post exchanges, and even in social clubs, as well as to remove "whites only" and "black only" signs. Though soldiers voluntarily segregated themselves, the military before the war's end was implementing desegregation, but gradually. Desegregation began broadly in the outer fringes or zones of military life and gradually coursed its way to the inner and final realm—the fighting unit—a process that took years to finally unfold. The unit was the last bastion of separation in the military, and separation was still the norm at the conclusion of World War II.

Fourth, most soldiers were skeptical about desegregation. Fifth, only through an executive order in 1948 did separation throughout the armed services in all areas officially end, and the Korean War (1950–53) was the first conflict where desegregated fighting units took the field and fought the enemy, nearly 4,000 days after Pearl Harbor. Sixth, desegregation of military units did not lead to massive disciplinary problems, racial strife, or unusual levels of interracial conflict. In fact, the more military the environment, the more productive the racial interaction. Seventh, co-mingling of racial and ethnic groups has become part of military custom and tradition, and is now ingrained within military society. Eighth, irony abounds in that integration in the military began so fitfully and yet today the U.S. military is probably the most desegregated free world social institution in American society.

Conclusion

The brief case histories presented in this chapter on desegregation in the Dallas Independent School District and the U.S. military illustrate important facets of what one might expect when a policy of desegregation is mandated for a large state prison system. It goes without saying that neither public schools nor the military exactly mirror the prison situation. Yet all three social institutions share two critical similarities worth underscoring: all three involve some exposure to batch living, and all three involve situations wherein the individuals in charge have no control over prejudices that individuals bring to the setting.

Based on the experience of desegregation in the Dallas public schools and the U.S. military, we might expect the following steps to unfold in the face of efforts to desegregate the Texas prison system: (1) efforts to desegregate the prison system will be adamantly opposed; (2) prison managers will stress the need for the status quo; (3) prison managers will engage in abject intransigence and use threats of prisoner violence and conflict as rationales to avoid compliance with orders to desegregate; (4) external pressures will force compliance with efforts to desegregate the prison system; (5) desegregation of the Texas prison system will unfold over the course of decades of legal maneuvering and eventually will become ingrained in tradition; and (6) desegregation will occur in the outer zones of prisons (e.g., work and programmatic settings) first and slowly move inward toward areas of the most intense and potentially the most combustible interaction—prison living areas, specifically two-person cells. We turn now to the Texas prison system—a place that by and large was insulated from the great social upheavals that roiled across America in the 1950s, 1960s, and 1970s.

PART II

THE INSIDE

CHAPTER 4

The Color Line Persists

The Color Line in American Prisons, Pre-1968

One of the persistent and enduring issues in prisoner management is maintaining control and order. Keeping the peace is critical when confining criminals. Inmate classification is the key to keeping order, and sorting and splitting the inmate population into similar groups enhances order, safety, and predictability. Even inmates like predictability.

In early American prisons, particularly among male convicts, the population was typically split along age and criminal sophistication. Young were kept from old, and the hardened criminals were kept from the "rubes" or less experienced offenders. Most important, prison managers separated prisoners by race. The classification and treatment of prisoners based on race emerged early on as one of the most persistent features of prison regimes across the country.[1] Indeed, one of America's earliest experiments with the penitentiary, Eastern State Penitentiary in Philadelphia, was rife with racial segregation. More than 100 years after this penitentiary admitted its first prisoner, inmates at Eastern State remained grouped and sorted by race. As Johnston remarked of Eastern State in the 1940s: "The institution was largely segregated. In the late 1940s African Americans—whose number rose from less than a third of the population before the war to more than half in 1948—were housed in cellblock four and the ground floor of cellblock five. . . . Cellblocks seven and twelve were entirely white."[2]

Segregation by race was not limited to housing arrangements, and it pervaded every aspect of prison life in Eastern State and at other early U.S. penal institutions. Prisoners were routinely segregated by race in work and field assignments, grooming facilities (e.g., inmate barbershops, showers), and dining areas.[3] Even recreational activities, such as prisoner sports teams and glee clubs, were segregated by race. For example, a 1913 article from Eastern State's weekly prison newspaper, *The Umpire*, reported the score of a convict football game between "whites" and "light blacks."[4] In the 1930s Texas prison system, same-race baseball games were routinely held. Former Texas prison manager Lee Simmons recalled the games:

> I got a heap of fun out of the Negro ball games. . . . The first game I want to tell you about was between the Negroes of Central Farm (Sugar Land) and the Negroes of Clemens Farm (Brazoria). . . . The hotter it got, the more the pitcher mopped his face on his sleeve. Miles [assistant manager of the Clemens Farm team] took one startled look at that pitcher and shouted: "Flanagan [captain of the Central Farm team], you old son of a sodalitarian, you've got your white pitcher and catcher in there! Get 'em out!"
>
> Flanagan had had his stage-show man get out his make-up kit and blacken the two white players to match the complexion of the rest of the team.[5]

Racial segregation of varying degrees existed in prison systems across the United States prior to 1960, but this practice was most extreme in the South.[6] There, entire prisons were racially segregated well into the 1960s and beyond in some states. Undoubtedly linked to the legacy of slavery and post-slavery forms of racial subjugation, the southern value system imported from the "outside" mandated that prisoners of different races on the "inside" could not be housed (or worked or recreated) together under any circumstances. According to one noted prison scholar, state laws in the South providing for prisoner segregation before the 1960s

> did not reflect the judgment of prison officials that blacks and whites could not be integrated without jeopardizing safety and security, but a societal and legislative judgment that blacks and whites should not share the same facilities. Racial segregation in the South, like all other pre-1954 segregation, was part of the total sociopolitical system whose aim was to keep blacks separated, subordinated, and exploited.[7]

Perhaps the most egregious examples of racial segregation come from states in the Deep South.[8] A 1940 Alabama law, for example, provided for the strict segregation of white and "colored convicts" in state prisons and local jails. The statute read:

> [In the state's penal institutions] there shall be proper separation. . . . White and colored convicts [shall not be] chained together or allowed to sleep

together. . . . Arrangements shall be made for keeping white and colored convicts at separate prisons and they shall not be allowed to be kept at the same place. . . . Each county jail or city prison must contain separate compartments for whites and negroes and racially segregate both facilities.[9]

Much of the same was found in other southern prison systems. The infamous turn-of-the-century plantation prison, Parchman Farm in Mississippi, was officially divided into racially segregated field camps until the early 1970s, when federal judge William Keady ordered Parchman officials to "eliminate all racially discriminatory practices at the prison," including the segregated field camps.[10] Arkansas's Tucker and Cummins prison farms were racially segregated as well—white inmates were incarcerated at Tucker and black inmates at Cummins.[11] This practice extended well into the early 1970s.

Any deviation from the segregation tradition in the Arkansas prison system received immediate negative reaction—even beyond prison walls. In January 1968, when Tucker prison warden Tom Murton bused over several black and white female inmates from the Women's Reformatory (located at Cummins Prison Farm) for a prisoner dance at Tucker, the backlash was harsh. As Murton recalled, the "reaction of the immediate community, and the whole state, was anger. I had committed three offenses: I had let dances occur at the prison, I had let prisoners dance, and I had allowed Negroes to dance with whites."[12] One angry Arkansas citizen wrote to Warden Murton and provided his thoughts about the interracial prisoner dance:[13]

Well Mr. Murton

By what we see in the paper seems like you are all have a fine time at the Tucker Farm. I did not know when a person was sent to prison he went there for a good time. If he commeted a crim he was to pay for it by being in confinement you are latting them dance and have fun leading u to no telling what.

Fine thing for a white women and a white girl dance with a stinking NEGGER. What on earth is the world coming to I am glad that I have seen the only good times on this earth as I am noy 75 years of age but I am a 100% white man and can not stand the stink of a NEGGER. Some time there will be a time when the white race will be Mollatos we will have no pure white blood.

From a white man to a bunch of fools.

Female prisoners were not immune from racial segregation in the South, although segregation was not as extensive as that found among male convicts. Female prisoners of different races were allowed to coexist at the same prison, yet they were strictly housed in racially segregated cell blocks or dormitories. When Alabama's Julia Tutwiler Prison for Women was completed in 1942, five cell blocks were reserved exclusively for black female prisoners and two cell blocks for white female prisoners. Like housing arrangements and other functions of the prison, separate dining halls were provided for the different races.[14]

Racial separation characterized the prison routine in the northern states as well, but the practice was slightly different than the total racial isolation found in the South. Prisoners of different races in the North were housed in the same prison units (much like females in the South), but they were often strictly segregated by race *within* these facilities. Barnes and Teeters summarized the practice in 1959: "Negroes have been segregated from whites in most prisons where they appear in appreciable numbers. . . . Few northern prisons exercise the courage and social insight to break with outmoded customs of racial segregation."[15]

The Persistence of Racial Segregation in American Prisons

Racial segregation was a defining feature of American prison life before the 1960s, and to various degrees afterward. Racial segregation in prisons and jails was authorized, indeed mandated, in numerous states prior to the U.S. Supreme Court's generalized prohibition of segregation in its 1954 *Brown v. Board of Education* decision.[16] Little changed, however, following this landmark decision with regard to racial segregation in prisons. Even after the Court's 1968 dictate (in *Lee v. Washington*) that racial segregation in prisons and jails was unconstitutional under most routine prison circumstances, this practice endured. Such segregationist policies and practices continued with little fanfare or outside criticism.

Change would come to prisons of the 1970s regarding racial segregation—prisoners of different races by this time were allowed to coexist in the same prison institutions—yet it was still the practice of prison administrators in the South that inmates of different races be housed in racially segregated cell blocks, cell block tiers, and cells.[17] Inmates at this time also remained segregated in outside field squads, dining facilities, shower areas, and nearly every other aspect of prison life.

Change would continue to occur over the ensuing decades concerning racial segregation, but it was slow and uneven. By the 1980s and 1990s, for example, inmates of different races were commonly housed in the same cell blocks, worked side-by-side in the fields, and were mixed in other aspects of prison life—progress of a fashion. With only a few specialized exceptions, however, there was little large-scale mixing of the races within cells.

At the turn of the new millennium, prison systems had instituted official policies proscribing racial discrimination in housing assignments and other aspects of prison operation. Yet few had required the racial desegregation of prison cells.[18] While there has been progress toward the desegregation of prison inmates over the last several decades, it is far from uniform and vestiges of this practice are still found in prison systems across the country today.[19]

Over time, racial segregation to one degree or another emerged as part of the fabric and culture of most prison systems in America. Yet as the character of racial segregation changed over the decades, so too did the rationale for this practice. Pre-1960s racial segregation in prisons was heavily influenced by the racial and economic caste system that characterized life outside of prisons in all areas of the country—particularly in the South. When these reasons for racial segregation on the outside were ruled unconstitutional by the 1950s U.S. Supreme Court, racial segregation continued on the inside because prison administrators were relatively insulated from criticism from outside entities. Because the targets of racial segregation were prisoners, few took notice or even cared.

When insulation from public scrutiny eroded by the 1970s, racial segregation persisted in prisons because it was a long-held tradition in the type of institution where tradition mattered—it was just what was to be done. A total institution like a prison relies on tradition to bring a measure of routine and predictability to an unpredictable environment filled with unpredictable individuals—according to prison administrators.[20] But when the traditional justification for racial segregation came under criticism by the late 1970s and 1980s, segregation was instead justified as necessary for the avoidance of race-based prisoner violence. This is a justification that still resounds today in various prison systems across the country.

The persistence of racial segregation in prisons came to symbolize the last vestige of government-imposed racial segregation in America. Perhaps the single most important reason for the maintenance of the racial status quo, despite its erosion in the wider society, had to do with the status of prisoners.

Courts and the Changing Status of Prisoners

As numerous prison scholars have noted, prisons prior to the 1960s were closed in the sense that prison officials were given considerable deference to run their institutions with little interference from legislatures, courts, or other outside influences.[21] Provided that prisons were not overly burdensome on public funds and that prisoners were pacified and contained, prison administrators had almost unlimited latitude in the day-to-day management of the inmate population.[22] For all intents and purposes, prisons prior to the 1960s were out-of-sight and out-of-mind places with little scrutiny from outsiders.

In the sense that prisons were closed institutions operated on the whims of administrators, prisoners themselves were largely an invisible lot. In what has become a now well-known expression, prisoners prior to the 1960s were relegated to the legal status of "slaves of the state."[23] Such a status meant that prisoners had little redress to challenge the conditions of their confinement and the overall operation of prison institutions. At the most basic level, prisoners were an excluded class not eligible for the rights and privileges enjoyed by free citizens. Fueled by this logic of exclusion, prison administrators took advantage of the slave status of prisoners, and employed harsh methods to keep them subservient and controlled.

By the 1960s, the unchecked administration of prisons was being challenged. The primary change agent came from the momentum of the civil rights movement of the 1950s and 1960s. During this movement on the outside, "one marginal group after another—blacks, poor people, welfare mothers, mental patients, women, children, aliens, gays, and the handicapped—pressed for admission into the societal mainstream."[24] Much, though certainly not all, of the transformation in the societal place of the marginalized came as a result of Supreme Court action in which it created public policy and demanded remedial action.[25] This movement was also heavily influenced by the Civil Rights Act of 1964 and other significant federal initiatives that not only prohibited discrimination by race, color, religion, sex, and national origin, but in general were meant to equalize status in American society.

In a progression of change which originated outside of prison walls and moved inward, the remaining marginalized class in American society, prisoners, sought inclusion into the mainstream. The road to societal inclusion of prisoners was heavily influenced by the rulings of the Supreme Court, just as it had been for other marginalized groups in the backdrop of the civil rights movement.[26] Among all Supreme Court actions, none was perhaps as important to prisoners' efforts at social inclusion as the Court's efforts at incorporation. Incorporation is a process whereby through Court rulings certain provisions of the Bill of Rights were incorporated under the due process and equal protection clauses of the Fourteenth Amendment. Once provisions of the Bill of Rights were incorporated, such as the Eighth Amendment's prohibition of cruel and unusual punishment, this allowed the federal judiciary to scrutinize the actions of state and local governmental officials under these amendments—and hence, the actions of state and local prison officials.

The importance of incorporation to prisoner efforts to obtain the basic rights of citizenship cannot be overemphasized. The Bill of Rights was originally meant to apply only to the actions of federal governmental officials. Therefore, violations of individual rights by state and local governmental officials could only be remedied by the provisions of state constitutions and laws.[27] This was problematic for state and local prisoners who sought redress from what they viewed as illegal treatment and violations of their rights. Because state court judges were usually elected or political appointees, "there is little indication that many judges were so inclined" to seriously consider prisoner complaints under existing state laws and constitutions. State judges' "close connections to and dependence on State and local politics made their independence suspect."[28]

One of the most significant actions by the Court to impact prisoners was the 1964 ruling in *Cooper v. Pate*.[29] This case involved an appeal from a Black Muslim prisoner incarcerated at the Illinois State Penitentiary (also known as Stateville) who claimed his rights to religious freedom were being violated. Cooper was denied access to his Koran and an opportunity to worship his religion by prison officials who felt that Islam's religious legitimacy was suspect. The Seventh Circuit Court of Appeals ruled in favor of prison officials' discretion to deny Cooper the opportunity for religious worship. The court remarked broadly that federal courts should not be the superintendents of state prisons—rather the operation of prisons should be left to prison administrators.[30] On a writ of certiorari, the U.S. Supreme Court reversed the Seventh Circuit and held that prisoners had a right to sue state government officials under Title 42, Section 1983 of the United States Code, for depriving them of their federal constitutional rights and/or those given by federal law while they were imprisoned.[31]

In a broader analysis, the *Cooper* decision constituted recognition by the Court that prisoners were persons under the Constitution, with constitutional rights (such as the freedom to worship one's own religion) that could be violated by state prison officials. The Supreme Court's opinions provided "a vehicle for litigation challenging correctional administration (Section 1983) . . . and a legal basis for judges' intervention in corrections (the Eighth Amendment and other elements of the Bill of Rights incorporated into the due process clause of the Fourteenth Amendment)."[32] The receptivity of the federal court to prisoner complaints "destroyed the custodians' absolute power and the prisoners' isolation from the larger society. And the litigation in itself heightened prisoners' consciousness and politicized them."[33]

The broader holding of the *Cooper* decision, along with the Court's efforts at incorporation, had a massive impact on the societal place of prisoners. The once marginalized, invisible, and excluded class of prisoners was now highly visible and charged. Predictably, hundreds of prisoners' rights lawsuits followed in the late 1960s and 1970s.[34] These lawsuits challenged virtually every aspect of prison operation from discipline and medical care to generalized conditions of confinement.[35] Unlike the hands-off stance of the federal courts prior to the 1960s, the federal judiciary now took an active role in shaping the administration of prisons in the ensuing twenty years following the *Cooper* decision. In one of its first decisions in the "hands on" era, the Court addressed racial segregation and discrimination in prisons.

The U.S. Supreme Court's Mandate to Desegregate Prisons, 1968

In 1966, a three-judge panel from the Middle District of Alabama scrutinized the 1940 state law (quoted in part above) that required "white and colored" convicts to be kept at separate prisons.[36] When held in county and local jails, prisoners of different races were to be kept in "separate compartments."[37] In an opinion which relied heavily on the U.S. Supreme Court's holding in *Brown v. Board of Education,* the three-judge district court struck down Alabama's segregation statute and remarked that "this Court can conceive of no consideration of prison security or discipline which will sustain the constitutionality of state statutes that on their face require complete and permanent segregation in all the Alabama penal facilities."[38]

On appeal, the U.S. Supreme Court affirmed *per curiam* (the Court acting as one voice) the district court's ruling in *Lee v. Washington* (1968):

> This appeal challenges a decree of a three-judge District Court declaring that certain Alabama statutes violate the Fourteenth Amendment to the extent that they require segregation of the races in prisons and jails, and establishing a schedule for desegregation of these institutions. . . . The remaining contention of the State is that the specific orders directing desegregation of prisons and jails make no allowance for the necessities of prison security and discipline. . . . We do not so read the "Order, Judgment and Decree" of the District Court, which when read as a whole we find unexceptionable.[39]

In concurrence, Justice Hugo Black, joined by Justices John Harlan and Potter Stewart, remarked:

> In joining the opinion of the Court, we wish to make explicit something that is left to be gathered only by implication from the Court's opinion. This

is that *prison authorities have the right, acting in good faith and in particularized circumstances, to take into account racial tensions in maintaining security, discipline and good order in prisons and jails.* We are unwilling to assume that state and local prison authorities might mistakenly regard such an explicit pronouncement as evincing any dilution of this Court's firm commitment to the Fourteenth Amendment's prohibition of racial discrimination. (emphasis added)[40]

According to the Court in *Lee,* racial segregation in prisons and jails was unconstitutional save for special and particular circumstances where segregation may be needed to maintain security and order. Yet this brief *per curiam* decision, along with an equally brief concurrence, led to several questions about the desegregation of prison inmates. For example, the Court never explained how desegregation was to be accomplished (e.g., voluntarily or by force) or which "particularized circumstances" might justify the segregation of the races as these circumstances were never defined (such as racial tensions, or a limited racial disturbance versus a full-scale race riot). The Court also failed to clarify whether such particularized circumstances, provided they were valid, implied a temporary or long-term policy of racial segregation or whether such segregation should then apply to an entire prison, a certain housing area within a prison, or simply to certain individuals. The Court also neglected a discussion of the degree of desegregation that would be required by prison officials, for example, in two-person or multiple-occupant cells, in dormitory housing areas, within all these areas, or if simply some aspect of broader desegregation would suffice—such as allowing inmates of different races to coexist in the same prison facility.[41]

Although the *Lee* decision was clear in an overall sense of prohibiting automatic forms of racial segregation behind prison walls, the lack of particulars meant that racial segregation would persist in prison systems across the nation. Without a court-ordered road map, prison administrators adopted a "wait-and-see" approach to racial desegregation.[42] Prison administrators believed the volatile clientele of the prison environment alone constituted the particularized circumstances situation announced in *Lee.* Therefore, racial segregation continued largely unabated in U.S. prisons with little criticism.[43]

While prison administrators waited to see what would happen, the particulars of racial segregation were left to the lower federal courts. On a case-by-case basis, the lower federal courts carved out what constituted the sort of special and particularized circumstances that might permit correctional administrators to employ racial segregation. They then attempted to force prison administrators to desegregate their institutions in the absence of these circumstances.

Lower Federal Court Rulings on Desegregation

Since *Lee,* there have been numerous federal court cases dealing with prisoner desegregation.[44] Some states have experienced multiple prisoner lawsuits on the issue, while others remain unscathed by the lower courts.[45] Across all these cases, the most consistent position taken by administrators, correctional officers, and some inmates was that desegregation would result in extreme racial violence kept at bay by racial segregation.[46]

Pre-1960s racial segregation in prisons was justified in the larger societal context of keeping blacks "separated, subordinated, and exploited" in all social arenas. Once this justification was invalidated by the Court in *Brown,* the legal rationale prison administrators, correctional officers, and inmates of the late 1960s through the 1990s offered to the lower federal courts was that racial segregation was necessary to prevent racial violence. Racial segregation in prisons was not a policy borne out of racism according to prison administrators and other segregation advocates; rather, it was to protect inmates' safety.[47] Such potential for racial violence, according to prison administrators, satisfied the "particularized circumstances" requirement announced in *Lee,* and thus justified the continued segregation of inmates by race.

In an overall analysis, courts have been reluctant to accept that "speculative" racial tensions and "vague" fears of racial violence constitute the sort of particularized circumstances warranting continued racial segregation in prisons.[48] In the aftermath of the *Lee* decision, several major desegregation cases in the lower federal courts espoused the "fear of violence" argument.[49]

In one of the earliest fear-of-violence cases, *Rentfrow v. Carter* (1968), the District Court for the Northern District of Georgia declined to issue an injunction to stop the desegregation of "all penal institutions within the state" as ordered by a previous three-judge panel in this same district court.[50] In *Rentfrow,* a group of white and black prisoners incarcerated in the Georgia State Prison at Reidsville, fearing racial violence in the face of forced desegregation, "pray that a 'strictly voluntary and freedom of choice' [desegregation plan] be substituted for mandatory desegregation."[51] In response, the court in *Rentfrow* remarked that racial tensions do not constitute a "license for 'violent resistance.' . . . Rather, the tensions generate a need for a higher degree of restraint, for those who follow the path of 'violent resistance' will not halt desegregation, but will merely bring their own conduct to a halt by disciplinary action and criminal sanctions."[52]

In *McClelland v. Sigler* (1971), racial segregation was held to be unconstitutional in a maximum security housing unit in the Nebraska Penal and Correctional Complex. Fifty white inmates were housed in "East Cell House" because they refused to be housed with black inmates. The Eighth Circuit Court of Appeals affirmed a lower district court decision and held that Nebraska prison administrators' refusal to desegregate based on fears of racial violence was unjustified. The court remarked: "If disruptions would occur as a result of the desegregation of this facility we would expect that administrators would take appropriate action against the offending inmates. . . . The image of the entire Nebraska penal system being held at bay by fifty prisoners is unacceptable. . . . To reward them [inmates] for their intransigent racial attitudes, cannot be legally sanctioned."[53]

Using this same rationale in 1973, the Tenth Circuit Court of Appeals held in *United States v. Wyandotte County, Kansas* that the speculative fear of racial violence in the Wyandotte County jail did not justify a racial segregation policy. The court remarked that segregation in the Wyandotte County Jail "finally boils down to . . . a vague fear on the part of the authorities that desegregation may result in violence. This is not enough."[54]

In *Mickens v. Winston* (1978), a Virginia federal district court ruled that fears of racial violence due to inadequate supervision levels (because of lack of funding) did not justify inmate racial segregation.[55] In *Stewart v. Rhodes* (1979), an Ohio federal district court held that prison officials of the Columbus Correctional Facility were unable to produce evidence to justify a policy of racial segregation based on the mere belief of possible racial violence. The court noted that "because integration has not even been attempted . . . within the past ten years, prison officials could not have had any experience with the effects of integration on which to base their apprehensions."[56]

In *Blevins v. Brew* (1984), a Wisconsin inmate sought monetary damages from a correctional officer who had a policy of segregating newly arrived inmates by race. The correctional officer allegedly based his practice on the growing number of race-based inmate gangs and fears of inmate-on-inmate assaults. The practice, as argued, was that segregating incoming inmates by race served to protect them from predatory attacks by other inmates. The court for the Western District of Wisconsin acknowledged that the correctional officer did not act out of racial prejudice, but nonetheless ruled in favor of the inmate plaintiff on the grounds that the officer had followed his racial segregation practice without proof that racial violence would result without it.[57]

A massive riot broke out in Ohio's Lucasville correctional facility in 1993, a year after prison cells were desegregated pursuant to a consent decree. One alleged reason for the riot was that prison administrators mistakenly believed that the consent decree required inmate desegregation without considering other factors to promote prison security, such as the criminal sophistication of inmates, prior incarcerations, racial gang affiliation, and prior prison behavior.[58] In response to the violence, in *White v. Morris* (1992/1993) the District Court for the Southern District of Ohio deferred to prison officials' judgment that segregation should take temporary precedence over the desegregation of offenders in light of the violent uprising.[59] This deference to prison officials permitted a temporary respite from desegregation, not a long-standing abandonment of this policy.

One of the most recent fear-of-violence cases comes from Louisiana, where the Fifth Circuit Court of Appeals ruled in *Sockwell v. Phelps* (1994) that Angola's prison cells be desegregated. Angola's prison was found to have racially segregated its double cells on the basis of generalized fears of racial violence, contrary to the particularized circumstances requirement enunciated in *Lee*.[60] After an earlier 1975 court order in *Williams v. McKeithen* (1975), which required that Angola be a completely desegregated facility, a prison official testified that it remained the policy at Angola not to desegregate two-man cells.[61] The basis for this policy was several interracial incidents that had occurred in the 1970s. However, only two incidents of interracial violence could be recalled by prison authorities, and it was never revealed whether racial tension or animosity precipitated these incidents. In attempting to demonstrate that their policy was supported by the types of "particularized circumstances" to warrant inmate segregation, prison administrators cited several factors: (1) prison guards were unable to visually monitor cells, (2) prisoners in Angola are the "worst of the worst," (3) two instances of interracial violence occurred involving integrated cell partners, (4) racial supremacy groups existed in the prison ranks, and (5) interracial conflicts may have triggered more generalized racial violence.[62] The court remarked that although the "particularized circumstances" exception in *Lee* had not been specifically defined, "the general rule is clear: a generalized or vague fear of racial violence is not a sufficient justification for a broad policy of racial segregation."[63]

Collateral Issues

There have been many other rulings on racial desegregation in prison facilities in which the issue of desegregation has been a component of a larger and more encompassing order against a state prison system. In *Taylor v. Perini* (1972), for example, Ohio prison officials under one portion of a 1972 order were ordered to eliminate racial discrimination in housing assignments.[64] In *Holt v. Sarver* (1971), *Holt v. Hutto* (1973), *Finney v. Arkansas Board of Corrections* (1974), and *Finney v. Mabry* (1982), various federal courts hovered around the issue of desegregation in Arkansas prisons and ruled that racial segregation could occur only under certain limited circumstances but was generally proscribed.[65] In Georgia, the District Court for the Southern District of Georgia in *Guthrie v. Evans* (1981), in one part of an earlier consent decree, ordered that the Georgia State Prison be desegregated despite claims by prison managers that desegregation would lead to severe racial violence.[66] Following compliance with court-ordered desegregation, racial violence erupted, leading to a temporary period of inmate segregation only after a special master's belief that racial violence would ensue with continued desegregation efforts.[67]

Other cases have been indirectly related to racial segregation, such as in the Arkansas cases of *Howard v. Collins* (1997) and *Jacobs v. Lockhart* (1993).[68] In *Howard*, an inmate of the Cummins farm brought suit against prison officials and claimed that they were involved in a conspiracy with white inmates to form a racially segregated protective custody unit. Although the district court denied relief to the inmate, the Eighth Circuit Court of Appeals reversed the ruling in part and remanded the case, citing *Lee*'s provision that an equal protection claim would be valid if such a conspiracy of racial segregation were found at the prison. In *Jacobs*, the Eighth Circuit Court of Appeals denied relief to a black inmate who filed a Section 1983 action alleging that a prison policy concerning the use of punitive and maximum-security cells was racially discriminatory. In dissent, Judge Henley of the Eighth Circuit rebuked the court for failing to remand the case back to the federal district court to determine if conditions and practices in the Arkansas prison system existed in violation of previous rulings on inmate racial segregation.

Additional cases involving inmate segregation came from *Thomas v. Pate* (1974) and *United States v. Illinois* (1976), which dealt with integrated inmate housing guidelines in Illinois.[69] A case dealing with numerous areas of prison operation, *Battle v. Anderson* (1974), also tackled desegregation in Oklahoma when the District Court for the Eastern District of Oklahoma ordered that cell and other housing assignments be made without regard to race.[70] This was one of the few cases that specifically addressed and required desegregated cell assignments. *Gates v. Collier* (1972), a prisoner lawsuit that led to the end of the trusty system of inmate guards and inmate corporal punishment in Mississippi's Parchman Farm, also addressed racial segregation in this facility where the court found such practices unconstitutional and ordered the facility to be desegregated.[71]

This discussion represents only a sampling of cases that lower federal courts decided with regard to racial segregation among prisoners.[72] The most frequently cited rationale for maintaining segregation in prisons was that segregation kept racial violence at bay—violence that would be unleashed by mixing the races. The lower federal court rulings were clear—vague or speculative fears of racial violence did not justify racial segregation of prisoners.

Legal rulings are one thing, but actual compliance with those rulings is another issue altogether. The reality of racial segregation is that prison administrators were not quick to desegregate prison facilities even after court orders that directed them to do so. Before we examine the Texas prison system and the court ruling that required the desegregation of its inmates, we first examine what is known about the aftermath of racial desegregation in prison systems that attempted this practice.

Anecdotal Evidence on the Aftermath of Desegregation, 1970s–1980s

Little systematic evidence exists regarding the aftermath of racial desegregation in those prison systems that either faced court orders requiring this mandate or voluntarily did so without court intervention.[73] Although numerous speculative reasons exist for the lack of evidence on the aftermath of desegregation, a primary reason is that large-scale desegregation of inmates was rare, even for those systems that faced early desegregation orders by the courts. Indeed, court orders were perhaps necessary for desegregation, but they were not entirely sufficient. In many cases, several years passed before any measure of desegregation became a reality, and even then it was on a relatively small scale.

It is also the case that well-organized and well-funded research and evaluation departments were almost unheard of in U.S. prison systems in the 1970s and early 1980s when the bulk of desegregation orders came down from the courts. Thus, even if desegregation was attempted, there was little in the way of standardization in reporting to accurately measure its impact on the prison setting. These two reasons were especially important in southern prison systems, where most of the desegregation cases originated. Although the details are sketchy, some anecdotal evidence exists on the aftermath of desegregation in systems that made an attempt at this practice—whether forced or voluntary.[74]

Leo Carroll was the first to systematically examine racial cleavages that exist in prison in his book *Hacks, Blacks, and Cons.*[75] In the Rhode Island maximum security prison he studied, desegregation efforts by prison administrators led to racial polarization and interracial attacks. His research documenting patterns of informal and formal racial self-segregation in the gym, movie theater, and housing areas are telling with regard to the attitudes of inmates and administrators on racial mixing. The consensus among them was that racial desegregation would lead to high levels of disorder and perhaps violence, which was otherwise being prevented by racial segregation.

Carroll's findings were generally supported by James Jacobs's study of Stateville Prison in Illinois in the 1970s.[76] Jacobs did not focus on desegregation per se, yet race relations among prisoners emerged as a major theme of his study on judicial and administrative change in the prison environment. In his observation of Stateville, he uncovered a prison world fraught with racial tension and violence, made worse with the importation of street gang members aligned along racial and ethnic lines. His outlook on racial desegregation, informed by his first-hand observations at Stateville, was best summarized in one of his subsequent works:

> It should hardly cause surprise to learn that relations among the racial groups of prisoners are extremely tense, predatory, and a source of continual conflict. Prison populations contain disproportionate numbers of the least mature, least stable, and most violent individuals in America. If that were not sufficient to make successful race relations unlikely, prison conditions themselves generate fear, hatred and violence. . . . Racial conflict, including extreme violence and riots, is a reality of institutional life in prisons around the country. . . . Such settings do not promote understanding among the races; on the contrary they are breeding grounds for racism.[77]

John Irwin, a former California prisoner and later renowned professor of sociology, offered one of the bleakest views of prison race relations and what to expect from forced desegregation in his book *Prisons in Turmoil*. He documented racially polarized inmate cliques and gangs who were responsible for numerous interracial assaults despite the almost complete segregation of inmates in the California prison system. In this tenuous racial environment, Irwin remarked that "at least Black and White prisoners were not allowed to cell together."[78]

Others have examined race relations in prisons and have generally given the indication that fear, violence, and hatred might be the likely outcome with forced prisoner desegregation. Some of these research efforts have documented racial tensions and violence in juvenile facilities, while other efforts have examined prison race relations and violence through the lenses of interracial sexual assault and rape.[79] Although none of the above studies provides a systematic empirical view of the aftermath of racial desegregation, their observations are rich in detail and seem to lead to the conclusion that racial desegregation would foment severe racial violence—more so than that experienced with racial segregation.[80]

Perhaps the most developed source of anecdotal evidence on the aftermath of forced desegregation comes from a stipulation of the *Gates v. Collier* deci-

sion in Mississippi where the court ordered Parchman Farm officials to eliminate all racially discriminatory practices, including the segregated housing of
inmates.[81] According to two noted scholars of the Mississippi prison system,
the end of inmate segregation led to high levels of interracial violence and disorder. David Oshinsky noted of Parchman Farm that "the end of racial segregation . . . led to a surge of gang activity in the cages, as Whites and Blacks
squared off to protect themselves, boost their status, and gain territorial control."[82] One inmate in Mississippi proclaimed, "Dis int'gration shit jis ain't
gon' go down. Black and White people be diff'rent, 'speshly dem wild town-
niggahs an' crazy 'necks." William Taylor noted that inmates were difficult
enough to control in "segregated cages," and that desegregation had turned
the Mississippi prison system into a "war zone . . . giving reign to the law of
th' jungle." Desegregated inmates were "facing off, shanks were everywhere,
and people 'be gittin' cut.'"[83]

As mentioned previously, Georgia experienced similar instances of racial
violence in the aftermath of the *Guthrie v. Evans* decision that desegregated
the Georgia State Prison. Following desegregation, a riot broke out that led
to the temporary resegregation of the inmates.[84] This situation was also found
in Ohio's Lucasville Prison following court intervention in *White v. Morris*
that mandated desegregation.[85]

While systematic evidence on the aftermath of desegregation efforts is
elusive, the available evidence suggests that efforts to desegregate were not
free from violence and disorder.

Summary of Court Intervention, Desegregation, and Outcomes

Since the *Lee* decision in 1968, federal courts have presided over more than
forty cases, in whole or in part, dealing with the racial segregation of inmates. Administrators, correctional officers, and inmates have all argued in
the lower federal courts for racial segregation policies, based almost solely
on the fear of racial violence. Some lower federal court cases dealt with desegregation in larger living areas such as dormitories and cell blocks. Other
cases dealt specifically with in-cell desegregation. Several cases dealt with
particular institutions and others involved entire systems. In still other cases,
the issue of desegregation was only a smaller part of a larger case that attacked
numerous areas of prison operation, or a case only narrowly related to racial
segregation.[86]

For those advocating racial segregation out of fear of violence, the courts
have consistently held that general, vague, and/or speculative fears of racial
violence are not sufficient reasons for racially segregating inmates; while seg-

regation may be necessary in some circumstances, it should only be a temporary expedient to the safe and secure operation of prison settings. Although evidence from the 1970s and 1980s suggested that racial desegregation would and did lead to racial violence in some prison systems, no study has specifically examined the aftermath of large-scale racial desegregation on an empirical basis in the long term. Additionally, no study has examined what happens when two-person cells are desegregated. As a result, we know little about whether the predicted scenario of doom and gloom following racial desegregation would eventually come true.

In less than five years following the *Lee* decision, during the same time that other prison systems were confronting the issue of racial segregation, Texas was in the early stages of one of the most massive prisoner lawsuits in the nation on racial and ethnic segregation and discrimination. We now detail the history of racial segregation in Texas prisons to provide the foundation for a story of change that unfolded over the course of more than three decades in Texas prisons.

The Color Line in Texas Prisons, 1848–1965

On the "outside," Texas had a long-standing tradition of racial and ethnic segregation. Laws were enacted that mandated separation, and whites, blacks, and Hispanics lived in three separate societies. The situation was little different on the "inside." In 1927, the Fortieth Texas Legislature created the Texas Prison Board and position of general manager of the Texas prison system. The legislature also authorized the manager of the Texas prison system to "make provision for the separation and classification of prisoners according to . . . color."[87] Well before this 1927 law was adopted, however, the practice in place since the 1848 birth of the Texas prison system was that "white and negro prisoners shall not be worked together when it can be avoided, and shall be kept separate when not at work."[88]

There is much more to Texas prisoner segregation than that formalized by the Texas Legislature in 1927. To understand the foundation for racial segregation in Lone Star prisons, one must look back to Texas society in the mid-1800s. Not unlike the history of segregation in other southern prison systems, racial segregation in the Texas prison system was clearly and directly related to the state's history of racial subjugation by way of slavery, lynching, and social exclusion. In this context, racial segregation in Texas prisons was simply a tradition continued from Texas's history of racial oppression in all aspects of public life.

More than twenty years after the 1848 passing of an "Act to Establish a State Penitentiary" in Texas, however, there was little need to be concerned with separating prisoners by race. Before the end of the Civil War and the eventual abolition of slavery (Texas did not ratify the Thirteenth Amendment to the U.S. Constitution until February 1870), two separate social systems existed in Texas—one for blacks (and Hispanics) and one for whites—and these racial divisions carried into the state's penal system.[89]

In the antebellum Texas prison system, racial segregation was automatic: blacks remained almost exclusively on slave plantations.[90] Law violations that might result in a penitentiary stay for a white criminal would not usually be met with a stay in the penitentiary for an errant slave. Transgressions perpetrated by slaves were addressed primarily through harsh plantation justice. Only the most serious white criminals of the time, such as horse thieves and bank robbers, ended up in a prison cell. These prisoners, usually well under 100 prior to and during the Civil War, were confined in the only penitentiary that existed in Texas before 1883, the "Walls" located in Huntsville, Texas.[91]

Following the Civil War and Texas's ratification of the Thirteenth Amendment in 1870, both the population of the Texas prison system and its racial dynamics changed. From 1865 to 1883, the Texas prisoner population grew from 165 to 2,301 prisoners, more than half of which were freed slaves. Whether this increase was the result of special laws (e.g., black codes) used to imprison freed slaves to aid in the reconstruction of Texas or whether the increase was simply a response to more crime is open to debate.[92] Regardless of the reasons for the increase, between the initial years after the Civil War through the end of the 1800s, a fairly steady 50 to 60 percent of all Texas prisoners were black, compared to roughly 30 percent who were white and 10 percent Hispanic.[93]

Despite the changing racial demographics of the prison system following the Civil War, prisoners did not experience any measure of racial mixing. The racial caste system characteristic of Texas prior to the Civil War remained strong in public and in prison life after the war. From the end of the Civil War to the early 1880s, the state routinely leased most able-bodied "second-class" prisoners to private farmers and railroad and mining companies for work in racially segregated work camps.[94] As opposed to the almost exclusively white, serious, and cell worthy "first-class" prisoners, the mostly black second-class prisoners, imprisoned for less serious offenses and for shorter sentences, were sent to racially segregated field camps under the lease.[95]

The lease system entailed an agreement between a private contractor and the state. Private interests would lease the entire prison system, including its convicts. The lessee would typically pay a price per convict or group of convicts to the state, and would be responsible for prisoner supervision, housing, and discipline.

The road to a formal system of leasing in Texas began in 1866 when the Texas Legislature established a five-member Board of Public Labor composed of the governor, secretary of state, comptroller, attorney general, and state treasurer, with the responsibility to retain contracts for the use of inmate labor. Leasing began because the state, like most southern states after the Civil War, was financially strapped and could not afford to fund or fully outfit a state prison. The job of organizing contracts and convicts to work for private entities fell to the prison's superintendent (changed to the title of manager in 1927).[96] In 1867, the board's first action was to lease 100 prisoners to the Airliner Railroad and 150 more to Brazos Branch Railroad. By the early to mid-1870s, the Ward Dewey Company of Galveston leased the entire penitentiary and its prisoners from the state and, in 1877, Burnett and Kilpatrick out of Galveston leased the penitentiary system for six months.[97]

By the close of the first decade of the convict lease system, criticisms pervaded that convicts were abused and mistreated by private authorities. Such claims led to numerous legislative investigations and inquiries into the lease system.[98] Because of these and other problems, Texas ended convict leasing by the 1880s and began entering into contract-lease agreements. Slightly different than a private lease system, contract-leases were arrangements made with private entities, such as railroads and lumber companies, where state prison officials and officers (instead of lessees) supervised, housed, and disciplined convicts at racially segregated work sites. Private entities were also allowed to lease the shops and materials inside the Huntsville "Walls" unit for goods to be manufactured by convict labor.[99]

Much like the convict lease system, the contract-lease also met with criticism concerning the treatment of inmates. Convicts were also strictly segregated by race in the prisoner field camps. Prisoners working in the field camps were subjected to harsh and unyielding labor by prison officials, worked from "can til can't" (from the time convicts could see at sunrise until the time convicts could not see after sunset), engaged in self-mutilation, attempted numerous escapes to avoid the fields, and were whipped and even killed by prison guards.[100] As one convict remarked of the convict-lease: "Surely, it is no sacrilege to say that a convict gets a foretaste of that awful place spoken of in the Bible as Hell."[101] These criticisms endured throughout the lease and contract periods of the Texas prison system, and by the early 1900s prison officials were already considering other options to deal with the inmate population.[102] As in the past, one new option would involve strict racial segregation.

A Plantation by Any Other Name Is Just a Prison Farm

Anticipating the demise of the lease and contract systems, Texas prison officials began to purchase large tracts of land for agricultural production.[103] This expansion began with the development of three "prison farms": Wynne in 1883, Harlem I and II in 1885 (now called Jester I and II), and Clemens in 1893.[104] The state also opened the second walled penitentiary in 1883, East Texas Penitentiary in Rusk, to help relieve overcrowding at the Walls in Huntsville.

By the official end of the contract-lease system in 1910, the Texas prison system had continued its agricultural expansion with the purchase of massive tracts of land in the eastern part of Texas for four additional farms: Ramsey I/II, Imperial, Blue Ridge, and Central.[105] The state also acquired land for farms at Darrington and Eastham in 1917 and Retrieve in 1919. These tracts of land were situated on former plantations, not unlike the penitentiaries found in other southern states such as Arkansas, Louisiana, and Mississippi. It was these former plantations that served as the backdrop of the plantation prison plan—an agricultural prison model focused on the use of inmate labor on state-owned land to benefit the state. No longer would convicts be leased or their labor contracted out to private persons while under supervision of state officials. Rather, by the early 1900s the state would employ convict labor to farm state-owned land for profit. Like the lease and contract system, however, convicts did not fare much better on the farms. As Walker noted:[106]

Unfortunately, it turned out that prisoners working in the state-owned camps fared little better. . . . The desire to reap rich returns from prison labor and make the state camps as profitable as possible led managers of the state farms to exact as much labor as they could from their charges yet return little to them in the way of adequate food, medical care, or proper quarters.

Early Texas prison farms remained strictly segregated by race with separate farms and work camps for white, black, and Hispanic inmates. Life on early Texas prison farms was still strongly connected to broader patterns of racial division and subjugation characteristic of the larger Texas free society. Indeed, the uniquely southern terminology for former Texas plantations, the "prison farm," was a clear reminder of the vestiges of slavery that remained for convicts in the Texas prison system.[107] If that were not enough, work at the farms was closely aligned with that of plantation slavery where "black prisoners were sent to the . . . river bottoms, including the sugarcane plantations.[108] White

Table 4.1. Racial Distribution of Texas Prison Farms, December 1, 1935

Prison Farm	Race	Number
Blue Ridge	Mexicans	465
Central	Whites and Negroes	648
Clemens	Negroes	526
Darrington	Negroes	352
Eastham	Whites	551
Ferguson	Whites and Negroes	168
Harlem	Whites	487
Ramsey	Negroes	848
Retrieve	Whites	318

Source: Annual Report, Texas Prison Board, 1935

and Hispanic prisoners usually worked on other farms."[109] Early Texas prison farms did not have cells, and most farms were divided into several camps that featured dormitory-style housing or "tanks" which were completely segregated by race.

The Texas prison experience during the lease and contract periods, and into the period of prison farm expansion of the late 1800s and early 1900s, was characterized by a racial caste system that predated the Civil War and the Thirteenth Amendment. For all intents and purposes, prisoners in Texas were slaves of the state. If a convict died or escaped, the prison farm would simply get another.[110] In short, life on Texas prison farms was "worse than slavery."[111]

As shown in Table 4.1, Texas convicts in 1935 remained almost exclusively segregated by race on the prisons farms, and on the rare occasion that different races coexisted on a farm, field camps were one race only. For those not at prison farms, such as those held in cells in Huntsville or East Texas Penitentiary in Rusk, "negroes occupy separate cells and are fed at separate tables."[112]

From Farms to Units

From the 1930s to the 1960s, the general theme of working convicts for state benefit did not change substantially.[113] Neither did the place of Texas convicts change when it came to practices of racial segregation. This consistency remained even after prison farms and their camps became referred to by the more innocuous term "units" by the 1960s.[114] This euphemism, perhaps meant to signify progressive penal practices, professionalism in corrections, and a distancing from the state's shameful history of racial oppression, was more terminological than real. The newly labeled units still carried on the legacy of plantation slavery and remained racially segregated as a matter of state law and official prison policy.[115] Writing on Texas prisons in 1963, A. B. J. Hammett, one-time publisher of the *Victoria Mirror*, observed the almost complete racial segregation of inmates on the newly named units, which he also periodically referred to as farms:[116]

- Retrieve Farm: Houses the second offenders, habitual criminals and Negroes over the age of twenty-five.
- Darrington Farm: Houses white, second offenders.
- Central Unit: The type of prisoners found at this unit are first offenders, white male prisoners under twenty-five years of age. In Unit II of this farm are male Negro, second offenders under the age of twenty-five.
- Harlem Unit: Unit I of the Harlem Farm, Latin American first offenders and the best rehabilitative prospects under twenty-five years of age are found. Unit II of this farm houses Latin Americans over twenty-five years of age.
- Ramsey Unit: In Unit I of this farm are white prisoners and Unit II houses the Negroes over the age of twenty-five.
- Clemens: Is a prison farm where first offenders, Negroes, are confined.
- Eastham: Is a prison farm containing mostly new units where white prisoners, mostly of maximum security classification, are confined.

The racial classifications observed in 1963 by Hammett were similar to the racial distributions on Texas prison farms nearly thirty years earlier, as shown in Table 4.1. Well into the 1960s, life in Texas prisons, at least concerning racial segregation, was completely separated from the advances toward racial desegregation in the larger society (as evidenced by efforts of the NAACP to break down racial segregation in various public areas in Texas). To prison officials, there was simply no comparison of the "outside" to the "inside" concerning racial desegregation despite periodic name changes to Texas's prison facilities.[117]

The practice of racial segregation in the Texas prison system from its inception is perhaps best demonstrated in the inmate culture during the time farms became known as units. This culture was highlighted by scholar Bruce Jackson. Jackson, a professor of English and comparative literature, was allowed unusual access to Texas prison farms in the early 1960s. His book on Afro-American work songs of Texas prisons, while not focused on racial segregation per se, sheds light on the segregated worlds of inmates that persisted in the 1960s Texas prison system.[118] The culture of segregation and its link to slavery was particularly salient among black convicts. This was clearly demonstrated through the slavery-era work songs they sang while picking cotton and hoeing the fields. According to Jackson, such songs were exclusively the province of black inmates in the Texas prison system, for "white and Latin-American inmates . . . do not sing these songs, nor do they have any body of . . . songs of their own used in similar fashion. The songs and the style of utilizing them are the property of black inmates exclusively, and they are clearly in a tradition going back beyond the importation of the first Negro slaves to the Virginia Colony in 1631"—and life on antebellum plantations.[119]

Although there were instances where inmates of different races were to be found on the same prison farms and units by the early 1960s, for all intents and purposes near complete racial segregation remained the practice in Texas prisons. Indeed, three separate race-based worlds existed in Texas prisons before 1965, and these racial cleavages were in no small way related to the history of slavery and racial subjugation both before and after the Civil War in Texas.[120] In fact, treatment by race remained one of the most persistent features of the Texas prison system from its inception, and little had changed in over 100 years. Yet this insulated society was about to change as a direct result of the civil rights movement in the wider society.

The Color Line Blurs, 1965

In 1965, Texas prison director George J. Beto desegregated individual units by allowing prisoners of different races to coexist in the same prison institution. Beto recognized that desegregation was in line with prison practices in many parts of the country outside the South, and was also in line with changes in the wider society as evidenced by the passage of the Civil Rights Act of 1964 that effectively ended the tradition of Jim Crow in American society. Beto also knew that completely segregated prison units caused logistical problems in terms of accommodating the growing number and diversity of prisoners. The year 1965 marked the first time that inmates of different races coexisted in the Texas prison system.

Although "wholly black or wholly white units" no longer existed after 1965, prisoners of different races remained housed in separate dormitories and cell blocks.[121] Prisoners of different races did not commingle in dining facilities or field squads. Prisoners were housed in all-black wings, all-white wings, and all-Hispanic wings, and labored in segregated field forces known as the "black-line, white-line, and Mexican-line."[122] Texas prison officials in the 1960s cited state law that allowed them to separate and classify prisoners based on color.

By the close of the tumultuous 1960s, Texas prison administrators had made important efforts to end racial segregation to be in line with developments in the wider society. Yet vestiges of the not-so-distant past remained.

Attention to the Color Line

Despite the fact that Beto desegregated prison units in 1965, it would be another decade before further change would alter the state sanctioned system of racial segregation in Texas prisons. Even by 1974, Texas law still authorized prison managers to use race to sort and classify the prisoner population. Excerpts from Texas Civil Statutes in 1974 demonstrate the authority given to prison officers:

> Title 108, Texas Civil Statutes, Penitentiaries, Article 6166j (1974): The Texas Prison Board shall employ a general manager of the prison system . . . with the consent of the Texas Prison Board, shall have power to prescribe reasonable rules and regulations governing the human treatment, training and discipline of prisoners, and to make *provision for the separation and classification of prisoners according to sex, color, age, health, corrigibility, and character of offense upon which the conviction of the prisoner was secured.* (emphasis added)

In 1975, however, Texas law governing penitentiary regulations was revised to prohibit discrimination among numerous areas protected by the U.S. Constitution, including race. The newly revised statute read as follows:

> Title 108, Texas Civil Statutes, Penitentiaries, Article 6166j (1975): The Texas Department of Corrections shall employ a director . . . with the consent of the Texas Department of Corrections, shall . . . make provision for the separation and classification of prisoners according to sex, age, health, corrigibility, and character of offense upon which the conviction of the prisoner was secured. *Neither the Department of Corrections nor the director may discriminate against a prisoner on the basis of sex, race, color, creed, or national origin.* (emphasis added)

What happened in the span of one year? This modification of Texas law can be traced back to two change agents involving Texas prisons in the 1970s—one that began outside of prisons and the other that originated within the prison system. The first was a massive investigation into prison system operations by a prison reform committee of the Texas Legislature. The second was a class-action prisoner lawsuit that challenged racial segregation and discrimination in the prison system. Although the investigation by the legislative committee helped change the law on racial separation in prisons, it was the class-action lawsuit that eventually facilitated massive changes in prison operations concerning the use of race in its administration. We first consider the impact of the investigation into the Texas prison system.

Joint Committee on Prison Reform

Effective September 1, 1975, the Sixty-fourth Texas Legislature prohibited the Texas Department of Corrections (TDC) and the director of the Texas prison system from discriminating "against a prisoner on the basis of . . . race, color, creed, or national origin,"[123] reversing the 1927 law that allowed prisoner segregation by color. The new legislation came twenty-one years or roughly 8,000 days after the U.S. Supreme Court held that racial segregation in all governmental facilities was unconstitutional, eleven years after the Civil Rights Act of 1964, and seven years after the Court expressly prohibited racial segregation in prisons and jails.

Surprisingly, the major impetus to change the 1927 law did not come from the U.S. Supreme Court or the Civil Rights Act of 1964. Rather, the impetus came from a December 1974 report by the Joint Committee on Prison Reform of the Texas Legislature. Based on a nearly two-year study of the Texas correctional system, the committee's ninety-three-page final report scrutinized several aspects of prison operations from classification and institutional life to living conditions and discipline, academic and vocational education, and racial segregation and discrimination.

The committee's final recommendations were heavily influenced by an incident that occurred at the prison system's Retrieve Unit on June 17 and 18, 1973 (where Albert "Race" Sample served time in the 1950s). In what became known as the Father's Day incident, several convicts rebelled against prison officers and refused to work in the fields, leading to violence. Once officials ended the rebellion and resulting melee, offending inmates were allegedly beaten, forced to run through a gauntlet of prison officials armed with ax handles, baseball bats, and rubber hoses. Soon after the incident became publicized, the committee formally notified Texas prison director W. J. Estelle that they would investigate the incident. Prison officials responded that they were forced to quell the rebellion through extreme measures, because rising tensions and the "revolutionary aims and goals" of some of the inmates involved.[124]

In the face of the committee's investigation and evidence of abuse concerning the Father's Day incident, among other occurrences, Estelle told the committee chairman, Senator Chet Brooks, that "I would much rather face the criticism of unknowing, inexperienced and ill-informed people for actions of that type than suffer the justifiable criticism that would be leveled at our agency for ignoring intelligence information and allowing a traumatic and violent incident to happen."[125] Soon after the incident, it also became clear that racial segregation and discrimination would be an important focus of the investigation. Indeed, two senators appointed to the committee noted that the Father's Day incident was a symptom of the brutality and racial discrimination that existed within the prison system.

Although the committee's report focused on numerous areas of prison system operation, one prominent area of the report focused on racial and ethnic discrimination within the prison walls. The committee's final report was supplemented by testimony and interviews from numerous inmates, many of whom described the practices of racial segregation and discrimination in the prison system. The committee's overall findings on racial segregation and discrimination provided stinging criticism of Texas prison system operation:[126]

Racial and Ethnic Segregation: The Joint Committee on Prison Reform has repeatedly requested a statement of TDC policy on the subject. The Department has refused to provide such a statement due to a pending civil rights suit which charges the Department with racial and ethnic segregation and discrimination.[127] However, indications of TDC's policy can be found through an analysis of TDC data on the wing assignments at each unit.

TDC figures compiled on unit assignments show that each unit has a mix of black, white, and Mexican-American inmates. Although some units have a disproportionately high percentage of one group or another, Texas does not maintain separate black and white units as it did in the past. At the unit level, wing and dormitory assignments are made by the Warden and Building Major. It is at this level that evidence of racial and ethnic segregation becomes apparent.

The degree of segregation in each of the units varied tremendously. Some units had so few segregated wings that it appeared to be insignificant. Other units approached and even reached 100% level of segregation. In the typical situation . . . the wing would be either all black or would be all white. . . . Throughout the entire Department, about 56% of all the inmates live in ethnically or racially segregated living units. . . . The units which have more than half of their inmates segregated are as follows in order of the degree of segregation: Ramsey II (100%), Central (97%), Clemens (93%), Darrington (89%), Jester I (86%), Eastham (85%), Ferguson (82%), Jester II (74%), Retrieve (71%), and Ramsey I (53%). Even in a wing that is racially and ethnically mixed, inmates who share a cell are almost always of the same race or ethnic background.

Racial and Ethnic Discrimination: Many inmates have written to the Joint Committee complaining of racial prejudice and discrimination on the part of some TDC personnel. The Committee staff has listened to Wardens and their employees openly display racist attitudes many times. One supervisory official was quoted in a Dallas newspaper as saying, "We don't practice discrimination here. We treat niggers just like whites." It can be assumed that if these personnel express their prejudices so openly to the Committee staff and to members of the press, these attitudes will affect their treatment of inmates.

Commentary: Discrimination, prejudice, and segregation do exist in the Department of Corrections to a significant degree. Despite the fact that many Department officials voice opposition to such practices and deny that they exist; the evidence is overwhelming. . . . In addition, some wardens use racial segregation as another method of punishment. Many instances were observed where an inmate of one race was assigned to live in a wing with inmates all of another race. This was done to a number of so-called "writ writers" as punishment. There is no excuse for this practice.

Rather than making an aggressive effort to stop discrimination and segregation at the unit level, the Department appears to tacitly support those practices.

Racial prejudice can only be dealt with effectively if top TDC officials make a firm determination that it will not be tolerated. At present, unit officials and employees do not fear repercussions.

In all, there were more than 160 recommendations in the committee's report, three of which pertained to racial segregation and discrimination against inmates.[128] These recommendations included the following: (1) the legislature shall compel TDC to end forever discrimination based on race, religion, nationality, or sex in its treatment of inmates and its employment policies; (2) the department shall order all unit wardens to eliminate racial and ethnic segregation in their units and take steps to enforce its directive; and (3) the legislature shall repeal those sections of the state law allowing separation of inmates based on race.[129] The color line was now under full assault.

Not all committee members endorsed the wide-ranging recommendations in the final report. As noted by committee chairman Chet Brooks, "It should be understood that although the recommendations and text were adopted by the full committee, not every member necessarily agrees with every word of commentary in the text."[130] As other Texas prison scholars have noted, "Political sentiment plus the traditional authority of the prison director were just too powerful" at the time to trigger a major change in the Texas prison system—whether it was racial segregation and discrimination or other areas of prison system operation such as discipline, medical care, and living conditions.[131]

The committee's investigation was one of the first inquiries into the Texas prison system in decades, and many long-held prison practices were now being openly questioned.[132] Significantly, the questioning came from a politically powerful group of legislators, not inmates. In fact, despite the more than 160 recommendations by the committee, the only legislation adopted by the Texas Legislature in the 1975 regular legislative session was the recommendation to change the 1927 "color" law and prohibit the segregation of prisoners by race.

Despite the committee's findings of racial segregation and discrimination in state prisons, and the reversal of the 1927 "color law" in the 1975 legislative session, prisoners in Texas would remain racially segregated to varying degrees for another fifteen years.[133] Changes in law and committee recommendations were perhaps necessary to foster change in prison practices regarding racial segregation and discrimination, but they were not entirely sufficient.

The committee's legislative report is a clear illustration of how large-scale change typically begins on the outer fringes and eventually weaves its way through the permeable walls of prison settings. Indeed, by the time the color law was changed in 1975, the prison system was embroiled in the beginnings of a class-action lawsuit that would ultimately change the tradition of over one hundred years of racially segregated Texas prison history.

CHAPTER 5

Cracks in the Color Line

In 1970, Dr. George Beto was nearly at the end of his tenure as director of the Texas prison system. At that time, he oversaw a prison system with roughly 15,000 prisoners, housed in roughly a dozen prison units scattered throughout East Texas. The system's operating budget was approximately $18 million. Under Beto's administration, litigation activity by inmates was sporadic and fundamentally a nuisance. For the most part, inmate life on any of the prison units was the same as it had been in the 1960s and even the 1950s. When the work bell chimed, the hoe squads hit the hallways, were counted, ran to the waiting trailers, and went to work in the fields "flat weeding" or picking cotton.

Prelude to Change

Only one month after Beto's retirement in 1972, roughly two years before the December 1974 final report by the Joint Committee on Prison Reform, the Texas Department of Corrections (TDC) faced a prisoner lawsuit that would have a massive impact on the system's operation. On October 17, 1972, black TDC inmate Allen L. Lamar filed a Section 1983 lawsuit (federal Civil Action for Deprivation of Civil Rights) in the U.S. District Court for the Southern District of Texas, alleging that system-wide practices of racial segregation and discrimination deprived inmates of their civil rights.[1]

As the Joint Committee's investigation entered its early stages, pretrial events in the *Lamar* case were gaining momentum and the case was expanding. Only weeks after Lamar filed suit with the court, on November 6, eight Spanish-speaking inmates (including David Ruiz, the plaintiff of *Ruiz v. Estelle*) moved to intervene as additional plaintiffs.[2] Two more black inmates then moved to intervene in the case in December.[3] In January 1973, the court granted these motions for intervention.

In what would turn out to be one of the most important developments in the case, on May 24, 1973, the U.S. attorney general directed the Department of Justice (DOJ) to file a motion to intervene on behalf of Lamar and the other inmate plaintiffs. This was granted on July 6. Soon after, two white inmates intervened in support of TDC, and two years later, on June 6, 1975, four additional black inmates and two Hispanic inmates also joined in support of TDC.[4]

By the time the committee issued its final report on the Texas prison system in December 1974, the *Lamar* suit had blossomed into a full-scale attack against alleged practices of racial segregation and discrimination in TDC. Although the claims made in the original 1972 complaint by Lamar were numerous, the case would continue to expand even further. Several months after Lamar filed his original complaint, two additional prisoner lawsuits with separate but related claims of racial and ethnic discrimination against TDC were consolidated with *Lamar*.[5] Once consolidated, the *Lamar* lawsuit was certified as a class action—*Allen L. Lamar et al. v. H. H. Coffield et al.*, Civil Action No. 72-H-1393—and became one of four major class-action lawsuits faced by TDC in the 1970s, in addition to numerous other non-class actions.[6]

Once certified as a class action, the *Lamar* suit pertained to "all past, present and future inmates of TDC" and placed scrutiny on the practices of the entire Texas penal system. The case was even more unique for having garnered the attention of the U.S. attorney general and the Department of Justice. Adding problems for TDC was that the suit came at the heels of the committee's investigation whereby long-held prison practices, once isolated from outside scrutiny, were now being openly questioned. The convergence of the above factors created a virtual perfect storm of prisoner litigation.

Lamar's Allegations

The *Lamar* suit was delineated among three different classes of inmates: (1) black TDC inmates who were plaintiffs, (2) Spanish-speaking inmates who were plaintiffs or plaintiff-intervenors, and (3) a mixed group of Anglo-American, black, and Spanish-speaking defendant-intervenors.[7] The allegations made by Lamar and the other inmate plaintiffs were wide-ranging. They charged TDC with racial and ethnic discrimination in the following venues:[8]

- In assignment to the various prison units within TDC.
- In assignment to living quarters within the various prison units.
- In assignment to agricultural work squads and other jobs within the various prison units.
- In the administration of inmate disciplinary procedures, both in charging minority inmates with disciplinary offenses and in assessing punishment.
- In selection of inmates for and in the administration of academic and vocational educational programs.
- In maintaining a predominantly Anglo-American employee staff.
- In providing medical care.
- In providing reasonable protection from harm within the various prison units.
- In providing recreational facilities and activities.
- In providing dining, showering, church, and other group activities.
- In the use by TDC staff of racial and ethnic verbal epithets and slurs.
- In the review and inspection of incoming publications.
- In forbidding Spanish-speaking inmates from speaking and writing in Spanish.

In their role as intervenors on behalf of the inmate plaintiffs, the DOJ sought to enjoin TDC from the following:

- Assigning inmates to cells, cell blocks, or dormitories on the basis of race, color, religion, or national origin.
- Failing or refusing forthwith to desegregate all TDC facilities.
- Failing or refusing to design and implement a standard system of prisoner classification and assignment not related to race.
- Failing or refusing to take prompt affirmative steps to correct and erase the effects of past discriminatory practices.

Taken as a whole, the claims made by Lamar and other inmate plaintiffs, as well as the DOJ, charged TDC with racial segregation and discrimination in virtually all aspects of prison administration. The remaining class of inmates, those supporting TDC as defendant-intervenors, denied that racially discriminatory practices existed in the prison system and they had no position concerning many of the claims made by Lamar and the other inmate plaintiffs or the DOJ. Their position as defendant-intervenors was limited to the fear that desegregating cells (as advocated by the DOJ) "will have an adverse effect on prison security and will bring about racial conflict which thus far has been avoided by non-integration of cells."[9] This was a claim that had been made before in other prison systems and institutional settings—a claim that set up cell desegregation as the most contentious issue of the *Lamar* suit.

Allen L. Lamar: From Child to Delinquent, 1936–1953

Allen Lawrence Lamar was born in Mertens, Texas, on January 5, 1936.[10] Located roughly seventy miles southeast of Fort Worth, Mertens is a rural Texas town with a population that barely exceeded 300 residents in the 1930s. Lamar entered the world the eldest child of Beulah Mae West and Allen Lamar Sr. He had one sister, Alene, who was born in 1938.[11]

Beulah Mae West was born in 1917. Her parents were tenant farmers and she was the seventh of fourteen children. She attended school through the seventh grade. In 1934, at age seventeen, she married thirty-seven-year-old Allen Lamar Sr. and soon after became pregnant with Allen Jr. According to Beulah, Allen Sr. was an abusive individual. Little else is known about him other than that he deserted the family sometime in 1936. The couple was legally divorced in 1942 and he reportedly died of natural causes in 1955.[12]

It was not long after his birth and presumably after Allen Sr. deserted the family that Beulah moved the children to Fort Worth, where Allen would spend his entire childhood. The same year that Beulah divorced Allen Sr., she married Horace Wilkins—the only real father figure that Allen would know throughout his childhood. In Fort Worth, the family resided in a modern, five-room home "in a Negro section" on the east side of the city. Wilkins was a licensed embalmer and worked as a mortician at a local funeral parlor. Unlike in her previous marriage, Beulah reported a stable home environment with Wilkins and described his relationship with Allen as "harmonious."[13]

Despite having an "epileptic spell" at the age of five, Allen had an uneventful childhood. He attended school regularly and earned fair to good grades. He also worked as a newspaper boy and a hotel bus boy and at various other odd jobs. When he misbehaved, he received the "average necessary amount" of control and punishment at home, according to his mother.[14] By all indications, Allen was on the path to becoming a productive member of society.

By age thirteen, however, Allen's trajectory of an ordinary and uneventful life began to veer. He was allegedly given dope at age thirteen, and then at age fifteen he started becoming more incorrigible at home. His school attendance started to fade, and he was fired from a job at a local drug store because he reportedly had difficulty taking orders and directions. Allen often left home without permission and just as frequently lied to his mother as to his where-abouts. Beulah attributed her son's behavior to smoking marijuana and re-marked during an interview with a juvenile court officer that "no normal boy would act like he does around home." She also said that by age fifteen Allen had a strong yearning to go to California.[15]

By age sixteen, Allen entered a more deviant path. His high school prin-cipal described him as a discipline problem in eleventh grade. His attendance continued to slide, and Allen was disciplined for petty thievery after stealing purses and bus cards from other students. Allen was also described by his principal as a defiant lad with "no respect for authority."[16]

At about the same time that his school progress began to decline, Allen had his first official contact with the justice system. Only months after turn-ing sixteen, Allen was detained by local authorities for the March 1952 bur-glary of a local drug store. Three days after he was released from the county jail on juvenile probation for this offense, Allen stole a car and was again detained by authorities. A social history report compiled by the juvenile court officer summarizes the car theft:[17]

Allen is charged with theft of over $50 in that on March 20, 1952, 9:55 AM, he willfully took a 1952 Buick Sedan, owned and operated by Bob Watts, who lives at 1211 Houston Street. This car was stolen from in front of Carter Paper Company on Calhoun Street. Allen told this officer that he had in-tentions of stealing a 1949 Mercury, but he was unable to start this car. So he left it in search of another. He saw the Buick, found it had keys in it, and so he took it from the above location and intended to drive it to California. He was unsuccessful in his attempt for he was apprehended [on the] above date, at Broadway and Henderson in company with a companion Charles Wesley Laster.

The social history report compiled by the juvenile court officer recounted Allen's previous delinquent involvement and a recommendation concerning the car theft:[18]

Allen's behavior and past adjustment is known to Mrs. Chatman, Probation Officer for Negro clients. On occasion Allen's mother made known to this person that Allen was a very ungovernable lad, he would not mind her, and all her efforts to get the boy to attend school and stay out of mischief were futile. The mother also stated that Allen admitted having taken dope and when this worker questioned Allen about this, he admitted that he had used a narcotic. The mother gave an account to Mrs. Chatman on how the boy would act at times when she was sure he was under the influence of dope; that the mother frankly admits she is unable to manage this boy and all her efforts to guide him have fallen on non-fertile soil.

Following the disclosure of these facts to the worker, Allen was apprehended . . . on March 9, 1952 by Detectives Lewis, Bush, Chandler, and Ruckman, charged with burglarizing the Ure Drug Store . . . and stealing in company with three other colored boys, one snub nose .38 cal. pistol and $185 cash after the owner closed for the evening. Allen hid out in the store, sitting until . . . [the] owner closed for the night. He was acquainted with the burglary alarm system and how it worked. He was able to open the door quickly and jump over the electric eye. Other boys were waiting outside to receive and divide the loot. After this the boys arranged to meet at a room which one Marvin Booker had rented and here the cash was divided. This done, the older boy, Marvin Booker, age 19, left town. Allen, together with three other Negro boys, were apprehended and at parents' request detained in County Jail awaiting disposition.

On [March 17, 1952] the boys and Allen were arraigned before Mr. McGee, Assistant Probation Officer, and at such time plans were made in accordance with parents' wishes; the boys were placed on Probation and a firm understanding made that they all would return to school and stay there.

But it was soon after this, in fact the day after Allen was released, he returned to school, ran off that night, returned to sleep in the family car, which was parked in the garage. Allen told this officer that his mother had threatened to call this Department and notify us that he was not willing to attend school. Allen told me in an interview [on] March 20, 1952 that he wanted to be on his own making big money. California holds this fascination for him and he does not want to go to school anymore and this officer feels that it would be futile to entertain the hope that Allen would remain in school for very long if allowed to go. Allen has expressed to this officer that he has had access to narcotics. He is familiar with its use and administration. He has knowledge of its source here in Fort Worth and it is known that he has taken dope on occasion. Allen, I feel, can best be assisted only by being made to understand that he is not old enough to assert his rights, rebel against the laws of society, and live his life in a belligerent and ungovernable manner. His mother has failed to do this job. Allen has failed and it is felt that Allen can only learn to do differently if made to do so.

Eight days after Allen was arrested for the March 20, 1952, car theft, and following this scathing recommendation by the juvenile court officer, he was adjudicated delinquent and committed to the State Youth Development Council for an indeterminate term. Three days later, on March 31, 1952, Allen (Ward #A-20696) was received by the State School for Boys in Gatesville.

The Gatesville State School for Boys was the first in a line of institutional destinations that would span Lamar's life. Located approximately two hours southwest of Fort Worth, the Gatesville State School for Boys was the first juvenile institution in Texas and considered the first juvenile training and rehabilitation institution in the southern United States when it opened in 1889. It was originally administered as a branch of the Texas prison system and known as the House of Correction and Reformatory. Prior to its opening, juveniles committed to the state were incarcerated in much the same way as adult felons in the Texas prison system. Able-bodied juveniles worked alongside adult convicts under the lease or were housed at one of the emerging prison farms.[19] If their crimes were sufficiently serious, such young offenders would be held in the Walls Unit in Huntsville or, if very young, intermixed with female prisoners.[20]

By 1909, the Texas Legislature changed the name of the House of Correction to the State Institution for the Training of Juveniles. Administration of this facility was also transferred to a five-member board of trustees. In 1913, the institution was renamed the State Juvenile Training School and by 1939 the facility had become officially known as the Gatesville State School for Boys. Not unlike adult Texas prison farms of the late 1800s and early 1900s, this facility rested on a 900-acre tract of state-owned land supplemented with another 2,700 acres leased by the state. Also similar to the early Texas prison farms was that this facility was largely segregated by race. Racial segregation in youth dormitories and other facets of institutional life would persist for years at Gatesville and as other youth facilities emerged in Texas. Name changes of this facility made little impact in the classification of state delinquents. Yet despite its cosmetic similarities to Texas prison farms, Gatesville was meant to be different than the adult farms, which became apparent as the institution and its governance evolved. Indeed, by the 1950s the Gatesville State School for Boys had long been disconnected from the Texas prison system and was being governed by the State Youth Development Council (later changed to the Texas Youth Council in 1957 and then to the Texas Youth Commission in 1983), which was more committed to reform than to punishment.[21]

At the time of Lamar's commitment, the Gatesville State School held roughly 500 boys dispersed among five separate housing units, all segregated along racial lines.[22] During his initial months at Gatesville, Lamar had problems. He reportedly had three escapes from the facility, and was also disciplined by staff for talking back and for sniffing gasoline. Nearing the end of his commitment, official reports by correctional personnel indicate that Lamar eventually made some progress in facility programming. He completed all the grades offered at the state school, and was enrolled in the wood shop taking carpentry classes. Allen was also a member of the basketball team. According to a summary report prepared just prior to his release, a state school caseworker noted:[23]

> Allen's adjustment here has been fair. It has improved somewhat in the last two months. He has appeared before the Disciplinary Committee on four occasions for relatively serious offenses.[24] Since Allen is beyond the academic grades taught here, he works in the wood shop. His instructor states he does very well. Allen gets along well with the rest of the boys and the staff. He participates well in athletics and currently is a member of the basketball team.
>
> It is felt by the staff who are acquainted with him that he has good potentialities but needs leadership that will direct his efforts into constructive channels. He reacts to anyone with leadership facilities.
>
> Allen's home appears to be adequate financially and he denies any tension in familial relationships. At present, he expresses a desire to complete High School and enter college. His parents should encourage and help him in this desire since he has that ability if applied.

The rather generic evaluation by the state school official prior to Allen's release suggests that his time in the Gatesville State School for Boys was not completely unproductive. Roughly one year after he was committed to state juvenile incarceration, Lamar was released under supervision on February 23, 1953, and finally discharged by the State Youth Development Council in February of 1954.[25]

Criminal persistence, 1954–1962

By age eighteen, Allen was able to realize his dream of going to California to make "big money." In California, however, he was arrested three different times in July 1954 (only five months after his discharge from the Texas State Youth Development Council) for the crimes of burglary, robbery, and grand theft auto. For the latter, Lamar was committed to the California Youth Authority for two to six years in November 1954. As a Youth Authority ward in the mid-1950s, Lamar spent his initial months in the Deuel Vocational Institution in Tracy, California, before being transferred to San Quentin. After a period there, Lamar was transferred to the Correctional Training Facility in Soledad, where he was paroled at age twenty. While incarcerated, Lamar continued his pattern of institutional maladjustment demonstrated during his early months in the Gatesville State School for Boys. He was allegedly punished for talking back to guards, smuggling letters, and instigating a riot.[26]

Following his release from the California Youth Authority, Lamar returned to Fort Worth by 1957. In October 1957 at the age of twenty-one, Lamar enlisted in the U.S. Army. Roughly one month after his enlistment, Lamar was arrested in Dallas for being absent without leave and spent roughly two months in the stockade. In January 1958, Lamar was arrested in Denver for auto theft. In June 1958, Lamar was detained by the U.S. Army for going AWOL a second time. Two months later, Lamar was arrested in Riverside, California, after having transported a stolen vehicle across state lines, which is a federal offense. On December 19, 1958, as federal authorities were proceeding with this case, Lamar received a dishonorable discharge from the army.[27]

For the offense of interstate transportation of a stolen vehicle, Lamar received a four-year prison sentence and was incarcerated in the Federal Bureau of Prisons (BOP) in October 1958. Lamar was incarcerated through October 1961 and served time in several federal institutions, including the El Reno, Oklahoma, Federal Reformatory, the United States Prison in Terre Haute, Indiana, and the La Tuna Federal Correctional Institution in Anthony, Texas. On October 23, 1961, Lamar was released from the La Tuna Federal Correctional Institution under mandatory release supervision.

Less than one month after his release from the BOP, Lamar passed a forged check in the amount of $112.35 in Fort Worth and was arrested. One month later, while apparently out of the county jail on bond, Lamar was arrested in Tyler, Texas, for stealing a purse from a thirty-six-year-old white woman.[28] During this criminal episode, Lamar and an accomplice netted $45 in cash and an $81 check. For the above crimes, to which he pled guilty on February 28 and April 3, 1962, Lamar received two two-to-four year sentences to run concurrently in TDC.[29]

Into the "Burnin' Hell," 1962–1966

Allen Lamar was admitted to TDC on April 10, 1962, at age twenty-six. His sentence carried a minimum expiration date of August 14, 1964, and a maximum of March 6, 1966.[30] According to his prison admission records, he was determined to be in good health and fit for work. Lamar also reported at his prison admission that he was a Methodist and was baptized at six years of age.

Lamar told prison officers that he grew up with little stability at home. He reported that he had used several drugs in the past, including but not limited to marijuana, red birds, yellow jackets, and morphine. Based on this and other information, Lamar was categorized as a 2-B in TDC terminology of the time—he was an intermediate rehabilitative prospect over the age of twenty-five. Concerning security and protection, Lamar was grouped as a Maximum-7, meaning he was to be placed in maximum custody but required no special protection.

The TDC admission process in the 1960s included a detailed background check that drew from both official and unofficial sources. In addition to a complete criminal background check, prison officers sent letters to Lamar's former employers, the U.S. Army, his mother, and institutions where Lamar had reportedly been incarcerated. Correspondence was received from a number of individuals and organizations, which helped classification officers come to a better understanding of Lamar's criminal and social history prior to his TDC commitment.

It was during this background process that an attorney named Elton M. Hyder, a partner in the firm of Tilley, Hyder, and Law of Fort Worth, wrote to the prison system to make a plea on Lamar's behalf, apparently at the request of the inmate's mother.[31] The letter read as follows:[32]

> Mrs. Beulah Wilkins, mother of Allen L. Lamar, is a sister of the office maid that has worked on the floor of this building for some ten years. I have known both our maid and her sister for nearly all of these ten years, and they have come to me from time to time with their problems. Both of them are wonderful mothers and extremely interested in their children and both are quite upset over what has happened to Allen. I should mention that I do not know this boy but I have seen his record and, of course, it is quite discouraging.
>
> Beulah tells me that the boy was somehow given narcotics when he was 13 or 14 years old and various people kept him on the narcotics during the intervening years by one device or another. Of course this is a terrible tragedy to befall any child and despite the good efforts of parents, I know that frequently nothing can be done unless the addiction is cured.
>
> I do not practice criminal law and never have, and I am writing this letter voluntarily to give you some idea of the background and character of Allen's mother. She has talked with me, of course, many, many times about this

problem and is quite convinced that unless he is placed in a hospital for the treatment and cure of the addiction his life will continue as it has in the past. This is a matter, of course, to be determined by those much more competent and experienced in these matters than I, but I do believe she speaks with sincerity and with knowledge.

They are colored, of course, and do not have the friends, money or knowledge that might be of help in presenting their case, but I do hope that you will seriously consider the recommendations made by the Criminal District Attorney in Smith County and the Criminal District Attorney in Tarrant County to the effect that he be transferred to a federal institution for treatment of narcotics.

Further information uncovered during TDC's intake process indicates that Lamar was involved in numerous institutional infractions in California state institutions and in BOP facilities. These included punishments previously noted for "talking back," "sniffing gas," "smuggling letters," and "instigating a riot." Lamar was also reportedly punished for "insubordination and instigating a riot," "instigating a mess hall strike," "writing a threatening letter to a federal employee," and "refusing to work." Lamar also admitted to "performing acts of anal sodomy as the active partner while incarcerated at FCI La Tuna."[33]

Following his nearly month-long intake and diagnostic evaluation, Lamar was transferred to TDC's Eastham Unit on May 3, 1962. Within one month of his arrival at the Eastham Farm, Lamar wrote to Richard C. Jones, Assistant Director for Treatment in TDC, and complained that his treatment needs were not being met:[34]

Sir, I am a narcotic user and have been addicted since the age of (14) fourteen and while I am confined under the Texas Prison System I would sincerely appreciate some consideration from this Staff with my paramount problem.

Sir, I have always been able to work and this is all that I have received. But my problem as I have stated is one very close to mental insanity. One that can neither be curbed or rechanneled by chopping cotton, or using my strength in the field that will serve to no avail to me when I am released from confinement.

It is not my intention directly or indirectly to show hostility or be disrespectful in any way. My only objective is to be given some type of program that is helpful to me on my return to society. For I am now of the mental age whereas I am concerned with my future as a constructive human being. And I only seek my Due.

While still at Eastham, on June 6, 1962, Lamar wrote to prison system director Dr. George J. Beto and requested a meeting:[35]

It is of utmost urgency that I be given an interview with you personally. I sincerely feel that I am asking you sir; to grant me this opportunity to help eradicate erroneous treatment and circumstances which I, as an inmate is subjected unto by certain members of this facility.

I have sent for my parents and attorney Elton Hyder to help bring about more favorable conditions under which I can receive a better opportunity to rehabilitate myself.

If sir; you can not grant me a personal interview, I would not care to speak on the matter with any other member of the department due to the fact that I do not feel that the situation can be handle by anyone except yourself, sir.

Therefore, I await the consideration which you feel the situation warrants.

Six days after he wrote this letter, on June 12, 1962, Lamar was transferred to the Ramsey II prison farm. Two days after arriving at Ramsey II, Beto wrote to Lamar acknowledging receipt of his letter. He also wrote: "When next I visit Ramsey Unit, I will talk with you."[36] Within a month, Beto spoke personally with Lamar at Ramsey.[37] Although the specific details of the conversation are unknown, Lamar apparently admitted to Beto that he was a Muslim.[38] The significance of this admission cannot be overemphasized.

Muslim prisoners as a whole were viewed as agitators and malcontents by Beto and other Texas prison officials.[39] It is not surprising, then, that in a July 2, 1962, internal communication, Beto advised prison classification director L. W. Hughes that Lamar was "an admitted Muslim. If the records do not already so indicate, they should be changed."[40] Handwritten on this inter-office communication was another note instructing Hughes to "put [Lamar] on the Muslim list."

At Ramsey II, Lamar worked on the "One Hoe" and "Five Hoe" squads and was housed in a "colored cell block."[41] Lamar's prison conduct was rated on a Point Incentive Program (PIP) evaluation chart, TDC's inmate grading system of the time that linked to outcomes such as custody level and time-earning rate and class.[42] Lamar's initial PIP evaluations at Ramsey II showed that he scored "below average" in areas of work, conduct, and attitude, but he soon improved to "average." In July 1963, however, Lamar's PIP evaluation at Ramsey II revealed consistent below-average marks and he was docked several time-earning points. It was at this time that Lamar was placed in solitary confinement for an unknown offense, the first known time he had been so placed in TDC. Roughly one month afterward, Lamar was transferred to the Harlem I prison farm in Southeast Texas (known today as Jester Unit).

From July through September 1963, Lamar was housed at the Harlem I and II prison farms, the first for about one month before moving to Harlem II on September 12. This movement was likely in response to Lamar being placed in solitary confinement for "laziness and impudence." Prison records indicate that while Lamar was in solitary, he became belligerent as the prison's medical assistant was checking on him. When the medical assistant advised Lamar to stand up, he refused. The medical assistant advised Lamar that if he wanted out of solitary, he "should show officers a little courtesy . . . and at least show the Warden some courtesy when he visited solitary." Following this exchange, the incident report reflects that Lamar proclaimed: "I haven't sent the Warden a God Damn invitation, and don't care if the mother fucker comes or not." For these offenses Lamar lost sixty days of good time (then called "overtime" in TDC), was demoted in time-earning class, and was recommended to be transferred to a "unit of his classification."

When the warden of the Harlem Farm, Virgle D. Starns, heard of this incident, he visited Lamar in solitary. Afterward, Starns reiterated the findings on Lamar's disciplinary report: "The above is true. I visited solitary and found the inmate belligerent and his impudent attitude remained the same. It is noted on his card that he is of the Muslim Faith, and all indications show that he could be."[43]

In late September 1963, Lamar was moved to the Ellis Farm near Huntsville—a unit more suited to his new classification as a malcontent and troublemaker. Just prior to his transfer there, Hughes, the TDC director of classification and records, sent Ellis Farm warden, Carl "Beartrack" McAdams, an interoffice communication on the matter:[44]

On this date Dr. Beto requested to this office that the above captioned inmate [Lamar] be transferred from Harlem #2 to Ellis Unit when released from Solitary. This inmate is presently in solitary confinement on Harlem 2 Unit. Records further reveal that Lamar is an admitted Muslim.

Lamar was received by the Ellis Unit at the end of September 1963 and assigned to the One Hoe field squad. At the time of Lamar's transfer, the Ellis

Unit was still being built; construction had begun early that year. The first building constructed at Ellis was the gymnasium, used to house inmates who toiled at the new unit. As opposed to Harlem, and to a lesser extent Ramsey, the Ellis Unit of the 1960s was the destination for the prison system's hard cases—multiple recidivists and those who were troublesome at other TDC farms.[45] Most inmates sent to Ellis in the early 1960s were assigned to the field, where the work was particularly difficult. Lamar arrived just in time to help clear the thick treed land and pave the way for the new Ellis building.

Lamar appeared to avoid major trouble during the initial months of his confinement at Ellis despite the fact that he was not considered a stellar inmate. Lamar's PIP evaluation in January 1964 showed average progress in work, but below average progress in conduct and attitude. Lamar received positive points for religious participation and for attending Alcoholics Anonymous, although his participation was rated as average. Several months into his stay at the Ellis Farm, however, Lamar's progress began to decline. Lamar's PIP evaluation for July 1964 showed below average progress in his work, conduct, and attitude, and average evaluation as to his participation in Alcoholics Anonymous.

Despite his lukewarm evaluations at Ellis, Lamar was able to avoid official sanction during his first year on this farm—but that is about as long as it lasted. On October 11, 1964, after barely a year at Ellis, Lamar was involved in another disciplinary offense. He was observed by a prison official and a building attendant as the active partner in an act of anal sodomy. Upon discovery of this offense, Lamar was ordered out of his cell by the prison official. According to the disciplinary report, as Lamar exited his cell he allegedly attacked the building attendant. For the offense of "sex perversion" and the attack on the building attendant, Lamar was placed in solitary confinement, lost all good-time points he had accumulated during his time in TDC, and was demoted to a lower time-earning class.[46]

In January 1965 Lamar was released from solitary and placed back on the One Hoe squad at Ellis. Because of his discipline problems, Lamar had earned a negative balance of good-time points and continued to receive average to below average scores in work, conduct, and attitude. This trend of minimum compliance and near defiance carried through to mid-1965, as indicated by his PIP evaluations.

In April 1965, Lamar appealed to Hughes that he might be elevated to a higher time-earning class. Hughes wrote back and explained that he would need the recommendation of Warden McAdams. Lamar followed up with McAdams soon after. In response, McAdams wrote: "You must keep a clear record for a longer time after looking at your disciplinary status. If you keep your record clear, I will consider this restoration at a later date."[47] This potential for restoration of time lost and an increase in a time-earning class appeared to motivate Lamar, and in the intervening months he made progress. By August 1965, for the first time ever in TDC, Lamar received a "good" evaluation for work progress, but he still received average ratings for conduct and attitude.

More than halfway through 1965, Lamar was nearing the end of his four-year maximum sentence. In early August 1965, Lamar wrote a letter to TDC director Beto and pleaded to have reinstated the sixty days of good time taken for the September 1963 offense at Harlem II. Beto replied that he would visit him the next time he was at the Ellis Unit. Beto eventually did meet with Lamar and was apparently impressed by his attitude—despite Lamar's previous admission that he was of the Muslim faith. On August 20, 1965, the prison's Disciplinary Committee reviewed Lamar's file and restored sixty days of good time following Beto's specific approval. With this restoration, along with other good time accumulated to that point, Lamar was eligible for discharge from TDC on August 21, 1965.

Although Lamar was eligible and approved for discharge from TDC custody, he was not released. Rather, he was held on a detainer by the United States Marshal's office. This detainer was a result of Lamar violating federal mandatory release guidelines from his previous federal conviction and incarceration for interstate transportation of a stolen vehicle. Lamar was physically released by TDC to the U.S. Marshal on September 20, 1965, and then transported to the Federal Correctional Institution in Texarkana, Texas. He was discharged from federal custody on April 2, 1966.[48]

Back in the Burnin' Hell

Following his April 1966 release from federal custody, Lamar wasted little time returning to TDC. On June 13, Lamar and an accomplice perpetrated an armed robbery in Big Spring, Texas.[49] Lamar's trial began one month later, and the next day he was convicted by an all-white jury in overwhelmingly white Howard County. While his case was on appeal, Lamar was held in the county jail. His appeal was affirmed on May 17, 1967. For this conviction, Lamar received a sentence of twenty-five years in the Texas prison system. He was received by TDC for the second time on July 6, 1967, and sent directly to the Ellis Unit.

During his second TDC incarceration, Lamar continued to appeal his conviction on several grounds. His major challenge centered on the jury selection process. He claimed the jury did not represent a cross-section of the community because it was composed exclusively of whites. It was during these attempts to appeal his criminal conviction that Lamar met lawyer Frances Jalet.

Jalet came to Texas in 1967 to work for the Legal Aid and Defender Society of Travis County. She quickly became interested in prisoner rights issues following correspondence and a subsequent visit with Ellis Unit inmate Fred Cruz in 1967.[50] Jalet continued corresponding with Cruz and soon became among the most active prisoner rights lawyers in Texas. (After his release, Jalet and Cruz were married in 1976.)

It was no surprise that Lamar would eventually come into contact with Jalet. First, she was a staunch advocate of prisoner rights, willing and ready to help TDC prisoners. Second, and perhaps most important, Lamar was incarcerated along with Cruz at the Ellis Unit in the late 1960s. Like Cruz, Lamar was building a reputation as a budding jailhouse lawyer. It was through his connection with Cruz that Lamar first contacted Jalet in 1969 while she was employed at Texas Southern's Legal Aid Clinic in Houston. He asked her for help with his criminal appeals. Jalet did some early research into his case and filed an amended habeas corpus petition for him, but said that she had neither the time nor the money to represent him fully during his appeals because of her involvement with other prisoner litigation.[51]

Jalet had not misled Lamar, for she was already very much involved with Texas prisoner litigation by 1969 and had by this time incurred increasing disfavor with TDC officials, in particular George Beto. In 1968, Beto allegedly had a hand in her transfer from the Legal Aid and Defender Society of Travis County and her dismissal from the Texas Legal Services Project in Dallas the same year. Beto also had her barred from TDC facilities in 1971 and allegedly organized a lawsuit against her on behalf of several TDC inmates and guards claiming that she was engaged in a conspiracy to encourage inmate uprisings.[52]

Although unable to help Lamar in his criminal appeals, Jalet eventually assisted him in various legal matters and would later become one of his confidants as he filed numerous lawsuits against TDC. She also contacted Houston attorney Edward Mallett on his behalf, writing that "one problem I do have, and in a sense it is of my own making . . . is seeking to aid Allen L. Lamar. . . . Mr. Lamar's family is not without means. . . . [I have] visited with them in Fort Worth, but they don't seem inclined to spend any money to help him. As you may know, he is now a 'jail-house lawyer' and has filed many cases against TDC."[53]

Jalet and Lamar also exchanged several letters in the early 1970s and she visited him in prison in late 1973. Notwithstanding her desire to help TDC prisoners in general, Lamar was equally impressed with Jalet's desire to help his causes, as evidenced in the following letter from January 9, 1974:

Allow me first to seek your compassionate kindness for the aggressive-ness exhibited in my many requests. I know that I have often said that I comprehend the time and energy these various requests consume and yet often repeat what I have sought your forgiveness for. But I really am not an overbearing person and why I show such tendencies really amazes me. . . . Nevertheless I sincerely pray your compassion in these matters as always. Frances, I realize that you have experienced many perplexing situations since your commencement of assisting the incarcerated. . . . That you have traveled some 800 miles simply for me gives further illustration of the human goodness and diligent representation you have always bestowed upon me. My indebtedness to you magnifies each day.[54]

By the early 1970s, Lamar had become well known as a writ-writer and filed numerous cases against TDC with varying levels of assistance from Jalet. Although most of Lamar's lawsuits were unsuccessful, he had no fewer than nine pending civil rights lawsuits in the early to mid-1970s against TDC. Lamar challenged the denial of vocational training in TDC and claimed that the parole board's lack of minority members prejudiced it against black and Hispanic inmates. Lamar also filed suit against TDC concerning a regulation prohibiting inmates from speaking Spanish. This case was eventually con-solidated with Lamar's claims of racial discrimination in *Lamar v. Coffield*. Lamar also challenged racial segregation in the Harris County Jail in Hous-ton, the punishment of minority inmates by white TDC staff, the use of building tenders, and arbitrary mailing procedures implemented against Ellis Unit inmates. As a result of these and other lawsuits against TDC, and his continued associations with Jalet, Lamar and other writ-writers associated with Jalet were placed on the Wynne Unit's Eight Hoe Squad in November 1971.[55]

The Eight Hoe Squad comprised twenty-seven prisoners throughout TDC, most from the Ellis Unit, whom Beto transferred to a separate wing at the Wynne Unit for maintaining attorney-client relationships with Jalet and for various writ-writing activities. The so-called "writ-writers" were widely regarded by prison staff in the 1970s as "the lowest form of life," requiring close watch, hence their central placement on the Eight Hoe Squad. Indeed, from November 1971 until October 1972, prisoners of the Eight Hoe Squad, all of whom were considered writ-writers and thus agitators, were integrated with prisoners of other races in double and triple cells as a form of punishment, were denied access to their attorneys, had privileges restricted, received less desirable job assignments, and were "constantly reminded that their circumstances could be improved if they simply gave up their association with Frances Jalet."[56]

Beto's attempts at concentrating the agitators backfired. Putting all the writ-writers in one place constituted a "who's who of TDC writ-writers . . . which thereafter produced virtually all the major reform litigation in TDC."[57] Almost immediately after his October 1972 release from the Eight Hoe Squad, Lamar filed his racial segregation and discrimination lawsuit with the court. *Lamar v. Coffield* emerged as one of four major class-action lawsuits of the 1970s that originated from the Eight Hoe Squad prisoners, among countless other non-class-action lawsuits.

Why Challenge the Status Quo?

What was the point of Lamar's lawsuit? What was he trying to accomplish? While his claims were straightforward, little evidence exists as to the motivation of the suit in the first place — particularly the complaint that inmates should not be subject to racial and ethnic discrimination in housing assignments. Anecdotal evidence of the time suggests that most TDC prisoners did not have a problem with racial segregation in terms of housing; in fact, a group of white, black, and Hispanic inmates intervened in the case with a specific interest in preventing racial desegregation for fears of racial violence. Insight into Lamar's motivation can perhaps be found only by examining the experience of his previous incarcerations.[58]

By the time of Lamar's second commitment to TDC, he had already been incarcerated in the Gatesville State School for Boys, countless local and county jails, three separate California state penal institutions, the U.S. Army disciplinary barracks, four federal correctional institutions, and four separate TDC units. Indeed, from age sixteen to thirty, Lamar had spent time in no fewer than ten correctional institutions spanning nearly every level of incarceration: juvenile, local, county, state, federal, and military facilities.

In each of the above incarcerations, Lamar had been segregated by race to one degree or another. Not only was Lamar classified and segregated according to his race, but this segregation often translated into less desirable treatment at the hands of correctional authorities than that experienced by white inmates. Black inmates generally received less desirable job and living assignments, fewer privileges, and heightened levels of punishment when they committed an institutional infraction. It is no secret that minority inmates as a whole were generally treated worse than other inmates during the 1960s and 1970s:[59]

> In many respects, prisoners were to officers what blacks were to whites in the antebellum south. . . . Many TDC officers brought to the job the prejudices toward criminals and minorities, especially blacks, that prevailed in the rural, conservative communities from which they usually came. Accordingly, TDC officers often called inmates simply 'nigger' or 'meskin.' Clearly, black and Mexican American prisoners were doubly subordinate.

Prison officers at the time of Lamar's first and second TDC bids were even instructed how to handle inmates based on their race or ethnicity. Whereas a white inmate should never be given "anything he doesn't ask for" and "Mexicans require close supervision," black inmates were to be treated like "children."[60]

Black prisoners who identified themselves as Muslims were viewed with an exceptional amount of suspicion by TDC administrators. Muslim prisoners received heightened attention to their behaviors and equally heightened reactions. In fact, it was during his first incarceration that Lamar was placed on the "Muslim list" and, as recounted by one prison official, "all indications show that he could be." This passing quote on Lamar's 1963 disciplinary report at the Harlem II Farm implicates that Muslim inmates were treated differently. For all intents and purposes, Lamar had three strikes against him when it came to life in TDC of the 1960s and 1970s. Lamar was black, a Muslim, and a writ-writer—attributes that generated a generous amount of disdain from prison officials.

The differential treatment Lamar experienced based on his race, faith, and prison activities might provide some insight as to his motivation to file the segregation and discrimination lawsuit during his second TDC incarceration. After more than five years of his second TDC incarceration, Lamar was becoming more and more disenchanted by what he viewed as extremely differential treatment against racial minorities, in particular black inmates. Once Lamar was released from the Eight Hoe Squad and shortly after the initial discrimination suit was filed, he wrote a quasi-manifesto titled "Imperialism Means Imprisonment," complaining of the unequal treatment he and other racial and ethnic minorities received in TDC.

He began this document with a quote from "Comrade George Jackson," the militant Black Panther prisoner from California who was gunned down in 1971 by San Quentin prison officers after an escape attempt. Among other writings, Lamar recounted numerous specific instances of "oppression" he had witnessed by Texas prison officials.[61] Lamar's lawsuit challenging racial and ethnic discrimination in TDC may have thus been motivated in part to remedy what he viewed as disproportionately oppressive conditions against black inmates in TDC. Accordingly, Lamar's view was that separate was certainly not equal in the 1970s Texas prison system. He felt that if blacks were integrated with whites, perhaps the unequal treatment would diminish.

Alternatively, Lamar's specific challenge against racial segregation and discrimination in TDC housing may have been no more complicated than a sincere desire to remove the barriers that kept prisoners of different races apart. This may have been motivated by his placement on the Eight Hoe Squad. Indeed, the separation, isolation, and harassment of the Eight Hoe Squad prisoners "encouraged the formation of a brotherhood."[62] This camaraderie among the isolated and harassed Eight Hoe Squad prisoners "transcended racial and cultural barriers to produce an environment in which . . . prisoner mutual assistance in legal matters flourished."[63] Thus, the racial integration of the Eight Hoe Squad members, which was meant to be a punishment because it was believed the prisoners would be stigmatized by other inmates of the same race, may have spurred Lamar and others to see the positive effects of racial desegregation.[64]

The fact that Lamar was part of the Eight Hoe Squad also indicates that his motivation may have come from a desire to be an "innovator," to be part of a full-out legal assault on the Texas prison system, regardless of the nature of the litigation. Placement on the Eight Hoe Squad fomented an "us against them" mentality and, as a result, institutional litigation was the only way Eight Hoe prisoners could fight back against the paternalistic and sometimes violent TDC. Thus, the Eight Hoe Squad's broad spectrum of complaints was motivated by a desire to cripple TDC, with perhaps little regard for the specific nature of the litigation. From his earliest days of incarceration in TDC, Lamar saw little use in TDC's incarceration process and made no secret of it. He did not agree with what he viewed as the lack of treatment programs, he did not like the field work, and he made it known to Beto that he disagreed with the way TDC operated. By his second TDC incarceration and placement on the Eight Hoe Squad, it is clear that Lamar had become extremely embittered by TDC. As a result, Lamar and the other "eight-hoe prisoners spent countless hours during the eleven months of confinement improving their legal skills, strategizing and coordinating their efforts, and assisting one another in the drafting of petitions."[65] It was perhaps by happenstance, then, and not by design that Allen Lamar and not one of the other Eight Hoe prisoners was the one to file the suit that would challenge racial and ethnic segregation and discrimination in TDC. Perhaps countering the views that Lamar's motivation for filing the suit was driven by removing the barriers of segregation, eliminating the unequal treatment of minorities in TDC, or besieging and exhausting the prison system with inmate litigation, in December 2000 the authors received a communication from a TDC inmate claiming to have been imprisoned alongside Lamar in the 1970s. The inmate, responding to a survey placed in the Texas prison newspaper the *Echo* asking for opinions on racial desegregation and the *Lamar* suit, also wrote about Lamar himself and the motivation for the lawsuit:

> First . . . Lamar did *not* care one bit about "equality" in prison housing, nor did he believe segregated housing really "disadvantaged" black prisoners. [Lamar] had a white, homosexual lover called "Kiki" (who was eventually assigned to Eastham and worked in the garment factory). [Lamar] wanted "Kiki" to share a cell with him—normally back in those days a couple packs of smokes or a bag of Max (coffee) to the Major's Bookkeeper BT would "fix" a cellmate assignment as long as the "punk" you wanted in your cell was the same race, and was the same custody level. Even if a different custody level, a carton of smokes would get a "fix" on the papers and get housing changed. The sole exception that could *not* be "fixed" is if the "punk" was a different race. Since Lamar was black and "Kiki" was white, no bribe would get Lamar's lover in the same cell with him . . . so Lamar, after consulting a "writ writer" named Donald Chastien, filed the suit on segregation. By the way—even though Lamar won the suit—he never did get "Kiki" in the cell with him, because administration made sure they went to separate units. Now, *that* is the *true* facts behind the *Lamar* suit on segregation.[66]

Although we cannot be sure the writer's account is true, it is documented that on two separate occasions Lamar was caught in the act of anal sodomy as the active partner. There is, however, no specific evidence to confirm or refute the inmate's claims. With regard to Lamar's ultimate motivation, we will never know for sure.

At the most basic level, perhaps Lamar was motivated by all these factors. We know that it was while on the Eight Hoe Squad that Lamar was first placed in the same cell with a member of another race. Just as the concentration of writ-writers on the Eight Hoe Squad backfired, the forced desegregation of Lamar with prisoners of another race, coupled with his belief that racial minorities received unequal treatment, may have had a large impact on his desire to force TDC to abandon its race-based practices.[67] If nothing else, placement on the Eight Hoe Squad spurred inmates to begin a massive legal assault on TDC. Whether Lamar was ever truly motivated by a desire to change the practices of racial and ethnic discrimination in TDC is unknown.

Conclusion

Our examination of Lamar's biography thus far has shown that he was no angel, nor a Rosa Parks–like trailblazer who sought to pull down a long-standing barrier for the benefit of humankind. From all indications, Lamar was a career criminal, an aggressive convict who probably enjoyed being a malcontent and derived pleasure and satisfaction at throwing a wrench into the well-oiled gears of the world-renowned Texas prison system. Lamar was a nobody in the free world, but by his second TDC incarceration, he emerged as a marginal somebody in the penitentiary who was smart enough to know how to file a lawsuit against the prison system. This lawsuit would constitute a full assault on the color line in Texas prisons.

CHAPTER 6

Full Assault on the Color Line

Early Developments in the Case, 1972–1977

In October 1972 the Eight Hoe Squad was disbanded, and in the same month, Lamar filed his *pro se* (without the assistance of counsel) segregation and discrimination complaint with the court. On September 25, 1973, Lamar and the black plaintiffs' class were assigned Gerald Birnberg as counsel. On February 26, 1974, the Hispanic class was assigned separate counsel, David T. Lopez, and on June 5, 1974, TDC inmate defendant-intervenors opposed to racial desegregation in cells were assigned their own counsel, Ernest Caldwell. Harry Walsh and later Ed Idar of the Texas attorney general's office represented members of the Texas Board of Corrections and the director of TDC. Gail Littlefield represented the U.S. Department of Justice (DOJ) as plaintiff-intervenors.[1]

From 1973 to 1977, routine court procedures unfolded, including voluminous discoveries, depositions, interrogatories, motions to intervene, requests for production of documents, requests for extensions of time, and objections. All parties in the case were accumulating information and developing strategies that would be used in the event of a trial.

During pretrial maneuvers, the DOJ took perhaps the most active role in the case—a role that would continue in the long term and would become one of the most important aspects of this case. Gerald Birnberg, attorney for Lamar and the black plaintiffs' class, explained: "The most crucial thing that happened during this period of time was that the United States Department of Justice agreed to intervene on behalf of the plaintiffs. . . . It was just absolutely impossible for solo practitioners . . . to be able to match the resources of the state."[2]

Lacking the resources to decipher discovery data and documents requested of TDC, Birnberg helped work out a strategy:

The individual lawyers would focus on the legal issues that were involved in the case . . . but that the USA [Department of Justice] would take the lead on the accumulation of evidence. . . . If it had not been for the United States . . . the plaintiffs probably would not have been able to prove their case other than anecdotal evidence.[3]

In the late 1960s and 1970s, it was not uncommon for the DOJ to intervene in prisoner rights cases, including the few prisoner desegregation cases occurring at this time involving other prison systems. Section 902 of the Civil Rights Act of 1964 gave the U.S. attorney general the power to intervene in any legal action where there is a denial of rights based on race, color, religion, or national origin as long as the attorney general classified the case as one of "general public importance." The *Lamar* suit was so categorized by the attorney general, and this led to DOJ intervention.

The rationale for providing the DOJ intervention power in civil rights complaints was based on Congress's belief that individual parties could not accomplish their mandates alone when faced with the resources and experience of other entities, in this case, the State of Texas and TDC.[4] The *Lamar* court docket prior to the scheduled trial in 1977 shows the active role of the DOJ through their numerous requests for discovery and depositions of inmates and staff of TDC. Throughout the duration of the case, the plaintiff classes in *Lamar* received significant assistance from the DOJ in these and other matters.[5]

After nearly two years of pretrial discovery and motions, on September 3, 1974, the DOJ put forth interrogatories for TDC defendants designed to force prison officials to provide evidence, other than anecdote and opinion, that racial desegregation would foment problems among inmates. The interrogatories and the responses provided by TDC officials also shed light on their position concerning the desegregation of inmates—a position that would remain relatively unchanged for more than fifteen years.

The Wagons Circle, 1974

In response to the DOJ interrogatories, prison administrators issued an inter-office communication in September of 1974 instructing all system wardens to complete two requests. The first request was that wardens list the date, location, and circumstances of any inmate disturbances in institutions under the management or control of TDC since January 1, 1970, and whether such incidents were racially motivated. Below are some incident descriptions from wardens.[6]

Incident Description I: On July 5, 1972, at 10:30 P.M. a disturbance started in the black dormitory. Approximately 300 black inmates assigned to A Dorm, and cellblocks I, II, 12, 6 and 2 were involved. The disturbance consisted of these inmates shouting, cursing, and throwing objects at employees. There was also some burning of bedding and other articles. Many windows were broken by inmates using locks attached to their belts. The inmates were given a time limit (riot act) to discontinue their activities and when they did not, the disturbance was quelled by the use of tear gas.

An investigation into the disturbance revealed that it was the result of an attempt by the administration to integrate some of the cellblocks, which failed due to the boycotting of the dayrooms by white inmates and some Mexicans assigned to these blocks. The administration, feeling that the attempt had failed, again segregated the cellblocks according to race which, when picked up by a few black (and white) agitators resulted in the disturbance.

Incident Description 2: The Ellis Unit has had several fights and disturbances since Sunday, April 12, 1970. The information I have received indicates that most of our trouble-makers attended Sunday School on Sunday, April 12, and voiced themselves to the effect that "Now is the time to get our demands. All concerned have been given notice." According to my informants, the inmates making these remarks Sunday were: B. B., J. F., N. J., and W. R.

B. B. has been telling his followers that they must act now and act fast. He also says that they cannot secure any help from the white population, accordingly, they must try to get supporters from the Mexicans. W. R. seems to be the recruiting sergeant, for he has enlisted three or four Mexicans who would follow anyone as long as trouble and stabbings were their aim and goal.

B. B., as their leader, started trouble Monday night as he was going to the writ room. He called turnkey F. K. a wetback snitching son-of-a-bitch. He apparently picked this inmate since he had been told F. K. had been in considerable trouble in the past but was currently trying to keep a clean record. But F. K. could not take the abusive language and turned on B.

Incident Description 3: Upon completion of our new facility on Clemens in 1969, I integrated one dormitory wing with older blacks, Mexican-Americans and whites. They got along fine. In 1971, the Clemens Unit began receiving a large number of younger inmates. . . . Consequently, older inmates were replaced by younger inmates in this integrated dormitory. They continuously had arguments and disturbances over the one TV set. The blacks wanted to watch movies and certain variety shows, and the white inmates wanted to watch variety shows and country western music. On some units, blacks are in the majority, and naturally a majority vote means that soul music programs and sports would be seen. The Mexican-American inmates in the wing always demanded to see a "Chicano" program at 2:00 p.m. on Sundays, which conflicted with a Dallas Cowboy game, or some other important sports event.

I was never able to come up with a suitable solution that would please everybody. It is my opinion that initially the inmates could not cooperate over the TV programs because of their basic immaturity, and not due to race; however, eventually, it resulted in the separation of the races in the wing, and we began to receive information that a serious disturbance was about to take place. I felt like that I had done everything in my power to make this integrated wing work in this dormitory. A number of inmates from all three races in the wing requested that they be reassigned to a segregated wing. I had no alternative, but to return the wing to a segregated status.

Incident Description 4: A Mexican-American knifed a black inmate at the medical window for allegedly patting him on the buttock in the shower. This caused some unrest among the inmates.

The second request asked wardens to furnish the name, race, and current unit and cell assignment of each TDC inmate who has been determined by prison officials to pose a security problem if housed with any inmates of a different race or national origin and the reasons for such determination. Below are some inmate descriptions by wardens.[7]

B. A.: Subject is a 3 time loser and expresses a hate for blacks and a dislike for Mex. Racist.

E. B.: A malcontent and trouble maker. His own race does not like him, much less the white or Mexican.

D. B.: About half-crazy. Made the statement before the Disciplinary Committee [that] the darn niggers is running the squad and I ain't going to work in that squad. If you send me back I'll kill me a nigger.

J. B.: A loner. Does not get along very well with his own race. Racist. Hates Blacks and Mexicans.

R. F.: Troublemaker, malcontent, and agitator. Racist. Would be killed if housed with a white or Mexican. Is despised by both races.

J. L.: A three time loser. Racist. Believes very strongly in his own race. Could not be housed with other race without violence occurring.

C. T.: Racist, malcontent, trouble maker, and agitator. No white or Mexican would put up with subject. Would be killed or beaten badly.

Prison wardens were also asked to address what percentage of the different racial or ethnic groups at their unit, in their opinion, would not want to be integrated with other inmates or would cause problems if integrated. Overall, TDC wardens believed that most members of different races would prefer segregation. In their own words:[8]

Opinion I: In my opinion the following percentage of the ethnic groups *could not be integrated.*

Mexican ———— 100%
White ———— 90%
Black ———— 80%

Opinion 2: In my opinion a very small percent of White, Black or Mexican inmates would want to be integrated. I would say 5% or less of our white population would desire integration, while approximately 15% of our black population would desire integration. . . . There is no question in my mind that our problems would be increased through forced integration. . . . The vast majority of our inmates do not desire integration and the administration supports their feelings.

Opinion 3: I have 11½ years experience in corrections, 10 of which have been in a supervisory capacity, and I have completed a B.S. degree in Sociology with a minor in Psychology. I consider myself an expert in inmate behavior and relationship.

It is my expert opinion that [the] substantial majority of the TDC population would prefer to be housed in the cell with inmates of their own race and national origin. If I were to hazard an educated guess, I would estimate that 95% of the Blacks, Anglos, or Mexican Americans would bitterly oppose living in a cell with someone of a different race or national origin.

Opinion 4: It is a consensus of opinion that we would encourage problems if we tried total integration.

Opinion 5: It is my opinion that 95% of Mexican-American inmates do not want to live with black inmates, 60% of whites would not want to live with black inmates, and 75% of black inmates would want to integrate with other races as long as they were in the majority in a wing.

Opinion 6: It is my considered opinion that the majority of inmates do not want to be housed with other inmates of different races of national origins. The security and tranquility of the institution would be at stake.

Opinion 7: After careful study I feel there could be serious trouble if possibly fifty to one hundred inmates were made to live in the same cell. I am not speaking of a dormitory or cell block, but the cell itself. Also, this will be a conservative figure.

The DOJ interrogatories were a way to force prison administrators and their lawyers to document the prevailing belief that segregation was necessary for the prevention of race-based violence. According to the DOJ, there was simply little evidence on the record that would suggest that racial mixing would foment violence in TDC. The "Justice Department took the lead in rejecting that notion" and placed the burden on TDC to put forth evidence showing why racial desegregation could not be accomplished.[9]

In some respects the DOJ was successful. Although most wardens believed that racial desegregation would "encourage" problems and that most inmates preferred segregation, several wardens were not able to specifically name inmates who would pose a security problem if desegregated, nor were many wardens able to identify any racially motivated incidents that had occurred at their unit during the requested time frame. As one warden remarked, "At present there are no inmates . . . who have been determined to pose a security problem if housed with any inmates of a different race or national origin."[10] Despite the competing perspectives of the DOJ and TDC on the likely outcomes of the desegregation of inmates at any level, especially within cells, pretrial discovery and procedures continued into 1976 concerning all aspects of the case in preparation for the eventual trial.

A Last Minute Maneuver, 1977

The *Lamar* trial was scheduled for July 14, 1977. Three months before the scheduled trial date, however, a draft consent decree was submitted to the court by TDC and the DOJ. In the meantime, negotiations continued between the DOJ, the Texas attorney general's office, and prison administrators on the specific aspects of the consent decree.

On July 13, 1977, on the eve of the trial, Judge Robert O'Conor held a pretrial conference in his chambers and addressed the provisions of the consent decree. Along with DOJ lawyers, the inmate plaintiffs and defendant-intervenor inmates were present with their counsel. TDC director W. J. Estelle and his counsel from the Texas attorney general's office were also present. The *Lamar* jury was selected and the trial was set to begin.

The next day, the case was called to order without the jury present, and stipulations of the consent decree between TDC and DOJ were stated. Judge O'Conor recessed for further negotiations. That same day, the jurors were brought into court, were informed that a settlement had been reached in the case, and were dismissed.[11] The settlement almost never happened, however. While TDC was willing to address and develop a plan to remedy most complaints, there still remained disagreement on the issue of desegregated housing, specifically the desegregation of double cells. To keep TDC from skirting the issue, the DOJ insisted that TDC "bring about the maximum possible integration of the cells." Prison administrators rejected this blanket wording; they wanted exceptions to be added into the consent decree, one in particular: "In no case, however, will an inmate be housed in the same cell with another inmate or inmates when such assignment would constitute a clear danger to security, control and rehabilitation." Birnberg recalled:

> On the eve of trial we entered into a consent decree . . . and the thrust of it was that the consent decree provided that the prison system . . . would be permanently enjoined from segregating on the basis of race. . . . The Justice Department was insisting upon that because they realized that any lesser standard would give too much wiggle room to the prison. . . . I thought that until the very few days before trial . . . that the case was going to go to trial and it was over the wording of that standard because the prison system . . . was completely convinced, I believe in good faith, that the result of desegregating the prison would be terrible turmoil, and ultimately at the last minute they agreed to this particular standard.[12]

Despite this last minute wrangling, the parties agreed to the stipulations of the consent decree. Two months later on September 22, 1977, the consent decree and an agreed judgment was approved by the court:

> The Order to be entered as hereafter set out does not constitute a finding that the Defendants have engaged in a system-wide pattern or

practice of past or present racial or ethnic discrimination or denial of equal
protection of the law or due process of law to black or Spanish-speaking
inmates; nor does it constitute an admission of liability on the part of
Defendants.[13]

Elements of the Consent Decree

The consent decree covered numerous aspects of TDC operation as they related to racial segregation and discrimination. The first provision required that
TDC develop an affirmative action plan designed to implement the provisions
of the decree, including a timetable for completion and periodic reporting to
the court of progress made toward the plan. Along with the development of
an affirmative action plan, the specific provisions of the consent decree called
for the following actions:[14]

1. Inmate Housing Assignments
   a. The assignment of inmates to dormitories, cell blocks, or other living
   quarters shall be made on the basis of rational objective criteria and
   shall not be made on the basis of race, color, religion or national origin. With respect to individual cells, the Plan shall provide guidelines
   for the exercise of discretion by the appropriate Warden or other TDC
   official so as to bring about the maximum possible integration of the
   cells consonant with the factors of security, control and rehabilitation.
   In no case, however, will an inmate be housed in the same cell with
   another inmate or inmates when such assignment would constitute a
   clear danger to security, control and rehabilitation. The following additional guidelines shall be employed:
   i. The proportion of each racial or ethnic group in each prison unit
   shall be at least 70 percent of that group's proportion of the total
   TDC population.
   ii. The racial and ethnic composition of each housing unit (excluding
   cells but including floors and tiers of cellblocks and dormitories)
   shall approximate the overall racial and ethnic composition of the
   unit's inmate population.
   Inmates are not to be concentrated by race or ethnic background
   in any one section of any particular housing unit.
   iv. The Plan shall provide for the orderly integration of any inmate
   facilities, including floors and tiers of cellblocks and dormitories.
   . . . It shall include an inmate classification program for each unit
   employing valid criteria for assignment of inmates to living quar-

ters, including such factors as age, physical characteristics such as weight and height, seriousness of offense, violent or passive tendencies, homosexual (both active and passive) tendencies, criminal sophistication and other factors used in the field of corrections in the assignment of inmates to housing within a prison unit.

2. Inmate Job Assignments

a. The assignment of inmates to jobs or work squads shall not be made on the basis of race, color, religion or national origin. All inmates shall have an equal opportunity to be considered fairly for assignment to and advancement within all job or work squad assignments. To assist in insuring that this is achieved the following guidelines shall be employed:

i. The racial and ethnic composition of each job category and work squad assignment shall approximate the racial and ethnic composition within each prison unit.

ii. Voluntary transfers and job or work squad reassignments will only be allowed if this racial and ethnic balance is maintained.

iii. No preference shall be given in future job or work squad assignments to an inmate's previous work within the prison system where such preference would have a discriminatory effect.

iv. The Plan shall provide for the orderly integration of all job and work squad assignments.

3. Inmate Discipline

a. Inmates must be informed of the disciplinary rules and regulations as are prescribed by the inmate handbook. . . . Race or ethnic background must never be the cause of any inmates or group of inmates receiving more frequent, severe, or disparate punishment.

b. Minority personnel shall, whenever and as frequently as possible, be assigned to sit on the unit disciplinary committee.

4. Education

a. Race, color, creed, or national origin has not and shall not be a factor in the selection for or administration of any educational program offered to inmates in TDC. No educational activities shall be segregated on the basis of race, color, creed or national origin.

5. Medical Care

a. Inmates shall not be deprived of medical care because of race, color, creed, or national origin. An effort will be made on a continuing basis to hire minority civilian personnel.

6. Recreational Activities

a. Inmates shall not be segregated or discriminated against in any inmate

group recreational and/or cultural activities such as movies, gymnasium, library and church services.
7. Racial Epithets
   a. Defendants shall inform their employees that the use of racial and ethnic epithets and slurs toward inmates will not be tolerated.
8. Discrimination Regarding Incoming Publications
   a. Race, color or national origin shall not be a consideration in the administrative review of incoming publications.
9. Punishment for Speaking Spanish
   a. Spanish-speaking inmates shall not be punished or in any way disciplined for speaking or writing Spanish.
10. Grievance Procedure Regarding Racial Segregation and Discrimination
   a. All persons confined to facilities of TDC shall be informed that they may raise complaints of discrimination through the inmate grievance procedure. In acting upon grievances which raise the issue of discrimination, the Director of TDC or unit Warden shall appoint, as their designees, persons who are sensitive to the issues of racial and ethnic equality.
11. Staffing
   a. To assist in the implementation of this Order and of the Plan to be formulated. . . . Defendants shall designate an affirmative action officer. One of this officer's primary functions will be to continue to recruit minority personnel and attempt to resolve equal opportunity grievances.

The *Lamar* consent decree and agreed judgment called for massive remedial action and covered eleven separate areas of TDC operation. In short, it required the elimination of racial segregation and other discriminatory practices in every aspect of TDC operation. At this point, the *Lamar* consent decree and its stipulations constituted the single greatest assault on TDC operation ever. While the *Ruiz* litigation (discussed later in this chapter) would hold the most prominent place in TDC legal history, the breadth and depth of *Lamar* was simply unparalleled, and perhaps set the stage for the massive changes wrought by *Ruiz*.[15]

While there were few specific timelines in the consent decree and agreed judgment, the affirmative action plan was to be submitted to the court by November 1977. Despite the breadth and depth of the consent decree, the most disputed issue would center on the desegregation of inmate housing areas, and in particular double cells. The following sections focus on this contentious issue.

The First Move: TDC Submits Affirmative Action Plan to the Court

Two months after the consent decree and agreed judgment was accepted, TDC submitted its affirmative action plan to the court. The affirmative action plan addressed all eleven aspects of the consent decree and agreed judgment. In the preface to the plan, system director W. J. Estelle wrote:[16]

> It is the belief of the Texas Department of Corrections that the Plan as presented fully addresses the concerns of the Court and the best interests of the Texas Department of Corrections in providing for equal treatment and opportunity for all inmates without jeopardizing the security, control, rehabilitation or safety responsibilities of the Department.

> The Texas Department of Corrections shall, in completely good faith, implement the Plan to the satisfaction of the Court and in a manner equal to the high standards of performance for which the Department is noted in the field of corrections.

The objectives of the plan, specific to the desegregation of inmate housing areas, called for the orderly desegregation of every inmate housing facility, including floors, tiers of cell blocks, and dormitories. TDC's affirmative action plan also noted:

> In exercising correctional discretion, and in order to bring about the maximum possible integration of individual cells, the appropriate TDC official or Warden shall integrate with due consideration for security, control, rehabilitation and safety. No such assignment shall be made which constitutes a clear and present danger to security, control, rehabilitation or safety of inmates or staff.[17]

TDC's three-month targets for the desegregation of inmate housing areas called for the following: (1) a plan for implementation; (2) the establishment of training requirements; (3) a computerized reporting program to aid in reporting the ethnic and racial composition of unit housing facilities; (4) a study of present housing assignments which deviate from the 70 percent rule (that the proportion of each racial or ethnic group in each prison unit shall be at least 70 percent of that group's proportion of the total TDC inmate population); and (5) the development of guidelines for the assignment of inmates to housing based on rational objective criteria.

TDC's nine-month goals included achieving compliance with the 70 percent rule for each racial and ethnic group and the initiation of desegregation of floors, tiers of cell blocks, and dormitories. At fifteen months, TDC's affirmative action plan target was a "report to the court on the progress made toward cell integration."

Two months after the affirmative action plan was submitted, on January 24, 1978, the DOJ filed a motion with the court requesting a hearing on TDC's affirmative action plan, and they also offered comments on the plan. Specific to in-cell desegregation, the DOJ noted:

> The action steps [in TDC's affirmative action plan] are not sufficiently detailed to judge their adequacy. . . . The defendants propose that in-cell integration be accomplished at a slower rate than the other desegregation, not being completed within fifteen months. In-cell integration should occur contemporaneously with reclassification and integration of other living units.[18]

Following receipt of the DOJ's motion and after reviewing their comments on the affirmative action plan, Ed Idar, the assistant attorney general representing TDC, wrote Judge O'Conor on January 25, 1978:

> I received today from the United States its Motion for Hearing on Defendants' Plan as well as United States Comments on Defendants' Affirmative Action Plan. We are not in accord with the United States that a hearing on the matter is necessary. The Plan submitted is comprehensive and carefully tracks the provisions of the Consent Decree and the Agreed Judgment. It was prepared in full consultation with Mr. Sherman Day who was the very person suggested by the United States for this purpose. I believe the Court should enter an Order forthwith approving the plan and order that it be implemented.
>
> The black and Mexican American Plaintiffs have filed no objections or other comments; nor have the Defendant-Intervenors nor have any of them requested an extension for this purpose. Their time to do this has long since expired. The Defendants are ready to implement the plan once it is approved by the Court and its implementation is ordered. In my view there is no need for further loss of time and nit-picking may result in a tale that never ends and tear apart a carefully drafted and comprehensive plan.[19]

Despite Idar's pleas for an order accepting the plan and his disdain for further nit-picking, the court never issued such an order. Rather, on March 9,

1978, Judge O'Conor held a hearing where members of the DOJ and TDC met privately and came to an agreement per the provisions of the affirmative action plan. Following these negotiations, another agreed order was signed by the court. Per this order, certain aspects of TDC's affirmative action plan were modified, TDC was ordered to submit progress reports to the court in six- and twelve-month intervals, and all other objections raised by the DOJ were overruled. Presumably, the DOJ and TDC dealt with the issue of in-cell desegregation at this time, for the court's order modifying the original affirmative action plan made no mention of modifying TDC's fifteen-month target of reporting "to the court on the progress made toward cell integration."

Life for a Writ-Writer

Following his release from the Wynne Unit's Eight Hoe Squad in 1972, Allen Lamar was transferred back to the Ellis Unit. At his arrival and for the next several years, Lamar allegedly received harassment and retaliation due to his writ-writing activities and specifically his participation in the *Lamar* lawsuit. In late 1973, roughly one year after filing his lawsuit, Lamar was moved from one cell block on the Ellis Unit to another. Concerned with this move, attorney Frances Jalet wrote TDC Director Estelle and requested that Lamar be transferred to another prison unit:[20]

> On the occasion of my first visit to my client, Mr. Allen Lamar just prior to Christmas he informed me that the atmosphere where he is assigned cell-wise and in the hoe squad was such that he feared there was some plan to harm him. He does not, however, wish to be segregated given the type of "protection" that entails segregation status and loss of privileges and normal prison comforts. He has merely requested that this be brought to the attention of the appropriate authority, whom I deem to be you, in order that his removal to another Unit might be considered.

> Today I received a letter from Mr. Lamar indicating his concern for his well being has not changed although he has been assigned to a different Wing (G-15) and put in a different hoe squad (5-hoe); the same persons who he noticed as possibly having designs against him were moved along with him. There is, therefore, no actual change.

> I would appreciate it if you would inquire into this matter and advise me of your findings, taking whatever precautions you may deem necessary short of segregation of Mr. Lamar.

Often I wish it were not necessary to advise you of so many various problems, but they seem to rise and must be met.

Estelle replied on January 18, 1974:[21]

Please be assured that we are as interested as you in the welfare of Mr. Lamar. However, he was moved from one cell block on the Ellis Unit to another not for his own protection, but to protect the other inmates from him. Thus, we cannot consider transferring him at this time.

We have in the past, and will continue in the future, to endeavor to insure the protection of all inmates of the Texas Department of Corrections.

Lamar allegedly continued to experience problems during 1974 at Ellis. In a letter he wrote to Jalet on April 24, 1974, Lamar complained of the consistent harassment he had received from prison officers:[22]

This acknowledges your recent correspondence of April 19, 1974 as always I am most happy and concerned.

My most recent incarceration in solitary confinement was for the charge of contraband. It was alleged by Captain L. A. Steele that five .38 bullets were found in my legal documents in the Unit Writroom. He presented those to the committee and recommended solitary confinement as my punishment. He also signed the disciplinary offense report as the Officer who made the charge and as a member of the Committee. This infraction however has the effect of disqualifying me for restoration to Class I status, restoration of lost overtime, participation in the College program; and, makes my upcoming Parole Review in June meaningless. So you see my position is the same as always. After a period that exceeds seven (7) years it would appear that they would give up, however, this is not the case and regardless everything must come in order. . . .

You are aware that my position with you is as firm and everlasting as always. I comprehend the situation fully and will expect you when the opportunity presents itself. You are still my small and mighty counsel.

Lamar was still at the Ellis Unit in 1976 when he was subject to further retaliation by prison officers. As a result, Lamar filed a lawsuit against Building Major Len Arthur Steele (who also had found Lamar in possession of several

.38 bullets in April 1974), complaining of harassment received during 1975 and 1976. In his suit, for which he offered some materials as proof, Lamar alleged that Steele, who had "manifested a distaste for Lamar's activities," had burned his legal documents, asked one inmate to assault him and another to kill him, invited him to pick up and attempt to use a small knife while Steele held a large hunting knife in his hand out of view, and promised to send him home in a "pine box."[23] The suit was successful, and after appeal for various issues, the Court of Appeals for the Fifth Circuit noted that "Steele's actions constituted punishment for Lamar's past activities and intimidation aimed at his future activities. . . . The conduct laid at Steele's door was a flagrant disregard of these constitutional rights."[24]

While prison system lawyers and TDC administrators were working on the particulars of the affirmative action plan, an attempt on Lamar's life was made at the Ellis Unit on January 3, 1978. Little is known about this attempt, although a letter to Frances Jalet from Joyce Armstrong, assistant to State Senator Oscar Mauzy, confirms that an attempt was made. In 1979, Lamar and several other TDC inmates who testified or who were otherwise involved in *Ruiz v. Estelle* and other pending TDC lawsuits were transferred to the Federal Bureau of Prisons for protection from retaliation by other inmates and staff. Lamar was then transferred to Ft. Leavenworth, Kansas, to continue his incarceration. In the meantime, TDC was progressing toward compliance with several areas of the *Lamar* consent decree.

Progress toward the Consent Decree, 1978–1980

In compliance with the court's order of March 3, 1978, between June 1978 and June 1979 TDC submitted progress reports to the court regarding the eleven areas of the *Lamar* consent decree. In an April 19, 1979, letter to TDC director W. J. Estelle, Dr. Sherman Day, a consultant assisting TDC to develop the affirmative action plan, noted that while "the system has made significant progress in all areas related to the plan . . . the one area where progress is extremely uneven is cell integration." Dr. Day noted that several TDC units needed significant cell desegregation to reach the minimum as established by the court, and ended the letter by noting that "the TDC has made a significant effort to comply with both the letter and spirit of the Consent Decree. The remaining months should be devoted to fine tuning of the compliance effort, as well as giving greater emphasis to cell integration."[25]

Roughly eight months after Dr. Day's evaluation of TDC compliance with the *Lamar* consent decree, on December 10, 1979, the court held a status conference on various matters relating to the case, including the issue of terminating the court's jurisdiction. The court did not terminate jurisdiction of the case, but rather, on December 20, 1979, ordered TDC to produce two additional reports detailing their level of compliance with the consent decree and affirmative action plan. These progress reports were to be submitted on February 9 and June 9, 1980, respectively. The court also ordered that additional discovery in the case be stayed pending TDC's filing of the required June 1980 progress report and that, if necessary, the court would set a date for an evidentiary hearing for the purpose of determining whether TDC was in compliance with the consent decree and whether the court should terminate its jurisdiction.

At the time of the December 20, 1979, court order, TDC had made significant progress toward many aspects of the consent decree, including the desegregation of larger housing units such as dormitories and cell blocks. The prison system had also made progress desegregating double cells. Data from TDC's twenty-two-month progress report submitted to the court on February 14, 1980 (which examined among other areas in-cell desegregation from May 1978 through January 1980), demonstrated the extent of double-cell desegregation. In May 1978, TDC had roughly 327 double cells desegregated among fifteen prison units as reported in the progress report (units listed were Central, Clemens, Coffield, Darrington, Eastham, Ellis, Ferguson, Goree, Huntsville, Jester II [formerly Harlem II], Mountain View, Ramsey I, Ramsey II, Retrieve, and Wynne). The prison system had desegregated 612 cells by August 1978, 621 cells by November 1978, 657 cells by February 1979, 899 cells by June 1979, and 970 cells by January 1980.[26] Although the total number of double cells available in TDC was not provided in this court report, nor did it take into account changes in TDC inmate population, TDC almost tripled the number of double cells desegregated from 1978 through the end of 1979.

When progress reports were filed with the court in July 1980, lawyers for TDC defendants filed a brief in support of termination of the court's jurisdiction. In this brief they argued that TDC was in substantial compliance with the consent decree and mandates of the affirmative action plan. The prison system's lawyers also opposed additional discovery by the DOJ and the inmate plaintiffs. At the same time that the prison system was submitting reports to the court and arguing for termination of the court's jurisdiction, the DOJ was also persisting in their efforts to document TDC's lack of progress toward the decree. One product of DOJ efforts was a survey of inmates regarding their views on TDC progress with desegregation.

A Time to Study Change

In February 1980, nearly eight years after the *Lamar* suit was filed, the DOJ and counsel for the plaintiff classes presented evidence to the court that TDC's progress with certain aspects of the consent decree did not justify termination of oversight. The DOJ produced results from a twenty-six-question survey administered to more than 100 TDC inmates. The survey inquired about various provisions related to the *Lamar* consent decree, from progress toward racial desegregation in housing and job assignments to the use of racial and ethnic slurs by TDC officers. Regarding desegregation of double cells, inmate responses revealed that TDC had made little if any progress.

Upon receipt of the survey and its results, prison administrators critiqued every aspect of the document from the methodology to the sampling procedure to wording of questions. They concluded:

The questionnaire itself is a poorly constructed document and is not aimed at the educational level of TDC inmates. Based on the responses given, many inmates did not understand the questions and valid answers were not available from all inmates. . . . Inmates responding to the questionnaire were not typical of the total inmate population at TDC. . . . Overall, this complete questionnaire was sent to an atypical group of TDC inmates in order to gain the responses which the Justice Department was anxious to hear.[27]

Notwithstanding complaints about the survey, it did provide a glimpse into how inmates viewed their progress with desegregation. Below are some responses from inmates:

In your own words, please describe the progress of racial-ethnic integration of housing assignments since January 1978 in the Units of the Texas Department of Corrections to which you have been assigned:

W. A. (Black): To the best of my knowledge it has been non-integrated from 1978 until now on Ramsey I during my stay. It's still a racist conflict going between the classes. The whites, blacks, Mexican Americans are trying to unite but job discrimination keep a separation and disciplinary committee action. Solitary confinement are always more blacks and Mexican/American than whites.

C. L. A. (Black): There is no progress because TDC Officials don't want racial integration, when they place an Inmate in an integrated cell or dorm it will be with someone that they know he won't get along with.

H. C. (Mexican/American): Basically it is still unchanged, because it is not done randomly. Men are not merely assigned to a wing. Race still has a lot to do with where one is assigned. TDC is handpicking a few and placing them here and there to get by the ruling. All in all, the ruling is not being complied with.

L. D. (Black): Basically there has been little or no progress as regard the dictates of the Court's Order, and at best, have been very slow in the implementation and enforcement thereof.

J. D. D. (Black): The racial-ethnic integration of housing assignments at the Darrington Unit has been very poor progress as a result of racial hostilities influence by the TDC correctional official by causing the racial conflicts between blacks and Chicanos or Mexican-Americans and Caucasian Americans by the use of inmate building tenders or floor-boys who advises inmates not to integrate in cells assignments with other inmates of different races because the correctional officials do not want integration.

J. J. D. (White): In March of 1978 the officials of the Eastham Unit passed out grievance forms and instructed inmates to file grievances against being placed in integrated quarters. These grievance forms are normally very difficult to obtain when seeking to use said forms for grievances against TDC policy or officials, but during this particular time the building tenders were passing the forms out and telling everyone to fill them out against integration. Hundreds of forms were filed during early 1978 and late 1977, these were filed at the request of TDC officials of the Eastham Unit. I refused to sign a grievance form and was called to the warden's office for telling other inmates not to sign the forms. Warden A, Asst. Warden B, and Major C cursed me, called me a nigger-lover, and an agitator who was trying to cause a racial riot. Everyday, I heard officials calling inmates niggers, wetbacks, Mexican in every derogatory tone of voice. . . . When I left Eastham 10-18-79—there were no integrated cells. Either all whites or blacks lived in individual cells although cellblocks were partially integrated.

A. L. L. (Black): Cell assignments are very few.

J. V. M. (Mexican/American): On the Ramsey Unit #1 cellblocks and dormitories have been integrated. This integration has done no good since unit officials in cahoots with the inmate-guard elite stir up the fires and racism every change they get, i.e., spreading rumors of forced cell integration, and refusing to inform the general population of all aspects of Lamar v. Coffield.

J. J. M. (Mexican/American): TDC had made progress in desegregation but only because of the prodding of the federal courts. Although I have heard of young whites and Mexicans having problems when placed with "big blacks" as a form of castigation. Personally I have had no problem as I'm consider dangerous to other inmates and no one is put in my cell for that purpose and then too, I don't want anyone with me in my cell.

L. C. P. (White): It is my belief that the TDC officials have been using the assignment to integrated housing, i.e., integrated two-man cells, or the threat of such assignments to harass and intimidate inmates who are writ-writers and/or witnesses or potential witnesses against TDC in cases such as Ruiz v. Estelle.

D. R. R. (Mexican/American): The guidelines and procedures did not meet with human treatment. To my understanding at Wynne Unit because of overcrowding, three to a cell, certain officials would inform inmates that the only way to get out of three to a cell was to agree to integrate and would be moved to a two man cell.

The DOJ received responses from over one hundred inmates regarding the desegregation of TDC's housing facilities and job assignments. Allen Lamar, Lorenzo Davis, and David Ruiz were three of those chosen for the survey, in addition to several other members of the Eight Hoe Squad and other inmates who were parties in lawsuits against TDC, including those involved with the *Lamar* suit.

The Perfect Legal Storm

Despite TDC's July 1980 request for the court to terminate jurisdiction of the case, court oversight would continue. In addition to the DOJ's survey results, a major reason court oversight continued was a direct result of *Ruiz v. Estelle*, another major class-action suit involving TDC and filed by former Eight Hoe Squad member David Ruiz. Filed in the same year as *Lamar*, *Ruiz* had been progressing simultaneously with *Lamar* (*Ruiz* was filed in the U.S. Court for the Eastern District of Texas, but the trial occurred in Houston at the Federal Courthouse for the U.S. Southern District of Texas, the court where *Lamar* was filed).[28] Just over one year after the *Lamar* consent decree and agreed judgment was accepted by the court, on October 2, 1978, the *Ruiz* trial began without a settlement. After 159 days of hearings, *Ruiz* became the longest civil rights trial in American history, concluding on September 20, 1979.

Fourteen months after the *Ruiz* trial concluded, Judge William Wayne Justice issued his opinion in the case and ordered changes in nine separate areas of the prison system's operation (overcrowding, security and supervision, health care, discipline, access to courts, fire safety, sanitation, work safety and hygiene, and unit size, structure, and location).[29] From 1980 to early 1983, as a direct result of *Ruiz*, little progress occurred in the *Lamar* case. Both TDC and the DOJ (which was also appointed by Judge Justice to assist the plaintiffs in *Ruiz*) were heavily involved in post-*Ruiz* issues and appeals.

Lamar Resumes, 1983–1986

In April 1983 the *Lamar* decree process resumed and Judge Robert O'Conor held a conference among the parties in the case during which TDC moved again for dismissal, as it had in July 1980. The court denied this request and ruled that TDC was to continue to file progress reports and that any motions to terminate jurisdiction of the case would be dealt with during a status conference in November 1983. At the scheduled status conference on November 11, the court held that a hearing on the termination of jurisdiction would occur in March 1984. This hearing was later rescheduled until July.

On July 17, the court entered a stipulation and order postponing a termination hearing for six months. The court ordered that TDC must submit additional progress reports and plans for compliance with the elements of the decree. Specifically with regard to in-cell desegregation, "no later than October 15, 1984, counsel for the parties will meet to discuss a plan to be submitted by TDC by that date for assignment of inmates to two-person cells consistent with the requirements of the *Lamar* decree."[30]

Following this order, between July 1984 and July 1985, TDC submitted twelve monthly progress reports concerning compliance toward the stipulations of the consent decree. Despite this compliance, in July 1985 the DOJ filed a contempt motion with the court due to TDC's failure to submit a timely in-cell desegregation plan. Roughly three weeks later, the court ordered, with the DOJ withholding objections, that TDC receive twenty additional days to submit a plan for the in-cell desegregation of inmates. In that grace period, TDC filed their plan for the assignment of inmates to two-person cells. Shortly thereafter, on September 6, 1985, the DOJ filed objections to TDC's plan for the assignment of inmates to two-person cells. According to the DOJ, TDC's "three-page document" was discretionary, vague, concentrated on what TDC would not do, and was noncompulsory.[31] In the plan, TDC proposed that inmates would be given a choice of whether to be assigned to a desegregated cell or not. The DOJ objected:[32]

In April 1977, over eight years ago, counsel for the defendant officials of the Texas Department of Corrections (TDC) and Texas Board of Corrections signed a Consent Decree requiring them to prepare a plan, which among other things, would . . . bring about the maximum possible integration of the cells consonant with the factors of security, control and rehabilitation. . . . In July 1984, having failed to achieve compliance with the cell desegregation requirement and other obligations under the 1977 decree and the plan, defendants signed a stipulation as an order of this Court, requiring, among other things, that on or before October 15, 1984, defendants would meet with the parties to discuss another cell desegregation plan to be submitted by that date. This stipulation represented a final compromise by the United States in its effort to end longstanding racial discrimination within TDC without recourse to litigation.

Despite this express commitment of the defendants, however, no plan was submitted by October 15, 1984. On July 11, 1985, the United States filed a Motion for Issuance or Order to Show Cause and for Contempt of Judgment. Defendants thereupon moved for an extension of time to respond, the United States agreed not to object, this Court granted an extension of 20 days, through August 14, 1985. On August 8, 1985, the defendants forwarded to the Court and to the parties a three-page document entitled "Plan for In-Cell Integration."

The United States strongly objects to the defendants' "plan" because it clearly does not satisfy the defendants' obligation . . . to prepare a cell desegregation plan. The proposal offers few details, is non-binding, and leaves most decision-making to the discretion of unidentified corrections personnel. It emphasizes what the defendants and TDC will not do, rather than provides details as to what they will do to rectify 8 years of non-compliance with this Court's 1977 Order. Truly, this document [TDC's cell desegregation plan] is no more than a plan to make a plan. . . . Apparently inmates

Table 6.1. Homicides in TDC, 1980–1988

Year	# of Killings	% Interracial	% Gang related
1980–1983	18	50	67
1984–1985	53	45	74
1986–1988	9	22	56

Source: Texas Department of Criminal Justice

will be given the choice of whether to be assigned to a cell with a person of another race. . . . It is difficult to believe that TDC's non-compulsory "system" of desegregation would be any system at all. . . . The circumstances of its submission strongly suggests that this "plan" is merely a hastily prepared effort to . . . avoid being held in contempt for failure to meet an essential element of [the] order.

While the lawyers for TDC defendants and the DOJ wrangled back and forth on the plan for in-cell desegregation, TDC was facing increased interracial gang activity and violence, which prompted emergency lockdowns on several of TDC's units. Indeed, from September through early October 1985, over 600 TDC inmates were placed in emergency detention and identified for single-cell status due to assaultive behavior and gang activity. A major reason for TDC's hesitation in providing the DOJ with a definitive plan was the onslaught of violence that rocked the prison system in 1984 and 1985.

Texas prisons had always had their share of violence and inmate murders. However, the remedies implemented as a result of *Ruiz* (e.g., removal of building tender system, hiring of more but inexperienced guards) put in motion near organizational chaos. Table 6.1 and Figure 6.1 present data on eighty inmate-on-inmate murders from May 1980 through July 1988. Implementation of the critical *Ruiz* stipulations by the prison system began in earnest in late 1983. Between 1980 and 1982 there were twelve killings. Six killings occurred in 1983. The years 1984 and 1985 (key years in the *Lamar* suit and the *Ruiz* implementation of remedies) witnessed fifty-three killings, the vast majority of which were gang-related. Interestingly, less than half of the 1984–1985 killings were interracial, despite the fact that 74 percent were gang-related.

The increased gang-related violence, in part, was attributed to TDC's January 1985 implementation of a newly developed classification plan promulgated as the result of *Ruiz* stipulations. After implementation of the clas-

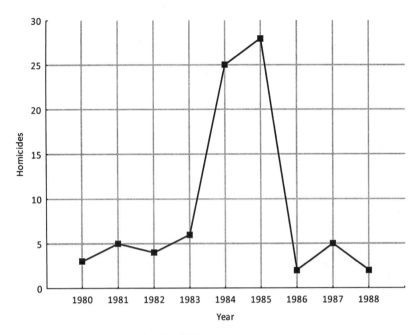

Figure 6.1. Homicides in TDC, 1980–1988

sification plan, several housing related problems occurred, which according to TDC impacted their ability to devise and implement in-cell desegregation. The new classification scheme revealed that many inmates required single-cell housing, but because TDC lacked the appropriate number of single cells, many assaultive and vulnerable inmates remained in the general population. According to prison officials, this created an "environment which would have made attempts at in-cell integration extremely difficult, if not impossible, and probably very dangerous as well."[33]

Nearing the end of 1985, and as a result of TDC's "inadequate" desegregation plan, the DOJ requested an expedited consideration of their contempt motion against TDC. Three weeks later, TDC filed an objection to the DOJ's motion. These and similar motions continued without answer from the court until 1986. At this time, Judge Lynn Hughes took over the *Lamar* case. On March 21, 1986, Judge Hughes presided over a status conference and set a plenary conference for May 5, 1986. It was at this conference that the trajectory of the *Lamar* case would change.

CHAPTER 7

The Color Line Breaks

Lamar's Prison Addiction Continues

As the lawsuit meandered through the legal system and facilitated animosities between the prison system and the Department of Justice (DOJ), life for Allen Lamar went on. It has been said that the best predictor of future behavior is past behavior. Based on this assumption, any street corner fortuneteller would have had no problem reading Lamar's lifeline etched deep in his palm. Bars, concrete, and confinement figured prominently in his past, and would do so well into his future. Lamar's future was an easy read.

In 1983, in his late forties, Lamar was discharged from his second TDC incarceration after serving nearly twenty years on a twenty-five-year sentence. In 1984, less than one year after his release, Lamar was convicted of murder with a deadly weapon and sentenced to life in prison.[1]

Lamar was returned to TDC on February 8, 1985. Three months later he was transferred to the custody of the Federal Bureau of Prisons (BOP) and placed at the United States Prison (USP) in Leavenworth, Kansas. Lamar's interagency transfer to Leavenworth, just as it had been in 1979, was to protect him from inmate enemies in TDC due to his status as lead plaintiff in the *Lamar* suit and as an inmate witness in the continuing *Ruiz* saga.

During his first year at Leavenworth, Lamar's life was relatively uneventful. Although he received a disciplinary infraction for possession of narcotics in his initial months there, he was rated as an average worker at his job in the clothing room and incurred no other incidents during his first year. In 1987, Lamar was again charged with possession of narcotics; he received forty-five days of disciplinary segregation and his social visits were terminated for one year. Outside of his persistent narcotics problem, Lamar received satisfactory work evaluations and federal authorities reported Lamar had "a very positive relationship" with staff members.

By 1990, Lamar was considered an "above average worker who shows initiative, responds well to his work supervisor's instruction, and his overall job performance is above average." Although Lamar received another disciplinary infraction at Leavenworth for using intoxicants, he was compliant according to federal authorities. This trend continued. Indeed, in an October 13, 1992, annual report to Texas authorities, a federal caseworker at Leavenworth noted that if "Mr. Lamar was a Federal prisoner, he would be receiving Meritorious Good Time for his work performance." He was no "jailhouse" lawyer in the federal system.

In April 1994, Lamar was transferred to USP Florence, Colorado, in order to increase that facility's population. His generally appropriate institutional conduct continued through 1994 and 1995 at USP Florence, with the exception that Lamar received a disciplinary report on June 8, 1994, for making a "sexual proposal." For this offense he received fifteen days of disciplinary segregation and a six-month loss of education privileges. In 1996, Lamar was returned to USP Leavenworth. Over the next several months, he received four disciplinary reports including two for possession of an intoxicant, one for possession of an unauthorized item, and one for threatening another with bodily harm. Although Lamar's conduct had declined somewhat by the late 1990s, generally he was an unremarkable federal inmate.

In October 1997 Lamar was transferred to USP Beaumont, Texas, to increase the population at this facility. Back in Texas, Lamar maintained a clear conduct record and was enrolled in several adult education courses including a counseling program in anger management.

In 1998, after nearly fifteen years in federal custody, Lamar's life came to an abrupt end when he died of unknown causes at age sixty-one.[2] While in the BOP, Lamar had little direct involvement in the civil suit that bore his name, or anything else for that matter. He filed no further federal lawsuits. He appeared to coexist well with staff and other inmates, received positive work evaluations, and was actively engaged in prison programs for most of his federal stay. Despite several relatively minor disciplinary infractions, he maintained an unremarkable disciplinary record. For all intents and purposes, TDC's lazy, impudent, and agitating writ-writer had been broken. After spending more than the balance of his life in correctional institutions and fighting the system for most of that time, Lamar's battle was done.

Lamar died more than a decade after Judge Lynn Hughes took control of the racial segregation and discrimination lawsuit. As he transitioned from

TDC to USP Leavenworth in 1985, the task of forcing TDC into compliance with the *Lamar* decree and judgment was still being fought by the individual plaintiff class lawyers and particularly the Department of Justice. A significant turning point in this fight would come from the persistence of Judge Hughes.

Turmoil and Transition in TDC

By the time Judge Hughes took over the *Lamar* decree, the Texas prison system was in turmoil. As a result of *Ruiz v. Estelle,* changes regarding the use of force and the use of building tenders (BTs), or inmate guards, had already taken place. The loss of the BTs, the system's inability to fill gaps in security staff, the hiring of young and inexperienced officers, and a burgeoning prison population led to levels of inmate-on-inmate violence (including a record number of homicides) never before experienced in the Texas prison system.

The loss of the BTs was particularly problematic according to some observers of the time, especially concerning race relations. According to one Texas inmate, prior to the BT system being dismantled, inmates "who tried to 'stir things up or get some shit goin','' for example, by forming racial cliques, were summarily punished." With the BT system defunct, however, "racial intolerance and animosities, once controlled and contained, became more overt, creating considerable tension."[3] For a time, the complete control that had once characterized the Texas prison system was lost. But the loss of the BTs, rising inmate populations, and the hiring of young and inexperienced staff were not the only obstacles confronting TDC in the 1980s.

At the same time *Ruiz* mandates were having their impact on TDC operation, the agency was also experiencing unprecedented transition in its leadership positions. For nearly four decades, TDC experienced remarkable stability in its top position of director. O. B. Ellis was director of TDC from 1948 to 1962. This leadership was continued by George J. Beto from 1962 to 1972, and then by his successor, W. J. Estelle, from 1972 to 1983. During the reigns of Ellis, Beto, and for most of Estelle's tenure, TDC enjoyed strong support from the Texas Legislature and the Texas Board of Corrections, headed by H. H. Coffield from 1955 to 1976. Even after Coffield's resignation in 1976, Estelle was still able to cultivate support from the board.[4]

By the early 1980s, however, the relationship between Estelle and the board became strained. Amid controversies resulting from the *Ruiz* litigation and the lack of support from the Board of Corrections and the Texas

Legislature, Estelle resigned in 1983.[5] What had once been an organization rich in tradition and marked by stability in leadership became characterized by transition and chaos. Following Estelle's departure, TDC weathered more directors in four years than had been experienced in four decades prior.[6]

The problems facing TDC were in many ways symptomatic of the turmoil borne from inmate litigation. By 1986, the prison system was besieged and exhausted by inmate litigation. TDC was involved in four major class-action suits involving everything from inmate mailing privileges and access to legal materials to racial and ethnic segregation and discrimination, in addition to a number of other non-class-action suits that attacked other aspects of TDC operation.[7] TDC was also still squarely involved in the aftermath of the *Ruiz* decision, which had massive system-wide impacts on TDC operation.

Despite the onslaught of prisoner litigation, TDC received little sympathy from the *Lamar* court. By the time Judge Hughes took over *Lamar* in 1986, nearly fifteen years had passed since the original complaint had been filed. Over those years, the TDC and DOJ were embroiled in a seemingly endless battle of legal maneuvers and negotiations, periodically stalled by *Ruiz*, and unable to come to an overall agreement concerning the desegregation of prison cells and other aspects of the decree. TDC was granted liberal extensions of time by the court to develop and then modify their affirmative action plan, and the DOJ and the court obliged most of these requests without strenuous objections. This was about to change.

With All Deliberate Speed, 1986–1991

At the May 5, 1986, status conference, Judge Hughes was not impressed with TDC's progress toward the *Lamar* consent decree. Gerald Birnberg, counsel for Allen Lamar and the black plaintiff's class, recalled the exchanges at this status conference between Judge Hughes, F. Scott McCown (Texas assistant attorney general representing TDC), and DOJ lawyers:

> Judge says Mr. McCown, the state of Texas was supposed to have filed a plan to desegregate the prisons some time ago, many months ago, and McCown said, well, we have your honor.

> What they had filed was . . . three pages of the most bland, you know, we are going to desegregate the prisons and, we are going to see that they are safe and secure in the meantime and . . . at the end of the day we will get the prisons all desegregated. Almost that bland and generic.

So he [Hughes] says where is this plan that you are talking about, and Scott [McCown] says well your honor, here is another copy . . . and the judge says, are you talking about this three page document, are you calling this a plan, and Scott [McCown] says well, yes your Honor, that's our plan. He [Hughes] says again, is this your plan. Well yes your Honor, as a matter of fact it is.

And he [Hughes] turns to somebody, sitting there in the courtroom on his staff, and says would you please call the Marshal, I need the Marshal here right now. And he [Hughes] turns to Scott [McCown] and says Mr. McCown, I don't believe that you would represent to this court that this is a desegregation plan. The court has issued orders and we expect the Attorney General's office to comply with that. . . .

The thrust of it was that you're fixin to go to jail. He [Hughes] turns to the Government's lawyers and says well what is the position of the United States. . . . This lawyer [from the Justice Department] stands up and looks him [Hughes] in the face and says we think you ought to commit Mr. McCown to jail right now. The Justice Department has been trying to get something workable out of these people for years and they haven't given it to us, and the only way we are going to get it is if this court shows its authority and quits accepting all this junk about security concerns and the best way to do that is to send somebody high up to jail today.[8]

At the end of this status conference, Judge Hughes found TDC in contempt of the consent decree without hearing further evidence or witnesses. Hughes delayed imposition of sanctions to allow for an agreement to be made between the DOJ and TDC. To facilitate such an agreement, he ordered TDC to comply with the "consent decree to the fastest extent possible."[9] He also ordered that within sixty days TDC was to meet with the DOJ to work through disagreements concerning the affirmative action plan and that TDC was to submit to the court and plaintiff classes a memorandum showing compliance with the decree.

The position of TDC following the May 1986 contempt finding was that the racial preference of inmates should be taken into account in any plan providing for the racial desegregation of double cells. Their position, based in large part on the violence experienced in the mid-1980s, was that forced cell desegregation would be a threat to security and control. Thus, following the May 1986 contempt citation, TDC's cell desegregation plan remained heavily predicated on inmate personal preference in the choice of cell partners.

Convict Opinions

On September 24, 1986, the Texas attorney general's office hired University of Texas sociologist Dr. Sheldon Ekland-Olson to study whether forced cell desegregation would threaten institutional security and safety—that a freedom-of-choice cell desegregation plan was the only way to ensure the safety and security of staff, inmates, and institutions. Ekland-Olson surveyed 750 randomly selected inmates dispersed throughout the prison system and asked inmates several questions, such as "Was your current offense committed against a member of another race?" "Have your ever been the victim of a racially motivated assault?" and "Do you object to having a cellmate of a different race or ethnic origin?"[10]

Of the 750 inmates surveyed, roughly 51 percent stated no objections to having a cellmate of a different race. Of the 49 percent who objected, only a small number held "very strong" objections. Inmates who objected were also asked which race(s) they objected to having as cellmates and the reasons for their objections. Below are some typical inmate objections:

V. G. (Hispanic): Blacks, I don't trust them, they try to take advantage of you.

K. S. (White): Black, because of the stigma in TDC when a white lives with a black.

L. R. (Black): Any race other than Caucasian. Would rather not be around them, it only increases tension.

W. S. (White): Would want no black in the cell, can get along with most Mexicans.

D. A. (Hispanic): Black, I'll kill him or he'll kill me.

D. M. (Hispanic): Black, just don't like niggers.

D. S. (White): I can't live with another race because I was raised to be prejudiced. Being in the penitentiary does not help alleviate those prejudices. I am Jewish.

V. G. (Hispanic): I could try it with a white guy, but I could not live with a black guy because I don't like them. I had a brother that was killed by some niggers.

A. B. (White): I wouldn't live with a nigger if my life depended on it.

J. J. (Black): Hispanics, because of gang activity.

Those inmates who objected to cell desegregation cited four main reasons: (1) general differences (religious, cultural, social, political), (2) feelings of incompatibility (preference, fear of other races), (3) specific problems experienced with other races outside of prison ("killed my brother"), and (4) specific prison-related concerns (prison stigma of living with another race, gang membership, contribute to prison tension).

Despite strong objections by some inmates, overall, Ekland-Olson's data revealed that most inmates either did not object or did not express strong objections to cell desegregation (like army soldiers four decades earlier). Perhaps because of these findings, a final report and recommendations were never produced and offered into evidence in the *Lamar* court. Indeed, the inmate responses countered longstanding staff beliefs and upended conventional wisdom on the likely outcome of cell desegregation.

While Ekland-Olson's survey was in the field, prison administrators conducted a study of nonfatal stabbings in the prison system expressly for the *Lamar* court. This retrospective analysis examined all nonfatal stabbings in TDC from September 1, 1984, through August 31, 1986, with a focus on interracial and intraracial dynamics of such incidents. Presumably, the goal of this study was to demonstrate that nonfatal stabbings in TDC would primarily cross racial lines, and, by default, that desegregating cells would increase the opportunity for cross-racial incidents.

During the time period of this study, TDC documented 359 nonfatal stabbing incidents. Roughly 45 percent of all incidents involved inmates of different races (interracial) and 48 percent of incidents were intraracial in nature (in roughly 6 percent of incidents the assailant's race was unknown). From the results of this study, and in preparation for further hearings on *Lamar*, TDC could not demonstrate with objective data that racial desegregation, in cells or otherwise, would lead to a disproportionate interracial violence. This was supported both by attitudinal evidence garnered through Ekland-Olson's survey and TDC's own analysis of official data.[11] This finding was also tacitly supported by homicide data presented in the previous chapter that found that between 1984 and 1985 twenty-nine of fifty-three killings, or 55 percent, were same-race killings. While freedom of choice was the preferred plan of desegregation for TDC, evidence did not conclusively show that forced desegregation would automatically lead to disproportionate interracial violence.

The lack of evidence supporting TDC's position was directly related to the fact that forced cell desegregation had never been attempted anywhere in the nation on a large scale. No one knew what to expect, and the stakes were high.

TDC Accused of Foot Dragging, 1986

In October 1986, roughly five months after the May 1986 contempt citation, the DOJ asked Judge Hughes to fine TDC $1,000 a day for failing to adhere to the court's previous orders.[12] In this contempt motion, the DOJ accused TDC of a "blatant disregard of even the most straightforward of court orders." The DOJ's main complaint was that TDC had submitted data and documents that made it impossible to determine progress toward the consent decree. According to the DOJ, the information provided by the prison system was only "raw data" and not enough to determine "the goal of . . . colorblind rational administration of prisoners."[13]

F. Scott McCown, Texas assistant attorney general, was "outraged" by the DOJ's contempt motion and allegations. He publicly remarked that there was "not a word of truth in the motion. It's a complete out-and-out fabrication. I'm going to be seeking sanctions against every Justice Department lawyer whose name is on the motion." The DOJ also noted in their contempt motion to the court that the "TDC has failed to comply with, and continues to disobey, virtually every substantive order of this court from 1977 to this date." McCown disagreed and replied that the "Justice Department has not written a single letter requesting additional information . . . nor have they written a single letter criticizing the information we provided. . . . In May [1986], we said to the court if this isn't what you want, tell us what you do want and we'll give it to you."[14]

Following these exchanges, Judge Hughes scheduled a conference for all parties on October 31, 1986. Prior to this conference, officials from TDC and the Texas attorney general's office traveled to Washington to meet with DOJ lawyers and to discuss a possible compromise concerning cell desegregation. By the October 31 conference, the DOJ and TDC were negotiating the finalization of a suitable desegregation plan. Here, the DOJ stipulated to withdraw a previous contempt motion contingent upon a proposed agreement with TDC concerning cell desegregation.

The next month, the prison system and the DOJ entered into a stipulation ordered by Judge Hughes. Per the stipulation, the court postponed a hearing on contempt sanctions against TDC. The specifics of the stipulation focused on remedying outstanding issues of the *Lamar* decree, such as racial discrimination in prison job assignments, but did not specifically address in-cell desegregation. Rather, the subject of cell desegregation was purposely excluded from the stipulation with the agreement that the DOJ was free to pursue its own remedies on the issue (e.g., pursuing further contempt charges), and TDC was free to implement its proposed in-cell desegregation plan.[15]

In December 1987, another stipulation was approved by the court. With the exception of cell desegregation, the DOJ and TDC reached an agreement that resolved all remaining aspects of the *Lamar* decree. In short, TDC was compliant with all issues in *Lamar*—the only outstanding issue by 1987 was the desegregation of double cells.[16] As it had in the past, the issue of cell desegregation would remain the most contentious and unaddressed aspect of the *Lamar* decree.

TDC Submits Revised Plan for In-Cell Desegregation, 1988

After several months of negotiations with the DOJ, on March 30, 1988, TDC submitted its revised desegregation plan. The overall structure of the plan called for the random assignment of inmates to two-person cells on the basis of legitimate and objective security-related criteria, without regard to race or ethnicity. TDC proposed that only inmates classified as minimum custody (excluding medium and close custodies, TDC general population custodies at the time) would be subject to random cell assignments. TDC also abandoned any reference to inmate personal preference in the cellmate assignments.

On April 11, 1988, TDC representatives and their counsel from the attorney general's office again traveled to Washington to discuss the cell desegregation plan with DOJ attorneys. Shortly afterward, the DOJ requested in a June 1988 letter that TDC provide evidence that medium- and close-custody inmates would be "inappropriate for integration pursuant to the plan's provisions." In short, the DOJ wanted prison administrators to prove that medium- and close-custody inmates would be unsuitable for random cell desegregation because of their potential for assaultiveness and poor institutional adjustment.

From June to October 1988, TDC and the DOJ continued to negotiate an agreement on cell desegregation. In October, DOJ lawyers made further revisions to TDC's proposed cell desegregation plan—changes that prison administrators considered to be "minor." According to court documents prepared by the prison system, the DOJ's October 1988 response to TDC's plan "indicated a clear acceptance of . . . limiting random cell assignments to minimum custody inmates." At this juncture, TDC believed "that the parties had reached agreement on the resolution of in-cell integration . . . and that only the formalities of signing and filing the proposed stipulation remained."[17] Under this assumption, TDC forwarded the revised cell desegregation plan to the DOJ on December 7, 1988, for the formalities of signing and filing.

Roughly five months later, DOJ lawyers returned the plan with substantial changes. Perhaps the most substantial change was the proposed requirement that the prison system randomly desegregate inmates in minimum, medium, and close custodies unless, upon a case-by-case determination, specific inmates were deemed unable to be desegregated based on their propensity for racial violence. Contrary to TDC assumptions, the DOJ rejected outright their blanket exclusion of all medium- and close-custody inmates from in-cell desegregation.

In a July 27, 1989, letter to assistant attorney general Michael Hodge (representing TDC at the time), DOJ lawyer Jeremy Schwartz wrote:

> Your verbal response has been that you have concluded, based solely on the perception of prison officials, that integration may increase violence and that no integration of the cells would be consonant with the factors of security, control and rehabilitation except as regards [to] minimum security inmates. You have stated that the Texas Department of Corrections will continue to segregate all others according to their race or ethnic background in making cell assignments, without fact-based, particularized determinations regarding the inmate, or inmates of a particular status or classification, demonstrating that racial segregation is necessary to maintain discipline and security within the prison. . . . Three years have passed since Judge Hughes found the State in contempt. . . . Please inform me within ten days whether the State is willing to accept our modifications to its proposed Plan for In-cell integration or to provide a statistically valid study to support its theory that racial segregation in necessary to maintain security at TDC.
>
> If I do not receive your written response within that time, I will assume that the State has rejected our proposal and does not have any legitimate basis for its continued segregation of all but minimum security inmates. I will then take appropriate action before the court to ensure compliance and, finally resolve this matter.[18]

On August 3, 1989, Hodge replied:

> We were surprised by your proposed revisions to the stipulation on two-person cells. . . . It had been the understanding of both the Texas Depart-

ment of Corrections Officials and Attorneys on our staff, based on conversations and negotiations . . . that the stipulation would be limited to
minimum custody inmates only.

In any event, we cannot agree to any plan that includes the medium custody,
close custody and safekeeping classifications. . . . It should be noted that
the cell blocks and work areas of these classifications are integrated but the
actual cells where they sleep are not. Even with this limited opportunity,
they account for the majority of the racial incidents in prisons. Not only
do they account for the majority of the racial incidents, the severity of the
incidents is much greater among these classifications than those that occur
in minimum custody areas. The day rooms of the cellblocks are, of course,
integrated and it is here that the majority of the incidents occur. Because
the majority of the incidents occur in the inmate housing area, one may,
therefore, conclude that increasing the contact in the housing area would
result in an even high incidence of violent behavior.

Under the consent decree entered in this case, the Texas Department of
Corrections must "bring about the maximum possible integration of cells
consonant with the factors of security, control, and rehabilitation." It is our
contention and our belief that the plan that has been previously presented
satisfies those requirements.

We are prepared to talk further with you about this if you so desire. If you
do not, we are prepared to litigate.[19]

As counsel for the prison system and the DOJ lawyers volleyed back and
forth concerning the particulars of cell desegregation, TDC was conducting
an analysis of interracial incidents to support their position (and offer proof
to the DOJ) that the desegregation of medium- and close-custody inmates
would encourage violence among the inmate population—TDC was trying
to prove that greater contact by way of cell desegregation among these higher
custodies would result in disproportionate violence not found among minimum custody inmates. This analysis would be the first systematic effort by
TDC to document empirically that desegregation would lead to racial violence that segregation allegedly prevented.

TDC Documents Racial Incidents, 1989

On October 26, 1989, lawyers from the Texas attorney general's office notified
DOJ attorneys that the prison system had finalized their analysis of inter-

racial incidents in minimum, medium, and close custodies—the proof that the DOJ had requested. Counsel for TDC believed that the report

> sufficiently documents racial as well as nonracial conflict in medium and close custody levels so as to show that the proposed Plan's provision for random cell assignments only in minimum custody levels satisfies the requirement to bring about the maximum possible integration of cells consonant with the factors of security, control, and rehabilitation.[20]

TDC's report consisted of an analysis of 1,105 incidents from October 1, 1988, through June 30, 1989, involving two or more inmates where at least one inmate received a major punishment. Data were collected on an Incident Data Form (IDF) prepared specifically for the *Lamar* negotiations (see chapter 8 for a copy of the IDF). Moreover, the IDF had fields indicating the location of the incident, whether the incident was intraracial or interracial, gang-related, and/or racially motivated, and the custody level of involved inmates.

The IDF was a valuable data tracking form for the measurement of inmate-on-inmate incidents. It significantly improved TDC's ability to document such incidents across all units. Prior to this time, TDC data collection process was fragmented, nonspecific, and not standardized across the various TDC units. The IDF served as an important tool as TDC attempted to provide evidence that racial desegregation in medium and close custodies would antagonize race relations and promote racial violence.

The pilot IDF data collection and analysis revealed that 55 percent of all incidents involved inmates of the same race. On its face, the IDF did not demonstrate that most prison incidents were interracial. Supporting their position that cell desegregation in medium and close custodies would result in disproportionate interracial violence (along with minimum, these custodies held roughly 80 percent of all TDC inmates at the time, more than 65 percent of which were in minimum custody alone), TDC revealed a substantially higher rate of interracial incidents in these custodies. The rate of interracial incidents in minimum custody was roughly 7 interracial incidents per 1,000 inmates. In medium custody, the rate of interracial incidents was 20 per 1,000, and in close custody the overall rate of interracial incidents approached 45 per 1,000 inmates in this nine-month reporting period. The TDC report also revealed that while medium- and close-custody inmates constituted roughly 12 percent of the prisoner population at the time, they were responsible for approximately 33 percent of all interracial incidents. Overall, the report noted that as "expected, the results of the data analysis indicate that a substantial amount of interracial activity is occurring in both medium and close custody."[21]

More than five months after the pilot analysis of interracial incidents, TDC received no correspondence from the DOJ. Then, in March 1990, DOJ attorneys arranged tours of several TDC units for basic compliance issues involving other aspects of the *Lamar* decree that had already been stipulated to by both parties. At that visit, the DOJ and their expert consultant, John J. Dahm (at the time warden of the Lincoln Correctional Center in Nebraska), toured five TDC units. According to court documents, DOJ counsel and Mr. Dahm were also allowed informal discovery concerning cell desegregation practices.[22] At the conclusion of the visit, DOJ counsel requested clarification of TDC's in-cell desegregation policy. In correspondence to counsel for TDC dated April 13, 1990, DOJ lawyers wrote:

> At the conclusion of our recent three day tour, you [TDC lawyers from the Attorney General's Office of Texas] promised that you would provide the Department of Justice with a statement concerning the Texas Department of Criminal Justice, Institutional Division's (TDC), current policy concerning assignment of inmates to two-person cells. As you know, during the tour we were informed by all staff involved in such assignments that the present policy is to assign inmates to these cells on the basis of race, i.e., blacks with blacks, whites with whites, Hispanics with Hispanics, unless an inmate specifically requests a cell partner of another race.
>
> Prior to the tour, the Department of Justice and TDC had been negotiating for more than a year in contemplation of entering into a stipulation addressing such assignments. It is my understanding that during these negotiations TDC had represented that it would randomly assign minimum security inmates to cells and that all such assignments would be based on legitimate safety and security criteria. . . . TDC's policy is clearly not consistent with that representation. Based upon what we were told and observed during the tour, TDC's policy is that inmates are to be assigned to segregated cells with inmates of the same race.[23]

Following this correspondence, TDC lawyers notified DOJ lawyers that a revised cell desegregation plan would be sent following a review by the Texas Board of Corrections in July 1990. In the meantime, lawyers for the DOJ wrote to the Texas attorney general's office and outlined the requirements for an acceptable plan, specifically, that any "new proposal from TDCJ-ID must incorporate the use of neutral classification criteria for medium and close custody cell assignments."[24]

Following the July 1990 review by the Board of Corrections, TDC submitted a revised cell desegregation plan to the DOJ. This revised plan stipulated
to the random cell assignment of minimum-, medium-, and close-custody
inmates. Following a critique by DOJ lawyers, TDC submitted another revised plan in September 1990. The next month, DOJ lawyers contacted the
Texas attorney general's office and expressed problems with the September
1990 version, also indicating via phone conference that they were contemplating another contempt motion against TDC. Following this phone conference, court documents revealed that lawyers for TDC were still under the
impression that negotiations would continue in good faith with the DOJ, and
that TDC would have further opportunity to revise their cell desegregation
plan into an acceptable compromise. According to attorneys from the Texas
attorney general's office representing TDC, "defendants certainly were not
operating under the belief that the parties had reached an impasse."[25]

Staff Resistance

While negotiations continued with the DOJ, TDC formed an "In-Cell Integration Committee" to work through the particulars of cell desegregation.
On this committee were several unit wardens, many of whom had serious
misgivings about cell desegregation. In a June 27, 1990, interoffice communication, one Texas prison warden expressed dismay that TDC would continue
to entertain cell desegregation plans:[26]

> Several months ago, this office was instructed to participate on a commit-
> tee to review the Department's position regarding in-cell integration as it
> pertains to the Lamar case. My initial position was that in-cell integration is
> not possible. . . . My original position remains unchanged and was recently
> stated through memo to this committee. While taking offense to my oppo-
> sition, the direction of this committee continues toward implementation
> of a cell-integration policy. My continued participation does not appear
> productive to this direction. I respectfully ask that my office be allowed to
> refrain from future participation in this process.

The communication above was perhaps indicative of the hesitation that
many TDC officials had concerning in-cell desegregation. Despite these hesi-
tations, however, TDC was on a path toward major changes concerning cell
desegregation.

DOJ Petitions Court for Contempt Sanctions, 1991

Just prior to submitting another revised in-cell desegregation plan, and still under the impression that the DOJ was open to further negotiations, TDC and their lawyers received, "without warning," a notice on January 25, 1991, that the DOJ had submitted a petition to the court for the imposition of contempt sanctions. In this petition, the DOJ requested that the court enforce a 1986 contempt finding by Judge Hughes and penalize the State of Texas and the prison system for failing to adhere to the consent decree.

The DOJ requested that the state be penalized $5,000 per day for each cell that was not racially desegregated, unless TDC agreed to desegregate at least 20 percent of their double cells by 1993. According to the DOJ, "It is necessary to impose sanctions upon [the state] in order that they correct the unconstitutional, intentional segregation presently practiced at TDCJ and to prod them into finally coming into compliance with the requirements of the consent decree."[27] Attorney Gerald Birnberg was quoted as saying that although progress had been made concerning all other areas of the decree, "an archaic mentality and lack of appreciation for the realities of the 1990s led to a lack of willingness to integrate two-man cells. . . . The state is simply reinforcing racial stereotypes and, more importantly, racial fears by not meaningfully dealing with this issue and having color-blind prisons."[28] David T. Lopez, attorney for the Hispanic inmate plaintiffs' class, advocated for a court-appointed special master to monitor and enforce the decree. Lopez did not believe TDC claims that racial segregation was necessary to prevent racial violence and remarked that when "you segregate by racial groups, you are encouraging those groups to coalesce into gangs. . . . When you keep them separated, you are not encouraging folks to learn to live with one another."[29]

On March 25, 1991, the Texas attorney general's office responded to the DOJ's petition for the imposition of sanctions, noting that the TDC had

in good faith continued to refine their proposed In-Cell Integration Plan to meet the parties' understanding of the requirements of the Consent Decree. . . . Since the court's order of May 8, 1986, defendants have been in communication with various representatives of the Justice Department in an attempt to work an amicable resolution to the in-cell integration issue. Defendants' delay in implementing a particular in-cell integration plan has certainly not been contemptuous. Rather, defendants have again and again put forth a good faith effort to settle the last remaining issue in this case—that of in-cell integration. . . . Nor has defendant's delay in implementing an in-cell integration plan been undue, but, as is illustrated by the history of this issue, has been caused by the natural course of resolving a complex issue among ever-changing players.[30]

History in the Making

DOJ pressure in early 1991 was the beginning of the end of racial segregation in TDC. In the face of stiff contempt sanctions, and a court that appeared willing to side with the DOJ on their contempt motions, TDC developed an in-cell desegregation plan that they believed would be acceptable to the DOJ and the court. In the plan, the prison system stipulated to previous requests of the DOJ and, by all indications, appeared to embrace cell desegregation. The color line had been broken.

The quick about-face of TDC concerning cell desegregation seems counter to expectations considering the system's general history with institutional litigation and their decade-long defiance to desegregating inmates in cells. Yet the TDC of the 1990s was in many ways different from that of the 1970s and 1980s. Several changes had impacted their ability to fully resist the *Lamar* court and DOJ pressure. One of the most significant factors was TDC's experience with *Ruiz*.[31]

By 1991, TDC had weathered numerous prisoner lawsuits, including four class actions. As prison lawyers admitted in the late 1980s, TDC was "besieged and exhausted" by litigation. *Ruiz* took a heavy toll. With *Ruiz* concluded, political pressure to get out from under court oversight was enormous. The Board of Corrections and the Texas Legislature learned from *Ruiz* that the only way to do that was to accede to the court. The new round of administrators that came after Beto and Estelle knew this as well—there was simply less support by the Texas Legislature and the Board of Corrections to fully resist court pressure. Stipulating to the DOJ and the court, despite a rich history of intransigence, was simply a product of a changing system that was much different than the system that produced these lawsuits.

Not only was political pressure great to stipulate to *Lamar*, but TDC was in the midst of a population explosion never before experienced. Beginning in the late 1980s and early 1990s, TDC was in the throes of adding more than 80,000 additional felony offenders. There was simply little time and perhaps less inclination to continue to drag out the *Lamar* decree process indefinitely—other pressing issues emerged that required TDC's time and resources. Ironically, this time period also represented TDC's best chance at cell desegregation. Indeed, the population explosion under way meant that the tight-knit and relatively isolated East Texas–centered prison system was now expanding across the state. New institutions were being populated with a new cohort of young officers who had not been groomed under the "old TDC." Old traditions and customs were lost upon this new crop of officers, and inmates did not know any different. By 1991 TDC had been desegregating inmates in all other aspects of housing and system operation. These forms of desegregation were met with little resistance by new prison staff and few problems emerged. If any time was right for cell desegregation, it was now.

On June 14, 1991, TDC submitted their desegregation plan to the court. The plan called for the random assignment of inmates to double cells in minimum, medium, and close custody—just as the DOJ had previously requested. Random assignment to cells was to be race-neutral, without taking inmate preference into account. So confident in this plan was TDC that prior to DOJ and court approval, TDC was already engaged in a massive statewide training of staff members on the in-cell desegregation of inmates.[32]

In the absence of an agreement and an approved court order accepting their desegregation plan, TDC took a risky move by designating a starting date for racial desegregation: August 1, 1991. Roughly two months before this start date, TDC began training in the southern region of the state, then the northern region, and finally the central region. After June 20, TDC wardens and their officers were allowed approximately one month to start random cell assignments and hence the racial desegregation of prison cells.

Inmates Are Put on Notice

On June 26, 1991, roughly one month before cell desegregation was to commence and one week after statewide training had ended, TDC director James A. Collins issued a communication to all inmates:

> This notice is to clarify any rumors you may have heard concerning the upcoming In-Cell Integration Plan. This plan is being implemented to fulfill the requirements of the 1977 Consent Decree. . . .
>
> All inmates in the TDC will be reviewed by the Unit Classification Committee to determine their eligibility for in-cell integration. Some inmates will actually be interviewed by the committee while others will have a paper review process only. All decisions will be made on a case-by-case basis after a thorough review of each inmate's records, in order to insure that the

integration of two-person cells in the general population is achieved in an orderly and rational fashion consistent with safety, security, treatment and rehabilitation of inmates.

Following the committee review process, the integration process will begin. There will not be a massive move of inmates to integrated cells in the existing population. As routine housing moves are made and as new inmates are received on the unit, these inmates will be randomly assigned to the first available cell that is consistent with their security and health-related needs. Race will not be considered when choosing a cell unless an inmate has been racially restricted by the classification committee.[33]

The First Available Cell

The specific elements of TDC's cell desegregation plan called for the random assignment of inmates in the general population (minimum-, medium-, and close-custody celled inmates) to the "first available cell" *consistent with an inmate's security and health-related needs* (in this context, the desegregation plan was more about finding the first available *and* appropriate cell than simply the first available cell).[34] To desegregate the cells, all first available cell assignments would be accomplished without regard to race, unless security required otherwise.

Random cell assignments would apply to all incoming inmates (arrivals from inmate reception centers), and existing inmates during the course of normal and routine cell movements (such as transfers from one cell, tier, or cell block to another, or transfers to another prison unit), but would not require a reshuffling of the existing inmate population. The operating assumption of TDC's plan was that all inmates were eligible for a desegregated cell unless rational and objective security related evidence suggested otherwise. Whether the first available cell wound up segregated or desegregated by race was completely up to chance.[35]

Several specialized populations were restricted from a desegregated cell. For example, death row inmates were automatically exempt due to their single-cell status (as were other single-celled designations). Inmates at reception centers and other "transient" inmates (e.g., inmates awaiting placement at a long-term unit) were also exempt from cell desegregation. For reception center inmates, prison officials argued that they needed time to observe and evaluate new commitments to accurately gauge their security needs and suitability for a desegregated double cell.[36] For all other inmates who were double celled in the general population, and inmates arriving at their long-term prison unit, racial desegregation within cells was a real possibility at one point or another due to the first available cell plan.

Accomplishing desegregation by way of the first available cell required a massive reclassification of all inmates. The reclassification process included inmate interviews, a review of all existing inmate records, and the implementation of new protocols for evaluating newly received inmates. Information from this reclassification review was recorded on a "Cell Assignment Form" to determine, among other things, each inmate's eligibility (or ineligibility) to be housed within a racially mixed cell.

Three general outcomes could result from this reclassification: (1) eligible for cell desegregation, (2) ineligible (or restricted) for cell desegregation, or (3) partially eligible (able to house with certain races but not others). This review focused on several security-related criteria in determining an inmate's eligibility status for cell desegregation:

1. Inmate enemies at the unit.
2. Homosexual tendencies (both active and passive).
3. Current or prior institutional adjustment problems where racial beliefs and attitudes were a motivating factor.
4. Inmate has been placed in, or requested placement in, safekeeping or protective custody, or has been placed in security detention, during current or previous incarceration for such occurrences as being affiliated with a gang or disruptive group, been the victim of a racial or sexual assault or threatened assault, and/or has received sexual harassment or extortion.
5. Current or prior offense(s) or conviction where racial beliefs and attitudes were a motivating factor in the commission of the offense(s).
6. Suspected or confirmed member of a group which advocates racial superiority and/or aggression towards other racial groups.
7. Statements made by the inmate which may indicate a potential safety or security problem relative to the inmate's assignment to cell housing, including statements which reflect racial beliefs and attitudes.[37]

The in-cell desegregation training manual for staff also clarified the stance of the new plan in terms of inmate preference and racial desegregation. The training guidelines noted:

A major distinction between this In-Cell Integration Plan and previous plans relates to the issue of personal preference on the part of inmates. Under this plan, personal preference statements made by an inmate in terms of which race or races he would like to live with or would not like to live with *cannot be taken into consideration when determining cell assignments status.* . . . the Cell Assignment Form does not contain any questions which solicit information from the inmate as to whether or not he expects problems from other races or would prefer to live with his own race. The fact that an inmate would prefer to live with his own race is not sufficient to restrict him from eligibility for in-cell integration. (emphasis added)[38]

In addition to these and other security-related criteria, the determination of the "first available and appropriate" cell placement would also hinge on factors such as age, height, weight, and health-related (including mental health) criteria. Taken together, all criteria would help to ensure that cell partners were as "equal" as possible on factors that mattered to safety and security.

Following the reevaluation of all inmates as to their eligibility for desegregation, the plan required that each inmate be assigned a "housing restriction code" or "Lamar code." The Lamar code was developed so housing officers could quickly identify those inmates restricted from a desegregated double-cell due to security-related criteria and those inmates who were deemed fully or partially eligible for cell desegregation. These codes included the following:

RW (Restricted White): Cannot be celled with a white inmate.
RB (Restricted Black): Cannot be celled with a black inmate.
RH (Restricted Hispanic): Cannot be celled with a Hispanic inmate.
RR (Racially Restricted): Cannot be celled with an inmate of any other race.
RO (Restricted Other): Cannot be celled with _____.
RE (Racially Eligible): Can be celled with any race inmate.

The Desegregation Procedure

Once inmates were reclassified and assigned a Lamar code, the actual desegregation of cells was a rather simple process. The officer making cell assignments at the unit level was responsible for reviewing an inmate's file and health summary to determine any special housing restrictions, including any security-based racial restrictions.

Following this review, the housing officer assigned the inmate to the first available cell on a tier in a chosen cell block—a cell most appropriate to the inmate's security, health, and other housing needs. The selection of the first

		CELLS														
	Tiers	1		2		3		4		5		6		7		8	
Cell Block A	Tier 1	B	W	B	B	W	H	W	W	-	-	B	-	H	W	W	W
	Tier 2	W	B	-	-	H	-	B	B	H	H	W	B	H	B	B	-
	Tier 3	B	B	-	-	H	B	W	W	H	W	B	B	-	-	B	W

Key

B	=	Black
W	=	White
H	=	Hispanic
-	=	Open Cell or Open ½ Cell

Figure 7.1. Sample Countboard Depicting One Cell Block

available cell was to be made on a race-neutral basis for those eligible to be desegregated. In this process, the focus would be on the first and most suitable cell as determined by rational objective security criteria, not the race of the inmate already in the cell.

The procedural details of the plan required the housing officer to consult a special "countboard" in the making of cell assignments. Countboards, roughly seven feet long by five feet wide, visually depicted all cell blocks on a unit, tiers in each cell block (typically three to six tiers per cell block), and cells on each tier. Each double cell on a tier was represented on the countboard by a square with two pegs (one peg for each inmate). On each peg was a plastic tag indicating the race of the inmate already in the cell (if already occupied), and other basic information such as the existing inmate's Lamar housing code, height, weight, and other pertinent housing information (such as a bottom-bunk restriction). Each tag was color-coded: clear for whites, blue for blacks, and red for Hispanics, allowing for a clear visual depiction of the race of inmates within specific cells. Cell squares without tags represented an open cell. Cell squares with one tag represented an open cell with room for one additional inmate. Cell squares with two tags represented a closed, fully occupied cell.

Upon inspection of the countboard, housing officers were required to begin at either the top or bottom row of a cell block and proceed from left to right until the first available cell consistent with an inmate's security and housing needs was found (see Figure 7.1). For racially eligible inmates (RE), the selection of the first available cell was to be completely race neutral but consistent with an inmate's security-related criteria. For example, finding the first available cell for a racially eligible inmate also meant matching him as closely as possible on several critical factors such as security-related criteria (not putting an active homosexual with a passive inmate) and health-related criteria (not putting an inmate with a bottom-bunk restriction in a cell where the bottom bunk was occupied). If the first available cell (or the inmate already in that cell, if occupied) did not mesh with these security and health-related criteria, the officer would proceed to the next available cell until an appropriate match was found.

The above process applied to those inmates who were classified in such a way that they required double-cell placement and were eligible to house with any race.[39] For those inmates deemed "RR," racially restricted from housing with an inmate of another race, or those with partial racial restrictions (a black inmate restricted from living with a white but not with a Hispanic inmate), the process of selecting the first available cell was to be essentially the same. The only exception was that race would be considered as one factor in finding the "first available and appropriate" cell, much like age or weight would be used.

It should be noted that even racially restricted inmates could be housed within a desegregated dormitory. If a restricted inmate required double-celling, he could also be housed in a desegregated cell block, a cell block tier, and even next to a desegregated cell. Being racially restricted meant only that the inmate would not be placed in a desegregated cell as determined by security-related criteria. Racially restricted inmates were not immune from racial mixing in other aspects of the prison routine either, including job assignments, dayrooms, and dining facilities.

The Reevaluation of Racial Restrictions

The desegregation plan also required the reevaluation of inmates initially deemed racially restricted from a desegregated cell. Inmate classifications, including the Lamar code, were to be reviewed semi-annually by a classification case manager at each unit. Thus, an inmate deemed racially restricted (or partially restricted) at one point would not necessarily be precluded from a desegregated cell during the duration of his sentence. Such determinations were to be periodically reevaluated and racially restricted inmates could eventually be reclassified as racially eligible—thus no inmate was altogether excluded from an opportunity at cell desegregation during their prison stay. The opposite is also true: a racially eligible inmate could later be considered racially restricted by the unit classification manager.

The September 1991 Order of the Court

TDC's preemptive strategy of implementing a desegregation plan prior to acceptance from the DOJ and a court order appeared to work. On September 4, 1991, roughly one month after the system's self-designated start of cell desegregation, Judge Hughes accepted TDC's plan. He also retained the option of contempt sanctions and held that if desegregation was not fully accomplished by a status conference set for February 16, 1993, "coercive sanctions will be imposed on the officers and the prison system of the State of Texas." The concept of "fully accomplished" meant that TDC would strive for the desegregation of 20 percent of the system's double cells by February 1993. In 1991, TDC housed roughly 24,000 inmates in approximately 12,000 double cells. This meant that by February 1993, TDC would have to present evidence that at least 2,400 double cells were desegregated; otherwise they would face potential contempt sanctions that had been delayed by the court since 1986 and stayed by the court's order of September 4, 1991.

TDC's Plan Gets Press: Desegregation as a Reason for Escape

The media paid special attention to TDC's response to the court mandate in 1991.[40] On June 22, 1991, the *Houston Chronicle* reported: "With the threat of millions of dollars in fines hanging over them, Texas prison officials . . . will begin implementing a racial desegregation plan that has some fearing inmate rebellion."[41] Yet despite the fanfare generated by the press, prison officials were straightforward in their dedication to the desegregation plan and made little mention of a fear of inmate rebellion or violence. Leonard Peck, assistant general counsel for TDC at the time, noted that prison officials were "committed to making this thing [cell desegregation] work." He also directed a message to inmates:[42]

> We don't care how you feel about it, we're going to do it. So go write your mothers about how miserable you are. But it is going to happen. And inmates who try to sabotage this are going to have to pay. We have lots of ways of dealing with insubordination—loss of good time, loss of classification status, and miserable work assignments.

Four days later, TDC director James A. Collins issued the June 26, 1991, communication to inmates on cell desegregation (see above). Two days after this notice was sent to TDC inmates, seven white inmates escaped from the Coffield Unit in Tennessee Colony, Texas. On July 23, 1991, almost one month after the escape and only days before cell desegregation was to commence, the remaining two escapees were caught. Headlines attributed the motive for the escape to integration.[43] This was based on interviews with two of the captured fugitive inmates, Roger Davis and Joseph Tigert, who said they felt forced to escape because of desegregation.[44] Davis added that many black inmates were also opposed to cell desegregation: "They don't want to sleep in a cell with a white boy who might stab them at any moment." He predicted severe interracial and racially motivated violence: "It just won't happen. . . . Because if they brought a black guy up there and rolled my door and said he was coming in there, I'd say well one of us is going out. One of us is going out hurt."[45] Both Davis and Tigert explained to reporters that their cell was their "house" and that they resented the state invading their home by pushing for cell desegregation. As Davis clarified:

> If I've got to live here for 15 years, I'm not going to live with a black or Mexican. It's bad enough I've got to shower with them. It's bad enough I've got to sit and watch TV with them. I didn't do it in the free world society, why would I do it in here. I'll tell you what. I'll integrate as soon as [Judge] William Wayne Justice brings a black to live with him in his house.[46]

Although the inmates incorrectly named the presiding judge at the time, what was not a mistake was that prison managers were committed to the desegregation of prison cells. According to one prison official: "None of the things said by inmates Tigert and Davis will exempt them from living in integrated quarters."[47] This 180-degree change in TDC's attitude would continue as the prison system embarked on something that had never been attempted anywhere in the nation.

The Right to Refuse?

During the first week of August 1991, TDC rolled out cell desegregation, starting with the units in the southeastern part of the state and gradually moving to the rest of the system within a few months. Prison administrators predicted that roughly 15 percent of the system's 47,000 inmates at the time would be racially restricted by the classification committee for security purposes or as a result of refusing a desegregated cell assignment.

Anticipating that some inmates might refuse a desegregated cell assignment, prison managers devised a stringent policy and procedure to deal with noncompliant inmates. If an inmate refused housing in the first available and appropriate cell because it contained an inmate of another race, the inmate would remain eligible for cell desegregation unless there was a legitimate reason for the refusal. But such legitimate reasons were few and far between. TDC policy, enumerated in "Procedures for the Management of Inmates Who Refuse Integrated Cell Assignments," emphasized "the fact that an inmate does not want to live in a cell with an inmate of another race is NOT a valid reason for refusing a cell assignment."[48]

Inmates who refused their desegregated cell assignment were to be counseled by the housing officer and given an opportunity to reconsider. If the inmate continued to refuse the cell assignment, he would be escorted to the "next available and appropriate cell" on the tier. This cell might again contain an inmate of another race as in the first instance. Although inmates could continue to refuse cell assignments, disciplinary actions were progressive. For the first refusal, the inmate was to be charged with refusing to accept a housing assignment. Punishments for such refusal, if convicted by the unit disciplinary committee, could include solitary confinement, loss of good time, reduction in time-earning class (resulting in fewer days of good time earned for each day served), and cell restriction with loss of privileges. Upon a second refusal, and subsequent conviction in a disciplinary hearing, TDC's policy called for a mandatory loss of an amount of good time and/or the time earning class status. Sanctions after a second refusal might also include solitary confinement and/or cell restriction, with loss of privileges.

After three refusals—again, provided the inmate was convicted by the disciplinary committee—mandatory punishments included loss of good time accrued up to two years until all good time was exhausted, a two-level reduction in good-time earning class, and cell restriction and loss of all privileges for forty-five days. A third refusal could also result in placement in solitary confinement with a reclassification into close custody.

Even after multiple refusals and convictions by the disciplinary committee, however, the inmate would still be placed in the first available and appropriate cell, regardless of race, and still be eligible for desegregation. Refusals simply would not result in racial restrictions unless such refusals clearly threatened security and control. Indeed, only after four cell refusal disciplinary convictions were inmates reclassified as a "chronic refuser of integrated cells." Upon this designation, the inmate would be reclassified into the highly restrictive close custody (the highest and most restrictive general population custody in TDC at the time) until which time the inmate agreed to abide by TDC's cell assignment policy. But even a "chronic refuser" label did not carry an automatic racial restriction. A chronic refuser was classified as racially restricted (RR) only when such a restriction was deemed required for reasons of inmate safety and security. The bottom line is that inmates face significant sanctions for refusing a desegregated cell assignment. Such a disciplinary policy was adopted by TDC so that inmates would face real consequences for failing to abide by housing procedures.[49]

Roughly two months after desegregation commenced, on October 31, 1991, prison officials completed a monitoring survey, requesting personnel at each unit to report the number of inmates who refused desegregated cell assignments. The results revealed that 694 inmates had refused desegregated cell assignments—just a fraction of the roughly 47,000 inmates in the system at the time, including the roughly 24,000 celled inmates in minimum, medium, and close custodies (or roughly 12,000 double cells). Of these 694 inmates, 155 had refused desegregated cells multiple times—fewer than ten multiple refusals per unit in TDC. Of those 155 multiple refusals, 75 inmates had been restricted from a racially desegregated cell. Overall, it appeared that most inmates accepted desegregated cell assignments. Even among those who refused, the majority complied with the desegregation policy after a few attempts. Only a small fraction of inmates "held out" and were cited for multiple refusals and eventually racially restricted because of security concerns.[50]

By the end of 1991, TDC had desegregated roughly 27 percent of its double cells in minimum, medium, and close custodies, up from roughly 2 percent at the start of in-cell desegregation. In March 1992, DOJ lawyers toured several TDC units (Beto I, Coffield, Michael, Goree, Ferguson, and Huntsville) to gauge the progress toward cell desegregation. By all indications, the tour was successful.

Several Months Later

By early 1992, all indications showed that TDC was on the path to full compliance with cell desegregation. A June 4, 1992, letter from Susan Bowers, senior trial attorney for the DOJ, to Nancy K. Juren, assistant attorney general representing TDC, indicated that TDC had made real progress toward compliance with cell desegregation:

> I am responding to your letter of April 29, 1992, in which you requested that we report any deficiencies that we observed during our March 1992 tour of units of the Texas Department of Criminal Justice-Institutional Division (TDCJ-ID). . . .
>
> As we told you and TDCJ-ID officials at the conclusion of the tour, we are pleased with the progress thus far in the implementation of the In-Cell Integration Plan ("Plan"). However, as your clients acknowledged, a few

minor problems remain. For example, we discussed our shared concerns as to the minimal integration of medium and close custody inmates at Coffield and the delay in integration of mentally retarded inmates at Beto. We have just received TDCJ-ID's most recent Integration Report and are gratified to see that the integration percentages of Coffield's close and medium custody cells have increased to 12.19 percent and 9.83 percent respectively and that random assignment of mentally retarded inmates seems to be underway at Beto. Clearly, TDCJ-ID has begun to address the problems that we identified. We anticipate that, at the February 1993 hearing, at the latest, we will join you in reporting that your clients are complying with the Plan and are achieving the objectives of the Consent Decree and Orders of the court. In order to be able to assure that that is the case, we expect to tour on or about December 1992.

I would like to restate that we have no specific integration percentage or numerical goal in mind as a measure of compliance. We believe that the integration that has been realized to date suggests that the State has begun serious implementation of the Plan. I agree that an informal approach to resolve this matter is appropriate and do not anticipate any "eleventh hour" surprises that would compromise our efforts.[51]

From 1992 to 1994, other than routine court motions and other court procedures, there was a virtual absence of activity in the case. A few inmates wrote the court and requested contempt citations against TDC or to intervene in the case, others asked for injunctions against in-cell desegregation, and some asked Judge Hughes to recuse himself from the case.[52] These efforts were routinely denied by the court. No matter: cell desegregation moved forward.

The Legal History of *Lamar* Is Finished

After years of motions and complaints by inmates about the *Lamar* decree, Judge Hughes issued a post-judgment opinion in the case in 1996. Hughes relayed that absent major and purposeful deficiencies with cell desegregation, inmates need not write to the court. He wrote:

In the early 1970s, a group of inmates in the Texas prison system sued the state for violations of their rights to be free from the arbitrary infliction of racially segregated facilities. This suit was supplemental to other suits about the way the prison was being run. The subjects of those suits ranged from unnecessary intrusion into inmate mail to staff sanctioned inmate violence as a management tool. In 1977, this court enjoined the state permanently from racially segregating inmate housing and other facilities, like jobs and recreation, unless an objective assessment showed that integration for a particular prisoner would pose a high likelihood of danger to him or others. . . .

Over the years, a series of hearings were held about compliance and modification. Those orders were expressly made dependent on the results of the classification system imposed in other litigation heard by my distinguished colleague William Wayne Justice of the Eastern District. In the last decade, occasional efforts by the plaintiffs have been necessary to keep the state's institutions moving toward full, spontaneous compliance with its obligation to be absolutely racially neutral unless a compelling legitimate interest can be shown in an individual case. The court discontinued the state's duty to make routine reports of in-cell integration. In recent years, the correspondence from individual prisoners has shifted from complaints about segregation to complaints about integration, which is progress of a fashion.

As 1996 begins, Texas prisons confine 126,000 people. Of those who are compelled to live with a person of a different race, a very small fraction write to the court asserting that, despite a stated preference for same race cellmates, they are forced to share a cell with an inmate of a different race. Frequently the preference is stated negatively as an animosity. Every socio-cultural type complains of every other one.

Bigoted prisoners have generated reams of complaints, including eighty-three requests to modify the desegregation decree. In the last three years alone, prisoners have filed sixty complaints requesting special race classification or re-segregation. Some of these communications are simply letters of protest. Others are couched as motions to intervene or modify the decree. Motions to modify the decree, to exempt individuals from it, or to intervene by individuals dissatisfied with desegregation will be denied routinely.

A prisoner or two who have not received rulings on their motions have applied to the court of appeals for writ of mandamus. For the benefit of present and future applicants to intervene, no intervention by individual inmates will be allowed. One intervenes in an active case, a case with undecided issues. . . .

The case began in 1972 and was settled in 1977. Nineteen years later, there is no need to address an individual inmate's bigotry through a modification of the decree. The problems in society that generated the legal contest persist. . . .

The court is wary of being seen to test the resolve of inmates who announce that their hate will make them violently disposed to other races if they are locked together. No amount of violence, large or small, to prove one's eligibility for a single-race cell will be rewarded by the state or by this court. An inmate who proves that he is both a bigot and violent will face consequences much worse than an undesirable cellmate (emphasis added).[53]

Judge Hughes's opinion was clear. The consent decree was being complied with and inmate requests for intervention, to modify the case, to enforce the decree, or to halt desegregation with injunctions were not going to be entertained by the court. After more than twenty years, or 9,000 days, Judge Hughes ended the legal history of *Lamar v. Coffield.*

Conclusion

The preceding chapters have examined the long road to racial desegregation in Texas prisons. Not unlike many prison conditions lawsuits, the *Lamar* case was dealt with by consent decree instead of trial. In this case, the consent decree process lasted years. Eventually, compliance was obtained.

By 2007, long after Allen Lamar had died, the "burnin' hell" had been in compliance with the *Lamar* stipulations for fifteen years. Unlike the majority of prison systems in the country, Texas prisoners are desegregated in one of the most unlikely and volatile places in a prison setting—the double cell. The next two chapters examine the aftermath of racial desegregation in Texas prisons. Chapter 8 first examines the overall level of inmate-on-inmate violence in Texas prisons from 1991 to 1999, with a focus on interracial and intraracial dynamics of incidents. Chapter 9 focuses specifically on incidents among desegregated cell partners. The goal is to uncover what happened when Texas inmates were forcibly desegregated within cells.

Picture I. The Waco Horror and the lynching of Jesse Washington, 1916.
Courtesy of The Texas Collection, Baylor University, Waco, Texas.

Picture 2. Black inmates arriving at Huntsville "Walls" Unit for processing in Black Betty, 1950. Courtesy Texas Department of Criminal Justice.

Picture 3. White inmates being processed at Huntsville "Walls" Unit, 1950. Courtesy Texas Department of Criminal Justice.

Picture 4. Single cell, Ferguson Unit, 1953. Courtesy Texas
Department of Criminal Justice.

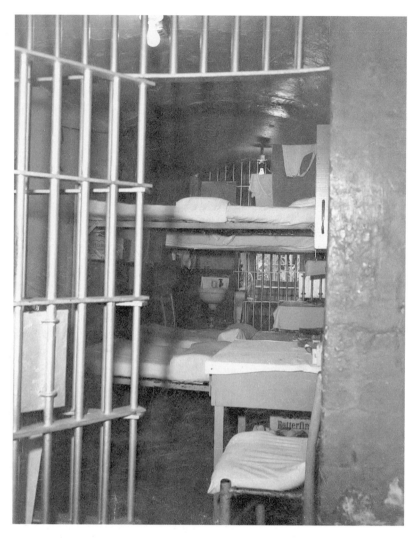

Picture 5. Double cell, 1950. Courtesy Texas Department of Criminal Justice.

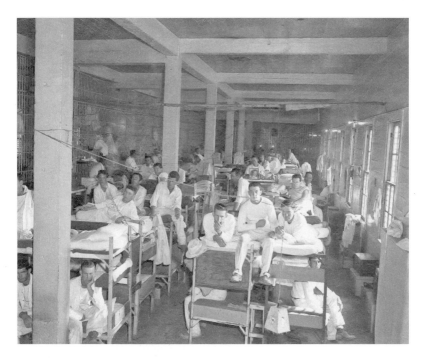

Picture 6. Segregated dormitory housing (white), old Eastham Farm, 1955. Courtesy Texas Department of Criminal Justice.

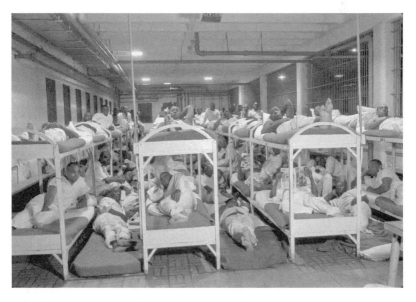

Picture 7. Segregated dormitory housing (black), 1961. Courtesy Texas Department of Criminal Justice.

Picture 8. Seven Row. Old death row, Huntsville "Walls" Unit, 1998.
Courtesy Texas Department of Criminal Justice.

Picture 9. Three-tier cell block, Ferguson Unit, 1952. Courtesy Texas
Department of Criminal Justice.

Picture 10. Segregated dormitory housing (black), 1960.
Courtesy Texas Department of Criminal Justice.

Picture 11. Segregated (black) "hoe squad" working the fields, Ellis Unit, 1966.
Courtesy of Bruce Jackson © 2008.

Picture 12. Inmate turnout at the back gate, 1966. Courtesy of Bruce Jackson © 2008.

Picture 13. Segregated "axe crew" in the Ellis Fields, 1966.
Courtesy of Bruce Jackson © 2008.

Picture 14. Inmates picking and dragging cotton from Ramsey Farm fields, 1968. Courtesy of Bruce Jackson © 2008.

Picture 15. Ramsey inmates picking cotton, 1968. Courtesy of Bruce Jackson © 2008.

Picture 16. Segregated field squad picking peas, Wynne Farm, 1960.
Courtesy Texas Department of Criminal Justice.

Picture 17. Segregated field squad picking and loading sweet corn, 1964.
Courtesy Texas Department of Criminal Justice.

Picture 18. "High Rider" supervising segregated (black) hoe squad in the fields, 1970. Courtesy Texas Department of Criminal Justice.

Picture 19. Segregated (black) hoe squad traveling to Clemens Farm fields on "Ellis Buggies," 1970. Courtesy Texas Department of Criminal Justice.

Picture 20. "High Rider" supervising white hoe squad in fields, 1970.
Courtesy Texas Department of Criminal Justice.

Picture 21. Ramsey I segregated (black) baseball team, 1950.
Courtesy Texas Department of Criminal Justice.

Picture 22. Segregated baseball team (Hispanic) at Huntsville "Walls" Unit in prison
rodeo arena, 1953. Courtesy Texas Department of Criminal Justice.

Picture 23. Segregated baseball team (white), 1953. Courtesy Texas Department of Criminal Justice.

Picture 24. Segregated (white) Huntsville "Walls" Unit Choir, 1961. Courtesy Texas Department of Criminal Justice.

Picture 25. The "Stringsters," Wynne Farm musical group, 1962.
Courtesy Texas Department of Criminal Justice.

Picture 26. Segregated (black) educational class, Clemens Farm, ca. 1952.
Courtesy Texas Department of Criminal Justice.

Picture 27. Segregated (white) classroom, Eastham Unit, ca. 1960.
Courtesy Texas Department of Criminal Justice.

Picture 28. Mess hall, Old Eastham Farm, 1952. Courtesy Texas
Department of Criminal Justice.

Picture 29. Segregated (black) "chow hall," Ramsey II, 1955.
Courtesy Texas Department of Criminal Justice.

Picture 30. White inmates in "chow line," Byrd Diagnostic Unit, ca. 1965. Courtesy Texas Department of Criminal Justice.

Picture 31. Aerial view of Eastham Farm, 1985. Eastham Farm was Allen Lamar's first destination in TDC. Courtesy Texas Department of Criminal Justice.

Picture 32. Eastham Unit entrance sign, ca. 1960. Courtesy Texas
Department of Criminal Justice.

Picture 33. Front of Ramsey I Building, ca. 1950. Courtesy Texas Department of Criminal Justice.

Picture 34. Ramsey II Building, 1960. Courtesy Texas Department of Criminal Justice.

Picture 35. Harlem I Farm (Jester I today), 1985. Courtesy Texas Department of Criminal Justice.

Picture 36. Aerial view of Ellis Unit, 1985. Courtesy Texas Department of Criminal Justice.

Picture 37. Aerial view of Wynne Unit, 1985. Courtesy Texas Department of Criminal Justice.

CHAPTER 8

7,000 Days Later

In the first chapter we discussed the zones of desegregation and how desegregation efforts often move from the outer fringes or zones inward—from the least to most contentious areas. We also showed, in Chapter 3, how U.S. military units were desegregated by way of social clubs, recreational areas, base transportation, and divisions first—efforts that paved the way for the racial mixing of fighting units, or the final zone.

The decades between 1960 and 1990 involving the Texas prison system clearly illustrate our theory about racial desegregation in TDC. Texas prison officials over these decades desegregated the prison units, work areas, field force and line squads, cell blocks, tiers, and dormitories—all areas except double cells. Prison desegregation was accomplished from the outside moving inward. Yet, by 1991, only the most contentious zone remained segregated, prison cells.

Predictions of a Bloodbath

Publicly, TDC administrators voiced a strong commitment to cell desegregation. There was a disjunction, however, between their public comments and the opinions of unit level personnel, including wardens, officers, and staff. With some variation, those at the unit level responsible for implementing desegregation on a day-to-day basis were highly skeptical of this court-mandated policy. These cellblock level bureaucrats believed that cell desegregation would result in "blood on the tiers," that the racial mixing of the most violent and least stable individuals in Texas was a recipe for disaster. As one warden expressed to a racial desegregation committee as late as 1990, "In-cell

integration is not possible."[1] The violence that followed the mid-1980s implementation of *Ruiz* remedies was still fresh in the minds of security staff.

Unlike desegregating a field squad or dormitory (which prison staff and
lawyers did not staunchly resist), desegregating cells was different.[2] This is because prison officers would have little control over what occurred within cells.
Moreover, cell partners or "cellies" had little opportunity for self-segregation
and avoidance, something that routinely occurred in dormitories and on yards.
Old-time wardens and more experienced officers, relying on their gut feelings
and years of experience, predicted that cell desegregation would become a
miserable and violent failure. Those new to the system did not know what to
expect.

The perspective taken by many seasoned custodial staff was not surprising
if one considers the massive transition and pursuant chaos that had been
weathered only a few years earlier in the aftermath of *Ruiz*.[3] To those in the
system, tradition was a stabilizing force, bringing a level of predictability and
standardization to an unpredictable environment filled with unpredictable
individuals.[4] Cell desegregation, as with any major affront to tradition, would
destabilize the system. Just as the stipulations of *Ruiz* disrupted existing inmate social arrangements and were blamed for the wave of lethal violence in
the 1980s, a similar belief abounded with the prospect of cell desegregation.
This belief was that the tenuous racial environment held at bay by cell segregation would explode once the final zone was penetrated.

At the same time that unit-level personnel were questioning cell desegregation, upper-level administrators publicly favoring the plan nevertheless
had no real idea what to expect. Officially, TDC was ready to attempt cell
desegregation—7,000 days after *Lamar* began—and then wait and see.

Documenting the Aftermath

By 1991, TDC had officially implemented the Incident Data Form (IDF)
to track the outcomes of cell desegregation. The IDF was originally developed for the *Lamar* litigation in 1988-1989 to document TDC's belief that
cell desegregation, specifically among medium- and close-custody inmates,
would result in disproportionate interracial and racially motivated violence.
Outcomes from the 1988–1989 pilot IDF data analysis revealed higher rates
of inmate-on-inmate incidents in these higher custody levels. Despite this
finding, the *Lamar* court and the DOJ rejected TDC's interpretation and
conclusion from the pilot IDF analysis—namely that higher rates of vio-

lence in medium and close custody warranted their automatic exclusion from cell desegregation. Eventually, the prison system stipulated to desegregate minimum-, medium-, and close-custody inmates within cells.

At the August 1, 1991, implementation of cell desegregation, the IDF had already become a part of TDC's official policy and procedure. Staff members from various units had been trained in its proper use, and IDFs with unique incident identification numbers had been used at all units for almost a year.[5] Per TDC policy, an IDF was to be completed for every incident involving two or more offenders in which an offense or disciplinary report was filed against at least one offender. The IDF was not used for inmate-on-staff, staff-on-inmate, single-inmate incidents (e.g., possession of contraband), or incidents in which there was no known perpetrator. The IDF officially adopted by TDC in 1991 is displayed in Figure 8.1.[6]

Following a qualifying incident at any TDC unit, prison officials collected and maintained IDFs from prison units across the state, and stored them at a central location: Classification and Treatment Headquarters, the BOT Warehouse in Huntsville, Texas. Incomplete or incorrectly filed forms were returned to the original prison unit for correction or completion in order to track the outcomes of desegregation as completely and accurately as possible. Once all forms arrived at Classification and Treatment, staff members entered the information into a database.[7]

The type of information captured by the IDF and the way it was implemented served numerous important functions for TDC. First, the IDF was a valuable tool for documenting what happened in the aftermath of cell desegregation.[8] Although the IDF was able to document all qualifying inmate-on-inmate incidents at prison units, it was unique in that it was specifically developed for cell desegregation. Second, if cell desegregation led to disproportionate interracial and racially motivated violence, the system could use such evidence in future *Lamar* court proceedings. Perhaps most important, the IDF provided a standardized way for prison staff to document inmate-on-inmate incidents, especially those crossing racial boundaries. Prior to the IDF, different units employed different procedures for documenting and resolving different types of incidents. Tracking the level of inmate-on-inmate incidents in any systematic fashion was therefore impossible prior to the IDF.

TDC officially collected data on the IDF from 1991 until early 2000, without substantive revisions.[9] In 2000, the system discontinued its use primarily because the *Lamar* court no longer required such reporting.[10] Although the prison continued to collect data on inmate-on-inmate incidents after the removal of the IDF, and still does so today, such data collection is not as detailed

IDF NUMBER: _____

INCIDENT DATA FORM

Attached Disciplinary Report #: _____

Bldg. Major	Hearing Officer
_____ Major _____ Minor	_____ Major _____ Minor

NOTE: IT IS VERY IMPORTANT TO PRINT CLEARLY OR YOU WILL BE REQUIRED TO REWRITE! This form is to be completed for all incidents involving 2 or more inmates in which a disciplinary report is filed on at least one of the inmates. All completed forms are to be mailed to Classification and Treatment Hdqtrs. (BOT Warehouse), Huntsville.

INCIDENT INFORMATION

1. This item is to be completed by the **REPORTING PERSON** reporting the incident and filing the Disciplinary Report:

Reporting Unit: _____   Date of Incident: ____ / ____ / ____
                                                   (Month) (Day) (Year)

(Print)   Reporting Person: _____ / _____ / _____
                            (Name/Title)   (Last)   (First)   (Title)

2. This item is to be completed by the BUILDING MAJOR OR DESIGNEE:

Was EAC contacted? Yes _____ No _____ | Was a Use of Force Report Completed?

If yes, was an incident report required by EAC? | Yes _____ No _____

Yes _____ No _____

3. This item is to be completed by the **REPORTING PERSON**:

From available evidence and the initial investigation provide: a brief description of what happened, who started it, etc. Example: "One white close custody inmate attempted to change the TV channel in the recreation area and one Hispanic close custody inmate walked over to the TV knocking the white inmate's hand off the TV dial."

_____

Did the incident involve cell partners as opponents?   Yes _____   No _____

4. To be completed by the **REPORTING PERSON**:
   Mark an (X) in the appropriate spaces:

   a. _____ No physical contact (verbal confrontation only)
   b. _____ Fist/Feet/Hands
   c. _____ Weapons: Type of weapon(s) used: _____
                         Number of each type of weapon: _____

5. To be completed by the **REPORTING PERSON**:
   Mark an (X) where the incident occurred. If housing location indicate housing custody code (see codes at bottom).

Custody Code

_____ Cell	_____	_____ Gymnasium
_____ Cellblock Run	_____	_____ Outside Rec. Yard
_____ Cellblock Dayroom	_____	_____ Work (specify location)_____
_____ Dorm Living Area	_____	_____ School
_____ Main Hallway		_____ Shower
_____ Dining Hall		_____ Other: (specify)_____

Custody Codes: A1-Admin Seg. Grp. A; A2-Admin Seg. Grp. B; AH- Admin. Seg.-Prehearing; AM= Admin. Seg. Management; AP-Admin. Seg. Protection; CC- Close; DS- Death Row Segregation; DW- Death Row Work Capable; II- Intell. (MROP); MB- Minimum in/out; MD- Medical; ME- Medium; MH- Mental Health; MI- Minimum in; MO- Minimum out; OT- Outside Trusty Camp; PC- Safekeeping Close; PE- Safekeeping Medium; PI- Safekeeping Minimum; SO- Solitary; TR- Transient.

Figure 8.1. Incident Data Form

as with the IDF. For example, after the IDF was abandoned, the prison system ceased making systematic determinations as to whether an incident was racially motivated and/or whether it involved cell partners as opponents.

TDC also restricted the definition of inmate-on-inmate incidents to be documented. Today, only inmate-on-inmate incidents involving an injury requiring medical treatment beyond first aid are documented.[11] This is much different than IDF collection (in which all inmate-on-inmate incidents were documented regardless of injury level) and thus underestimates the number

INMATE INFORMATION

6. Columns 1-7 to be completed by the **REPORTING PERSON**. Column 8 to be completed by the **DISCIPLINARY CLERK**.

COLUMNS 1, 2:	List every inmate involved in the incident by TDC# and full name.
COLUMN 3:	Race: use "W" or "B" or "H" or "O" (i.e. American Indian, Asian, etc)
COLUMN 4:	User custody codes provided on the bottom of the front side.
COLUMN 5:	Level of Injury "N" = No injury; "M" = Minor Injury (treatment provided by other than M.D.); "S" = Serious Injury (treatment required by M.D.); "D" = Death Result.
COLUMN 6:	Victim/Assailant Relationship: Enter "E" on top line if equal confrontation (no clear instigator or victim) If not, then for each inmate, enter "V" = Inmate was Victim or "A" = Inmate was Assailant.
COLUMN 7:	List all offense codes inmate is charged with.

COL. 1 Inmate's Name Last	First	COL. 2 TDC#	COL. 3 Race	COL. 4 Custody Code	COL. 5 Level of Injury	COL. 6 Victim / Assailant	COL. 7 Offense Code(s)	COL. 8 Disciplinary Report #

7. Items A and B below are to be completed by the **REPORTING PERSON**. Mark (X) on the spaces below which best describe the incident. Responses are required for both A and B.

A. _____ Gang Related (explain reason why) _____

_____ Unclear if Gang Related.

_____ Not Gang Related.

B. _____ Racially Motivated. Explain reason why (racial slur, etc.) _____

_____ Unclear if Racially Motivated.

_____ Not Racially Motivated.

C. **To be completed for major cases by the COUNSEL SUBSTITUTE:** Consideration for re-evaluation of 7.B above:

_____ No re-evaluation indicated.

_____ Re-evaluation indicated due to the following reasons: _____

D. To be completed by the MAJOR OR DESIGNEE:

_____ Determination same as reported in 7.B above (no change).

_____ Determination changed as follows:

_____ Racially Motivated

_____ Unclear if Racially Motivated

_____ Not Racially Motivated

of inmate-on-inmate incidents. Despite these changes, the implementation of the IDF was the first instance in the nation in which systematic data on the aftermath of prisoner desegregation were collected. Studying the data gives a relatively complete picture of the first decade of desegregation in Texas prisons.[12]

The Aftermath of Desegregation in Texas Prisons, 1991–1999

To more fully appreciate the prison system's progress toward cell desegregation in the 1990s, it is necessary to put our coming analysis into a larger context. In 1991, TDC incarcerated more than 47,000 male offenders (see

Table 8.1, which includes male and female totals; Table 8.2 includes only male population totals). In the 1990s, TDC received over 80,000 new felony offenders; by the end of 1999, TDC incarcerated more than 134,000 inmates— 126,280 of whom were males. By the end of 1991, TDC had 12,173 double cells, 25 percent of which (3,067 cells or 6,134 inmates) were desegregated. Nine years later, at the end of 1999, TDC had 23,831 double cells with 62 percent (14,805 cells or 29,610 inmates) desegregated.[13]

Also by that time, the Texas prison system had desegregated more inmates within cells than the entire correctional populations in the state systems of forty-one out of the fifty states.[14] Moreover, all non-celled inmates in Texas were desegregated in dormitory housing areas. Since 1993, the prison system has never fallen below 50 percent of double cells desegregated system-wide. Indeed, TDC averaged roughly 55 percent desegregation of all double cells from 1991 to 1999. While TDC desegregates on average 55 percent of its double cells in any given year, some prison units desegregate upward of 80 percent of all double cells.[15]

To summarize, from 1991 to 1999, there was nearly a threefold increase in the number of male prisoners in TDC, almost a 100 percent increase in the total number of double cells, and a nearly fivefold increase in the number of inmates desegregated within double cells. Overall, the level of desegregation in TDC, particularly within cells, is not matched by any other prison system in the nation.

Overall Inmate-on-Inmate Incidents

Table 8.2 examines all male inmate-on-inmate incidents in the Texas prison system between 1991 and 1999 as collected on the IDF (this includes all documented incidents among cell partners and non-cell partners from 1991 to 1999). Overall, there were a total of 35,995 incidents among male inmates, or roughly 4,000 documented incidents per year system-wide.[16]

Table 8.2 reveals that from 1991 to 1999 the raw number of intraracial incidents exceeded the raw number of interracial incidents (incidents among different races). Intraracial incidents accounted for roughly 55 percent of all incidents among male inmates in the prison system (19,708 out of 35,995), and interracial incidents accounted for 45 percent of all incidents (16,287 out of 35,995). In no year did the raw number of interracial incidents surpass the raw number of intraracial incidents. At the most basic level, data on the number of intraracial and interracial incidents provides some evidence on the impact of desegregation. The finding that, over the 1990s, interracial incidents

Table 8.1. Growth and Desegregation of Texas Prisons, 1991–1999

Year	TDC Population	System Race Percentages			Total Double Cells	Desegregated Double Cells	Percentage of Desegregated Double Cells	Inmates in Desegregated Double Cells	Inmates in Segregated Double Cells
		Black	White	Hispanic					
1991	49,413	48	29	23	12,173	3,067	25.2%	6,134	18,212
1992	50,895	48	28	24	12,378	5,141	41.5%	10,282	14,474
1993	59,750	47	28	24	16,706	8,759	52.4%	17,518	15,894
1994	68,804	47	28	25	18,800	10,490	55.8%	20,980	16,620
1995	103,342	47	27	25	21,794	12,371	56.8%	24,742	18,846
1996	123,862	46	27	26	24,361	14,382	59.0%	28,764	19,958
1997	127,007	45	27	27	23,935	14,556	60.8%	29,112	18,758
1998	131,408	45	29	26	23,957	15,041	62.8%	30,082	17,832
1999	134,114	44	30	25	23,831	14,805	62.1%	29,610	18,052

Note: Population Information obtained from Texas Department of Criminal Justice-Institutional Division (TDCJ-ID) Fiscal Year Statistical Reports, 1990–1999. Data on double cells and desegregation obtained from TDCJ-ID report "Number of Integrated General Population Cells by Unit and Custody," 1991–1999. Totals are reflective of yearly averages. Calculations by percentage may be slightly off due to rounding. Changes in the number of double cells, particularly small decreases from year to year, indicate housing and/or custody changes by the TDCJ-ID.

Table 8.2. Inmate-on-Inmate Incidents in the Texas Prison System, 1991–1999

Year	TDC Male Population	Total Number of Incidents	Type of Incident Intraracial	Interracial	Incident Racially Motivated Yes	No	Unclear	Rate of Incidents Per 1,000 Inmates Intraracial	Interracial
1991	47,262	3,906	2,269	1,637	323	2,879	704	48	35
1992	48,510	4,178	2,276	1,902	204	3,094	880	47	39
1993	57,038	4,183	2,325	1,858	163	3,352	668	41	33
1994	65,107	3,426	1,838	1,588	135	2,783	508	28	24
1995	96,847	4,149	2,291	1,858	143	2,937	1,069	24	19
1996	116,121	4,136	2,267	1,869	124	2,886	1,126	20	16
1997	118,752	4,069	2,191	1,878	105	2,714	1,251	18	16
1998	123,449	4,001	2,115	1,886	85	2,541	1,375	17	15
1999	126,280	3,947	2,136	1,811	95	2,582	1,270	17	14
Total		35,995	19,708	16,287	1,377	25,768	8,851		

Note: Population data obtained from the Texas Department of Criminal Justice-Institutional Division (TDCJ-ID) Fiscal Year Statistical Reports, 1991–1999. Male population totals are year-end averages. Incident totals for 1997 were derived from average of 1996 and 1998 because of missing data from the TDCJ-ID. Column totals not equal to the total number of incidents are the result of rounding for imputed 1997 data.

accounted for a smaller proportion of all incidents than intraracial incidents suggests that desegregation did not unleash the racial unrest feared, at least as officially documented.

Further evidence that desegregation did not unleash a wave of violence is found by examining the seriousness of incidents. Although not shown in the table, the overwhelming majority of incidents consisted either of an assault involving fists, feet, or hands or a verbal assault (92 percent).[17] Only 8 percent of all inmate-on-inmate incidents involved a weapon, and weapon use was no more prevalent among interracial incidents than it was for intraracial incidents. When a weapon was used, the most frequent weapon of choice was a razor, knife, or metal object, followed by a common tool (e.g., aggie or a hammer), liquid (including bodily fluids), or "other" (e.g., pork chop bone, wall, rock, etc.).

Another proxy for seriousness can be found by examining injuries sustained during an inmate-on-inmate incident. Ninety-five percent of all incidents did not result in an offender injury (55 percent) or resulted in only a minor injury (40 percent)—defined by TDC policy of the time as treatment provided by other than a medical doctor. Two percent of inmates received a serious injury (treatment required by a medical doctor). Finally, out of 35,995 documented incidents, there were twelve inmate-on-inmate incidents over the 1990s that resulted in the death of an inmate.

Incidents with Racial Motivations

Racial motivation is an important concept concerning the aftermath of desegregation in Texas prisons. TDC recognized in their training that an incident which happened to involve inmates of different races did not automatically signify the incident was motivated by race. In "Guidelines for Determining Racial Motivation," the TDC training manual for cell desegregation stated as follows:

The fact that an incident involved inmates of different races is not in and of itself sufficient to make the determination that the incident was racially motivated. There must be some indicator(s) that the incident was either the result of the racial attitudes or beliefs of one or more of the inmates involved, or that the fact that the incident involved inmates of different races was a contributing factor to the seriousness of the incident.[18]

The concept of "racial motivation" is subjective, an aspect that prison managers also recognized. The prison system implemented an investigative process to determine more objectively whether incidents that crossed racial boundaries were actually motivated by race. Investigators thoroughly examined the circumstances surrounding the incident; the context surrounding the incident; any and all statements made by involved inmates before, during, and after the incident; information provided by a reliable inmate informant about the incident; whether the involved inmates had a history of race-related threats of violence and/or expressed attitudes of racial hatred; and a pattern of interracial incidents (defined as three or more interracial incidents during the previous two years). In short, racial motivation labels were not automatically assumed for every interracial incident. Trained staff peeled away the layers of each incident to accurately ferret out those incidents truly motivated by race and those incidents that just happened to involve offenders of different races.[19]

Of the 35,995 documented incidents from 1991 to 1999, 1,377 incidents were deemed racially motivated. The overwhelming majority of incidents were not racially motivated (25,768), although there were a number of incidents where the motivation was unclear (8,851) and not conclusively determined by officers.

The 1,377 confirmed racially motivated incidents accounted for 4 percent of all male inmate-on-inmate incidents (1,377 out of 35,995) from 1991 to 1999. Putting these figures into context, there were a total of 1,377 confirmed racially motivated incidents, among numerous prison units, and thousands of inmates moving in and out of TDC from 1991 to 1999.[20] Even considering unclear determinations, the bulk of incidents were not considered racially motivated.[21]

An evaluation of the frequency of racially motivated incidents in Table 8.2 reveals two important perspectives. Considering TDC's stance on cell desegregation prior to 1991, it is not unreasonable to expect that TDC would have been quite liberal with describing interracial incidents as racially motivated. In short, a higher number of racially motivated incidents would have made TDC predictions correct. This did not appear to happen; while only speculation, the system's commitment to cell desegregation is demonstrated to some degree by their attention to detail in collecting what appears to be valid data on racial motivations.

Second, the initial years of cell desegregation produced the highest number of racially motivated incidents, much higher than later years, even following the massive prison expansion of the mid-1990s. There are several potential explanations. The observed trend of racially motivated incidents may have resulted from a new policy implementation and confusion on the part of correctional staff as to what the racial motivation label entailed. Therefore, in the early years prison officers may have been more liberal with racial motivation labels out of confusion. Alternatively, it is possible that in later years prison staff either ignored or failed to detect racially motivated incidents because of increasing populations. It is also possible that inmates in the early 1990s were simply responding to cell desegregation in a more violent and racially motivated way than in the later 1990s because they had not been "conditioned" to this practice. Regardless of these and other competing explanations, racially motivated incidents in Texas prisons, as officially documented on the IDF, were few and far between. The feared racial Armageddon did not materialize—there was no saturnalia of death.

The Overall Finding

The last two columns in Table 8.2 present the overall rate of intraracial and interracial incidents per 1,000 male inmates from 1991 to 1999. The rates are graphically depicted in Figure 8.2.[22] The data in Table 8.2 and Figure 8.2 reveal that the rate of intraracial incidents (same race incidents) was greater than the rate of interracial incidents in each year from 1991 through 1999. Between 1991 and 1993, the system-wide rates of intraracial and interracial incidents were more disparate, but by the mid- to late 1990s, they were virtually indistinguishable. Interestingly, the overall rate of incidents among TDC male population consistently dropped following the initial years of cell desegregation, and this trend in the rate of incidents was found for both intraracial and interracial incidents.

Two plausible explanations emerge for the overall drop in the rate of incidents system-wide from 1991 to 1999, beyond inmates simply becoming less troublesome. First, because of the increasing number of inmates over the decade of the 1990s, it is possible that correctional officers were limited in their ability to detect incidents that were not of a sufficiently serious nature. Or, perhaps, correctional officers simply could have ignored relatively nonserious incidents that would otherwise qualify for IDF reporting, choosing instead to informally resolve such incidents. We can only speculate, but if this actually occurred across Texas prison units, it is perhaps also the case that correctional officers failed to detect or informally resolved incidents consistently concerning both intraracial and interracial incidents. Thus, the documentation of incidents was consistent, even if some incidents were ignored, failed to be detected, or were simply informally resolved when they could or should have been officially documented on the IDF.

On the other hand, there were perhaps occurrences that equally impacted the likelihood of inmate-on-inmate incidents occurring regardless of whether

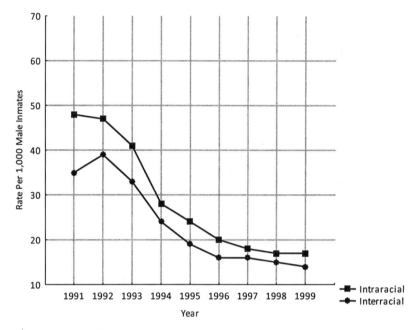

Figure 8.2. Rate of Intraracial and Interracial Incidents per 1,000 Male Inmates in the Texas Prison System, 1991–1999

they were intraracial or interracial. Rather than correctional officers ignoring, failing to detect, or informally resolving incidents that should have been reported on the IDF, larger organizational events during the 1990s may help explain the relative consistency in the raw number of incidents over time, and the consequent drop in the rate of incidents, despite massive increases in the offender population. Some evidence for this claim is the fact that the majority of documented incidents in TDC were not overly serious, most did not involve a weapon, and few resulted in serious injuries. Thus, it appears by that evidence alone that officers were doing a consistent job at detecting inmate-on-inmate incidents, regardless of their seriousness and despite the population explosion.

If the behavior of officers and/or the explosion of the offender population had a great impact on incident reporting, it might be expected that nonserious incidents would be neglected in favor of attention to more serious incidents. This did not appear to happen. Significant variations in incident totals from year to year would also be expected. This did not happen. Indeed, there was remarkable consistency. For now, the data do not appear to be an artifact impacted by changes in officer behavior over time in detecting and documenting incidents as a result of population changes, but rather the result of larger organizational dynamics impacting incident levels among all inmates—regardless of whether the incidents were intraracial or interracial.[23]

We more fully explore these larger organizational dynamics in the final chapter; however, a possible explanation for the consistency in incidents relates to population dynamics and unprecedented change that came to the prison system. Between 1980 and 2000, the Texas prison system added more than 80,000 new beds. It is within this unprecedented cycle of growth that the *Lamar* stipulations were implemented. The onslaught of new prisons, new prisoners, and new staff, in our view, probably helped to reduce incidents. In other words, the last vestiges of the old Texas prison traditions and customs were obliterated by the growth. New inmates and staff had no knowledge of the past and were amenable to desegregation—they simply did not know any better. The old "heads" (including both staff and inmates) were in the minority, talked of the old days, but "rolled with the flow." Among other speculations, we believe this factor not only helped to reduce incidents, but also helps to explain the consistency in incidents over time and the implementation of desegregation absent a race war.

Conclusion

This chapter has presented initial findings of the aftermath of desegregation in Texas prisons on a broad scale. Analyses reveal that there was remarkable consistency in incidents over the decade among the entire TDC population. Moreover, there appeared to be no race war as a result of desegregation. Interracial incidents occurred at a lower rate than intraracial incidents—despite the fact that more inmates were desegregated than segregated after 1993. To further examine the impact of desegregation in Texas prisons, the next chapter focuses exclusively on incidents among desegregated cell partners. It is at the cell level that the true impact of cell desegregation can be found.

CHAPTER 9

Life in the First Available Cell

Typically, most inmates begin their prison careers housed in cell blocks and living in cells, nine-by-six-foot compartments arranged in rows (or runs) along two and three story tiers. Most runs have between twenty and twenty-five cells, or "houses," as the inmates call them. Texas prison cells house two offenders, and two steel bunks (one over the other) are attached to the wall. Each cell has an open commode. Personal belongings are limited and life in the cell is cramped, noisy, and virtually devoid of any personal privacy.

Hot in the summer and cold in the winter, cells have few creature comforts. Inmates must also endure the constant smell of sweat, body waste, and such disinfectants as Pine Sol and other industrial strength cleaners. Into this setting, as a result of *Lamar*, inmates are randomly assigned to the "first available cell." Through this process, some cells are desegregated and some are segregated, all by chance. No matter: it is up to the "cellies" to figure out or adapt a routine whereby they can do their time. We devote this entire chapter to answer the question we posed in Chapter 1: What happened when Texas prison cells were desegregated?

Incidents among Desegregated and Segregated Cell Partners

From its onset, through its protracted path through the courts, *Lamar* was about cell desegregation. The cell was the target, and cell desegregation was no doubt the most contentious and drawn out aspect of the *Lamar* suit. To understand the impact of cell desegregation, one of the best barometers is by comparing the level of violence among inmates who were housed in a racially mixed first available cell to those who received a single-race cell. Tables 9.1 and 9.2 present the findings of this analysis. The focus is on one simple ques-

Table 9.1. Cell Partner Incidents in the Texas Prison System, 1991–1999

Year	Total Cell Partner Incidents	Type of Incident		Percentage of Total Cell Partner Incidents		Racially Motivated Cell Partner Incidents (Desegregated Cells)		Rate of Cell Partner Incidents Per 1,000 Inmates	
		Intraracial	Interracial	Intraracial	Interracial	N	%	Intraracial	Interracial
1991	411	275	136	67%	33%	22	16	15	22
1992	527	272	255	52%	48%	56	22	19	25
1993	533	275	258	52%	48%	35	14	17	15
1994	501	218	283	44%	56%	36	13	13	13
1995	747	341	406	46%	54%	47	12	18	16
1996	864	376	488	44%	56%	39	8	19	17
1997	860	367	493	43%	57%	35	7	20	17
1998	855	357	498	42%	58%	31	6	20	17
1999	900	380	520	42%	58%	28	5	21	18
Total	6,198	2,861	3,337	46%	54%	329	10		

Note: Rate per 1,000 intraracial cell incidents is the rate of incidents per 1,000 inmates racially segregated in double cells in each year indicated. Rate per 1,000 interracial cell incidents is the rate of incidents per 1,000 inmates racially desegregated in double cells in each year indicated. Incident totals for 1997 were derived from average of 1996 and 1998 because of missing data from the TDCJ-ID.

tion: Did racially mixed cell partners engage in a greater level of violence than offenders in single-race cells?

From 1991 to 1999, there were a total of 6,198 incidents involving all cell partners documented on the IDF. Incidents involving cell partners accounted for roughly 17 percent of inmate-on-inmate incidents in TDC from 1991 to 1999 (6,198 out of 35,995). Viewed another way, more than 80 percent of all incidents in Texas prisons *did not* occur among cell partners. Among cell partner incidents (6,198) in the 1990s, 54 percent occurred among mixed-race cell partners, and 46 percent occurred among cell partners of the same race.

The critical point of focus when gauging the impact of cell desegregation, however, is whether interracial cell partner incidents occurred at a higher level than would be expected relative to the level of desegregated cells. For example, if 50 percent of TDC's double cells are integrated in any given year, 50 percent of all cell partner incidents would be expected to occur among racially mixed cell partners, all else being equal. Alternatively, if racial animosities were a driving force for interracial cell partner incidents, it might be expected that mixed-race cell partners would engage in violence at a level much higher than their proportion of the double-celled population. For example, both same- and mixed-race cell partners experience the pressures and inconveniences of prison life that can lead to conflict, but mixed-race cell partners may have an added layer of frustration from being forced to cell with someone of a different race. Thus they might be expected to engage in a level of violence beyond their proportion of the double-celled population.

To answer whether racially mixed cell partners engaged in violence against each other at a greater than expected level compared to same-race cell partners first requires examining changes in the percent of double cells desegregated by TDC.

By the end of 1993 TDC had desegregated roughly 52 percent of all double cells (see Table 9.2). In each successive year more than half of all double cells were desegregated. The expectation following 1993 is that interracial cell partner incidents should surpass the raw number of intraracial cell partner incidents. Proportionately, more racially mixed inmates (or cells) should result in more interracial cell partner incidents, all else being equal.[1] With a few minor exceptions, the data show that as more inmates (or cells) were desegregated, there was a corresponding increase in the incidents across racial boundaries.[2] Thus, more desegregated cells resulted in more incidents among desegregated cell partners.

The final perspective is whether the level of violence among racially mixed cell partners was *proportionate* to the level of desegregated cells in any given year. There are three potential outcomes and three potential explanations that could arise from this examination:

Table 9.2. Desegregated Double Cells and Interracial Cell Partner Incidents, 1991–1999

Year	Percentage of Desegregated Double Cells	Percentage of Interracial Cell Partner Incidents
1991	25%	33%
1992	42%	48%
1993	52%	48%
1994	56%	56%
1995	57%	54%
1996	59%	56%
1997	61%	57%
1998	63%	58%
1999	62%	58%

If the level of violence among racially mixed cell partners is *proportionate* to the level of cell desegregation, the logical explanation is that the higher level of violence among desegregated cell partners was simply a natural consequence of increasing the proportion of desegregated double cells in the system.

If the level of violence among racially mixed cell partners is *disproportionately higher* than the level of cell desegregation, then something other than the routine pressures and inconveniences of prison life, such as racial animosities between cell partners, fueled the higher level of violence among desegregated cell partners but did not do so for single-race cell partners.

If the level of violence among racially mixed cell partners is *disproportionately lower* than the level of cell desegregation, than perhaps only the "best risk" inmates were desegregated, whereas the harder cases remained segregated by race within double cells. Another potential explanation is that something about desegregation actually decreased the level of violence among racially mixed cell partners, something not experienced by those who remained segregated by race in double cells.

Examining these competing explanations, the results of the analysis indicate that the level of violence among racially mixed cell partners was *proportionate* to the level of cell desegregation. As Table 9.2 shows, with the exception of 1991 and 1992, the proportion of interracial cell partner incidents was slightly *lower than or equal to* the proportion of desegregated double cells.[3] Thus, more cell desegregation resulted in more raw incidents among desegregated cell partners as the new policy expanded, but the violence was proportionate to, and appears explained only by, the increasing level of cell desegregation.

TDC's desegregation procedure highlights the importance of the finding that there was not a disproportionate amount of incidents attributed to racially mixed cell partners relative to the proportion of cells desegregated. Prison officers assigned inmates to the first available and appropriate cell, without regard to race. The factors that prison officers considered when choosing the first available cell were objective criteria such as age, height, weight, active or passive tendencies, and other security and health-related criteria.[4] Through this process, TDC matched the most compatible inmates together. In essence, prison staff tried to equalize status among inmates within *both* single-race and mixed-race cells.

The random assignment process resulted in both racially mixed and unmixed cells. Through this race-neutral process, individuals who by chance wound up in a single-race cell were perhaps equivalent to those who received an integrated cell assignment, at least in terms of the factors that may lead to an incident between inmates in a cell. The only difference was the racial makeup of cells in the mixed and homogeneous double-celled populations. That more raw incidents were found among cell partners of different races appears to relate only to the fact that there were more mixed-race cells than single-race cells starting in 1993. The data do not appear to support the notion that the slightly greater frequency of interracial cell partner incidents over the decade resulted from potential racial animosities or tensions as a result of being desegregated, factors not found among the cells with same-race inmates. The trend in the data is such that the same factors that led to an intraracial cell partner incident are probably the same factors that led to an interracial cell partner incident—and those factors were not likely due to race but rather the pressures and inconveniences of imprisonment experienced by all inmates.

An alternative perspective is that the slightly lower level of interracial violence relative to the proportion of desegregated double cells resulted from some sort of selection bias on the part of prison officials. Here, the interpretation is that only the best risks were desegregated (those favoring or at worst indifferent to cell desegregation). Such a perspective seems to belie what the data show and also what is known about TDC's desegregation protocol. Indeed, while interracial cell partner incidents were found at a slightly lower than expected level relative to the proportion of desegregated cells (see Table 9.2), this difference was extremely small and likely due to chance.[5]

A related aspect to the selection bias argument is the practice of racial restrictions in TDC. While it is true that inmates with racial restrictions were to be placed with a member of the same race, it is also true that racial restrictions were tightly controlled and were not simply granted to any inmate who desired to be in a same-race cell.[6] The bar was set high for an inmate to receive a racial restriction. Less than one-half of 1 percent of all inmates classified for double-cell housing received racial restrictions from 1991 to 1999—a mere handful of inmates dispersed across several prison units in the state.[7]

Moreover, provided an inmate received a racial restriction, such restrictions could occur for numerous reasons, such as if an inmate was the victim of a racially motivated attack or due to racially biased behavior on the part of the inmate—sometimes racial prey received racial restrictions, and sometimes the predators received racial restrictions. Thus, hard cases were racially restricted and segregated for the protection of others, but inmates were also restricted and racially segregated for their own protection. In any event, such restrictions were extremely few and far between and had little impact on cell assignments. As such, racial restrictions are unlikely as an explanation of the slightly lower proportion of interracial cell partner incidents relative to the proportion of desegregated double cells.

The finding that the level of violence among desegregated cell partners was closely associated to the proportion of desegregated double cells leads to the following conclusions: (1) a selection bias in which only the best risks were desegregated cannot explain the results; (2) race or racial animosities produced by simply desegregating cells is unlikely the driving factor behind most incidents among desegregated cell partners; and (3) the higher number of incidents among desegregated cell partners over the decade is explained by increases in the number of desegregated cells.[8]

Thus an initial answer to our original question is as follows: Desegregated cell partners did not engage in a greater expected level of violence than cell partners who remained segregated by race, taking into account increases in the proportion of desegregated double cells. To further explore the impact of cell desegregation, we now turn our attention to racially motivated cell partner incidents.

Racially Motivated Cell Partner Incidents

The fact that an incident occurred among different-race cell partners does not necessarily mean the incident was motivated by race. To further explore this issue, Table 9.1 presents data on whether interracial incidents among desegregated cell partners were racially motivated. Along with comparing the level of violence among racially mixed and racially homogeneous cell partners, interracial cell partner incidents with racial motivations provide more evidence on the true impact of cell desegregation. Indeed, cell desegregation provided the opportunity for such incidents to occur.

As shown in Table 9.1, a total of 329 racially motivated interracial cell partner incidents occurred from 1991 to 1999. This resulted in an average of roughly 37 racially motivated cell partner incidents per year across the sprawling Texas prison system. Viewed another way, 90 percent of all interracial cell partner incidents were not racially motivated—TDC experienced less than one racially motivated attack among desegregated cell partners, per prison unit, per year, from 1991 through 1999. Although such racially motivated cell partner incidents might arguably have been prevented with continued racial segregation, this is not the "blood on the tiers" that many had predicted.[9]

The 329 confirmed racially motivated cell partner incidents accounted for 24 percent of all racially motivated incidents system-wide (329 of 1,377 racially motivated incidents system-wide, as reported in Chapter 8). Because the majority of inmates are not housed in double cells, it is not surprising that most racially motivated incidents occurred among the larger population of non-celled inmates.[10] The bottom line is that racially motivated incidents in Texas prison cells were extremely rare relative to all inmate-on-inmate incidents.[11]

Rates of Intraracial and Interracial Cell Partner Incidents

The last column of Table 9.1 examines the rate of intraracial and interracial incidents per 1,000 inmates in the desegregated and segregated double cell populations of TDC. Although raw numbers and percentages are useful, they do not account for population differences among the desegregated and segregated double-celled populations. To account for these population differences, the use of rates allows a standardized point of comparison.[12]

With the exception of 1991 and 1992, the rate of incidents among desegregated cell partners was slightly lower than the rate of incidents among cell partners who remained segregated. Figure 9.1 graphically depicts the rates from 1991 to 1999. The data show that cell desegregation did not result in a consistently higher rate of incidents than did segregating inmates by race in double cells—in fact, the rate of cell partner incidents after 1992 was always less among desegregated cellmates. Even in 1991 and 1992, where the rate of interracial cell partner incidents did surpass the rate of intraracial cell partner incidents, the differences were negligible. In the same vein, in the years following 1992 when the rate of interracial incidents was equal to or lower than the rate of intraracial incidents, the difference was negligible.

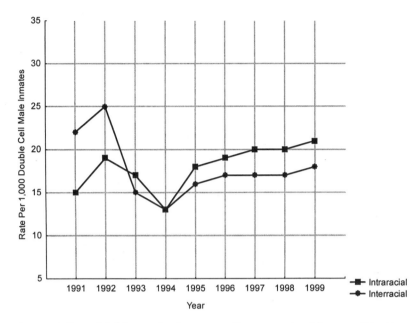

Figure 9.1. Rate of Cell Partner Incidents among Desegregated and Segregated Double Cell Populations, 1991–1999

It is important to note that in 1994, the rate of intraracial and interracial cell partner incidents were at their lowest level during the 1990s. From 1995 through the end of 1999, the rate of incidents among both same-race and different-race cell partners rose slightly. Despite these rises, the differences are extremely small. The intraracial rate of cell partner incidents rose from its lowest point of 13 per 1,000 in 1994 to a peak level of 21 incidents per 1,000 inmates in 1999. For the interracial rate, the increase over the same period was from 13 to 18 incidents per 1,000 inmates. Although the rates increased slightly from their lowest levels, in practical terms the differences are extremely small.

Summary of Official Outcomes of the First Decade of Desegregation

Of all inmate-on-inmate incidents in the Texas prison system, the majority (55 percent or 19,708 incidents) were among inmates of the same race, system-wide, over nearly a decade (see Table 8.1). During this same time period, inter-racial incidents accounted for roughly 45 percent of all incidents, or 16,287 incidents. Unfortunately, systematic data were not collected by TDC prior to IDF data collection. It is not known whether the incident figures during the first decade of desegregation represent an increase or a decrease in the total raw number of incidents in TDC. It is also not known whether the rate of incidents increased, decreased, or stayed the same after full-scale desegregation took effect. We simply do not know whether the period under focus was a constant or an aberration compared to the period before cell desegregation.

Of the 16,287 interracial incidents recorded by the prison system, 1,377 were confirmed by prison officers as racially motivated, or 8 percent of all interracial incidents. Interracial incidents absent racial motivations are simply incidents that happened to involve offenders of different races, perhaps being motivated by a number of things from a television program, debts, or cutting into a chow line, but not racial motivations. Prison is a dense, packed existence where disputes occur all day long. Without racial motivations, such incidents cannot be attributed to desegregation specifically, and could have occurred under any condition with the exception of complete and utter racial segregation of prison units—something that was abandoned by 1965.[13]

Specific to cell partners, there were a total of 6,198 incidents among cell partners from 1991 to 1999. Of the 6,198 incidents, 3,337 or 54 percent were among desegregated cell partners. Considering that by the end of 1993 there were more inmates desegregated within cells than segregated, it is not surprising that interracial cell partner incidents represented a slightly greater proportion of all cell partner incidents over the decade. Yet this proportion closely followed changes in the proportion of desegregated double cells. In raw numbers, there were only 476 more interracial than intraracial cell partner incidents, over a span of nearly a decade, even as more inmates were desegregated in cells than segregated by the end of 1993.

It is true that interracial cell partner incidents would have been prevented with continued racial segregation of cells. Prior to large-scale cell desegregation, cell partners were almost exclusively of the same race, thus precluding the very label of an interracial cell partner incident. Yet the possibility still remained that different race inmates could have engaged in interracial incidents (e.g., in dayrooms, dormitories, hospital, chapel, cell block, yard), including individuals who may have eventually become cell partners as a result of *Lamar*. The same rationale holds true for racially motivated cell partner incidents. Noting this consideration, perhaps the closest approximation of the true impact of cell desegregation was through an examination of interracial cell partner incidents with racial motivations.

There were a total of 329 racially motivated cell partner incidents from

1991 to 1999. In short, when an incident occurred among racially mixed cell partners, it was rarely motivated by race. The continued racial segregation of cells would have prevented 329 racially motivated cell partner incidents over nearly a decade system-wide.[14] Considering that from 1991 to 1999 TDC had an average of eighty prison units spread across the state, this equaled less than one racially motivated attack per prison unit per year during the 1990s. Even using the most liberal definition of racial motivations, and by including unclear racial motivation determinations among desegregated cell partners, the impact of racially motivated incidents across the entire system was extremely small relative to all incidents.

All evidence points to the conclusion that desegregation in general, and cell desegregation in particular, did not lead to massive racial unrest as initially feared by Texas administrators. While pre-desegregation data would have been useful, the analysis comparing incidents among desegregated and segregated cell partners in the aftermath revealed little if any negative *official* impact of desegregation.

At the most specific level, the impact of desegregation can be boiled down to 329 racially motivated incidents among desegregated cell partners, over a decade, in a prison system beset with massive change. While desegregation may not have helped, it did not appear to hurt in terms of escalating inmate-on-inmate violence. The major question, then, is whether the risk of one racially motivated cell partner attack per prison unit per year outweighs cell desegregation. Was the change worth it? It is possible that, with continued racial segregation of cells, the racially motivated attacks among desegregated cell partners would have been prevented, although such attacks may still have occurred without the cell partner designation. To some, this is the price of diversity: equal protection by race in a prison setting and a few non-lethal incidents have been worth the cost of the *Lamar* remedies. To others, the price has been too great among the most violent and least stable. These points are perhaps best illustrated by the voices of Texas prison inmates, those who live in color-blind "houses."

Inmate Views after a Decade of Racial Mixing

Official incident data collected by TDC demonstrated that cell desegregation did not lead to disproportionate interracial violence, rather a negligible amount of racially motivated violence among desegregated cell partners. Agency-collected data, however, presents only one side of the story of desegregation in Texas prisons. The other side poses the following question: Does the apparent success of desegregation as revealed by official data mesh with inmate views of this policy mandate in Texas prisons?

To answer this question, we placed a general survey with open-ended questions in the Texas prison newspaper, the *Echo*, in November 2000. The *Echo* has been published since 1928 and remains a central source of information for inmates.[15] It includes information such as system updates and regulation changes, reprints of prison-related stories, prison-related columns, staff editorials (some written by inmates), and other general types of information including but not limited to legal notices, articles submitted by inmates, and letters to the editor.[16]

At the time our survey was published in 2000, the *Echo* was typically printed every month or two and placed in prison libraries, cell block dayrooms, and other areas where inmates congregate. Inmates in administrative segregation or more restrictive custodies may request a copy as well. Thus, although not all inmates have the same access to the *Echo* (and it is not printed in Spanish), it is widely read throughout the Texas prison system.[17]

Our survey asked inmates to respond to three open-ended questions concerning desegregation:

1. Does racial integration, in your opinion, increase or decrease tension on your unit?
2. In your opinion, is integration a good policy, or would you prefer to be housed with members of your own race?
3. What are the limits and benefits of racial integration on your unit?

The survey appeared in the Letter to the Editor section and was approved and supported by Texas prison administrators.

As part of the survey, a brief overview of *Lamar* was presented. Inmates were also informed that official data on inmate-on-inmate incidents were being analyzed to document what officially occurs versus how inmates view and experience desegregation on a day-to-day basis. Inmates were asked to respond to the address provided and were required to use their own stamp, paper, and envelope. Inmates were also informed that their identities would be kept confidential in any presentations and/or publications and that they would be mailed a summary of all findings (including those concerning official IDF data) if they responded.

Over 300 inmates responded to this informal query, some with letters spanning numerous pages. The majority of responses were from white inmates, although there were responses from black and Hispanic inmates as well. Among the respondents were inmates who had been incarcerated in Texas prisons since before desegregation went into effect, those who were relatively recent prisons arrivals, and those who had been incarcerated numerous times and in different prison systems. Some responses were detailed, while others were more general, addressing certain aspects of the questions and then offering more peripheral insight about desegregation.

Overall, respondents believed that desegregation increased racial tensions, preferred to be housed with their own race, and saw few benefits to this policy. Although attitudes do not necessarily translate into actions, overall the respondents held a negative view of desegregation and of cell desegregation in particular. A representative sampling of responses to the survey is included below.[18]

Letter from R. S.: So, it's been about 10 years and here you are! Sure, I'll go ahead and throw in a 33 cent stamp, no big deal, this subject has already cost me a few years of my life (freedom). . . . Water and oil do not mix. It's as simple as that. Have you ever been to a zoo? Have you ever seen polar bears in the same cages as lions? Do you know why you haven't? Because it's not natural. Sure you could say the lion and the polar bear have no problems living in the wild together. That's right Chad, they don't. But you put those two mean fuckers together in a 6 by 10 cell and see what goes on. . . . Limits and benefits [of desegregation]. Such a strange question. Limits, hmmmm, ok, fuck you White boy, ho ass blue eyed devil, funky ass cracker, suck a niggers dick, give me some of your store you all White folks owe a niga. All of the above are over the limit.

Letter from L. C.: I was racially restricted until the last of 1998. I am still restricted against living with Blacks. I get along with most Hispanics but I will not live with a Black. Plain and simple, if they force it on me I will kill one for them. . . . I would rather be on death row, ready for the needle than to have to do my time in a cell with a Black. It is bad enough having to live with Hispanics, but they at least have a little respect for themselves and their celly.

Letter from T. R.: All this racial integration created in the early stages of the 90s was to cause a lot of fighting not by the opposite race, but within the offender's own race. For letting himself be housed with the opposite race. . . . There was intense pressure being put on by your own race. A lot of offenders caved in to the pressure and refused housing with the opposite race. The prison unit was forced to take action and give disciplinary case for refusing an order to house with the other race. Hundreds of offenders were stripped of all good time credit and dropped in level status and housed in close custody and ad-seg.

The ones that did stay in general population were ridicule[d] by their own race. Many that did refuse to be housed, started to pick fights with the opposite race in order for them to be given a racial restriction. Many were given a racial restriction. Mainly Hispanics fighting with blacks. So once the restrictions were in place, the atmosphere was some what a little better by the end of 93–94. Because by then new offenders were coming into the prison system, not knowing the history race living with their own race. They were unaware what had happened in past.

Letter from J. W.: I will assume you've read Lamar Judge Lynn N. Hughes' threatening, unprofessional, and uncalled for comment in his opinion on Post-Judgment Interventions, dated I/II/96. . . . Each time I watch callous, incompetent, hateful prison personnel place a white, weak, first-time young-ster in a cell with a black, huge, well-known predator, I want to watch Lynn Hughes raped repeatedly until he dies a long, slow death.

Letter from T. S.: I'd give one of my fingers to be housed with my own race, white culture and blacks does not mix in prison. No Way!

Letter from W. B.: There is no positive side to integration in prison. . . . On the unit I'm on, as well as lots of other units, blacks make up the majority. . . . When a new white inmate enters this unit and is assigned to a tank blacks pull what is called "checking" or "back dooring." That's to say 3, 4, 5 or 6 blacks form a line and the new white inmate must fight them all, one after the other, without rest and regardless of injury. If he fails to do so then he is labeled "a hoe" (whore) and forced "to ride" (pay protection) and/or grant sexual favors whose property he now is.

By integrating cells the situation became that much worse. Inmates are constantly being attacked and/or stabbed in their sleep by their cellies when problems arise between races on the Unit, or as the incident in Jasper spurred throughout TDCJ where several white inmates were attacked by black cell mates due to the dragging death of James Byrd by 3 white ex-mates of TDCJ. . . . Integration will never work in TDCJ. Only a blind fool would believe it could or would. It's a damn race war going on down here.

Letter from D. B.: I personally believe that most offenders get confused by what they really feel about integration because of the "homeboy" issue. Although each individual may or may not have a hatred of races other than their own, there is always an underlying element of racial tension because of the obligation to "stay down" for your race. We also have the gang element involved here which creates a lot of tension which on the surface appears to be racial, but actually gangs will prey on their own race if they are not "down" with them or an individual appears weak for some reason.

It would appear (on the surface) that integration has increased tension, but the real problem lies in the classification system. Anytime there is a larger portion of one race than another in housing areas, the race with the biggest percentile will attempt to dominate causing racial friction. Here again I would like to mention gang affiliation, if a percentage of "same gang" members are present in one area, they will also attempt to dominate causing tension which could be construed as racial.

In my opinion integration is an excellent idea!! Although different races have different cultures, we live in a world where we have to learn to "get along" and since our goal in here (mine anyway) is to someday re-enter society, we have to learn to get along here. I have been housed with Blacks, Hispanics, and whites and although we have different upbringings and cultures, I believe it all depends on the individuals not the color. I have had good and bad cellies of all races including my own.

Letter from C. F.: Having spent 15+ calendar years in TDC I decided to respond to your request for my opinion on Lamar v. Coffield. I spent 10/67 to 11/69 on the Ramsey I Unit—during this time the unit was fully segregated—we did not work, live, eat, or shower with blacks and Mexicans. I spent 6/79 to 10/86 at the Walls Unit and during that time (approx. 1985) there was only a brief period when several blacks and whites voluntarily lived together. I spent 87–90 at the Ellis I and though we worked and otherwise went to activities together, the Unit was integrated only in the dormitory housing. I was very surprised to be automatically housed in a 2-man cell with a black when I returned to prison 6/99.

Racial integration (forced) increases tension on any unit. My best cellie has been a very happy go lucky, considerate, and kind black man—at the same time my worst cellie has been a loud mouth, filthy, arrogant, inconsiderate, prejudiced black man. It was such an uptight existence that I stayed out of my cell as much as possible. I went so far as to try and reset my body clock to have any bowel movement while I was at work.

I have spent 5 years in prison in California and they don't mix races in the cells. There may be blacks on one side and Chicanos on the other and you all work and program together. Their system works fine and I don't understand why Texas doesn't leave it at that. I'm going to read Lamar and see if it specified integration in each cell.

Thank God I'm out of there soon—this new style prison system leaves very little hope and is gonna blow up in a few years, and I only want to see it on the news from my rocking chair.

Although some offenders did not overly object to desegregation, the overwhelming majority of inmates felt it was a negative policy—either in general, within cells, or both. The bottom line, based on the responses of inmates, is that desegregation was not desired among inmates. It is likely that the responses received were probably limited to those most in favor of or against desegregation. Perhaps the majority of inmates who did not respond have little issue with this policy, and thus simply chose not to respond. Regardless of interpretation, the survey responses above give some perspective on what some inmates think about this policy in their own words.

Several inmates spoke to more peripheral issues relating to desegregation as they experience it on a day-to-day basis despite their general attitudes for or against this policy. For example, desegregation within cells caused tension *within* the races instead of between races, especially during the early years. The pressure to "stay down" with one's own race may have been an unintended consequence of desegregation, and might explain why the overall number of incidents among same-race inmates were higher in TDC from 1991 to 1999 (see Table 8.2). Indeed, the raw number of intraracial incidents, the rate of intraracial incidents per 1,000 inmates in general, and the rate of intraracial incidents among same-race cell partners was, with few exceptions, always greater than the same figures concerning inmates who were racially desegregated.[19] This paradox, that desegregation actually may have led to more violence within racial groupings than between them, is an interesting claim that seems at least tacitly supported by the data.

Inmate respondents also had numerous comments about the findings of the data analysis. All were mailed an overview of the findings after their initial response. Several later wrote back to give their interpretation of findings. A number of inmates believed that the 35,995 incidents over the 1990s did not represent a true picture of what happens in prisons on a daily basis, in that many incidents are overlooked or never discovered. Undoubtedly there is some truth to this argument. Offenders also discussed a number of other areas concerning the policy: that desegregation was sometimes used in a retaliatory manner, that racial restrictions were exceedingly difficult to obtain, that some custodies were more closely scrutinized for incidents than others, that some races are more closely scrutinized than others, that racial desegregation has increased the exploitation of some inmates (in particular what they considered the less organized white inmates), and so on.

Interestingly, however, despite a stated preference against desegregation and numerous perspectives about how desegregation unfolds on a daily basis, very few inmates indicated that they had engaged in violence to avoid its effects. Although some claimed that they would rather lose a finger or be on death row than in a desegregated cell, few proclaimed that they would resort to violence to avoid it.

These inmate perspectives shed light on how desegregation is viewed by those who experience its effects on a day-to-day basis. Official data revealed that the first decade of desegregation did not lead to disproportionate interracial and racially motivated violence. Among other indicators, this finding is supported by the fact that the Texas prison system continues to desegregate its cells; by the fact that there are very few racial restrictions in the prison system; and by inmate views on desegregation—although they did not like it, most did not resort to violence to avoid it.

The above findings are perhaps the best that can be hoped for, considering the clientele and the issue. Indeed, the goal of desegregation promulgated by *Lamar* was never to promote racial harmony. Rather, desegregation was to accomplish race-neutral housing assignments with the related goal of coexistence without violence. Racial harmony is much different than coexistence without violence, and the former was certainly not mandated by the Constitution or the *Lamar* court. Any measure of racial harmony that may have resulted was an added benefit, but that was not an overt goal of this massive natural experiment.

Texas Prisoner Desegregation in the New Millennium, 2000–2005

By 2000, TDC had been desegregating offenders in double cells for roughly a decade, with over 60 percent of its double cells system-wide having been desegregated. This section presents what happened following the first decade of desegregation in Texas prisons, during the first six years of the new millennium.

Among the most significant changes in TDC since we first began studying Texas prison desegregation in 1999 has been with regard to the research approval process and data collection procedures. The research approval process in today's TDC has been highly centralized, as opposed to the largely informal and decentralized processes we encountered in 1999. This became apparent in 2005 when we approached prison officials again and requested IDF data from 2000 through 2005. What in 1999 had taken a matter of days took several months in 2005. In part, this was because the IDF had been discontinued.

We were instead provided data on all inmate-on-inmate incidents in TDC from 2000 through 2005, data on the number of double cells desegregated and segregated, and data on the number of offenders racially restricted from a desegregated double cell.[20] Despite the exceptional support we received from TDC, additional changes to inmate-on-inmate incident data and its collection made it difficult for us to compare data from 1991–1999 to that from 2000–2005. We examine these changes below.

First, TDC ceased making systematic determinations as to whether inmate-on-inmate incidents occurred among cell partners. This is a major limitation to the data analysis and prevents a specific examination of the rate of incidents among desegregated and segregated cell partners after the end of year 1999. Second, TDC ceased making determinations of the motivations of inmate-on-inmate incidents, racial or otherwise. Therefore, we were not able to determine if incidents occurred among desegregated cell partners and, if so, whether such incidents were racially motivated. These first two changes are particularly problematic, for cell partner status and racial motivation determinations are critical pieces of information concerning the aftermath of cell desegregation in the longer term.

Perhaps the most dramatic change to data collection procedures was that the types of inmate-on-inmate incidents required to be documented by line officers have changed since the IDF was discontinued. The IDF documented all inmate-on-inmate incidents in TDC as long as at least one inmate received a disciplinary report. Previously, this meant that almost all discovered inmate-on-inmate incidents would have been documented on the IDF. Today, however, data collection is limited to a "serious offender assault," defined as an incident resulting in an injury requiring treatment beyond first aid. The IDF was used to document inmate-on-inmate incidents regardless of level of treatment needed and/or injury level. Therefore, the new data collection protocol excludes a large number of incidents that would have previously been documented on the IDF.

Because of changes in documenting inmate-on-inmate incidents, the type of information collected, and the discontinuation of the IDF, it is impossible to compare the first decade of desegregation to the first six years of the new millennium with any real accuracy. As a result, this section presents an independent analysis of six years of desegregation into the new millennium with the data collection changes experienced in TDC.

The First Six Years of Desegregation in the New Millennium

Table 9.3 examines desegregation in Texas prisons from 2000 to 2005. It reveals that the prison system continued to progress with desegregation, such that by 2002 (the highest reported percentage of desegregated double cells) TDC had desegregated over 70 percent of all double cells system-wide—more than 35,000 double celled inmates desegregated in 2002–2003 compared to roughly 15,000 racially segregated inmates in double cells. Because information on the number of desegregated private prison double cells were not available after 2003, this resulted in a reduction of the percent of double cells. Provided such data were available, it is likely that the percent of double cells desegregated would have remained over 70 percent. Based on these figures, TDC has continued their progress with desegregation.

Inmate-on-Inmate Incidents, 2000–2005

Data analysis during the first decade of desegregation (1991–1999) showed that TDC documented roughly 4,000 inmate-on-inmate incidents per year on the IDF. From 2000 to 2005, however, TDC documented roughly 1,500 inmate-on-inmate incidents per year (see Table 9.4). It is likely that the new data collection protocol resulted in a significant drop in officially collected incidents in TDC—not that inmates were somehow less likely to engage in incidents beginning in 2000.[21]

Examining the racial dynamics of incidents, the data in Table 9.4 reveals that 51 percent of all inmate-on-inmate incidents occurred among offenders of the same race from 2000 to 2005. Although the percentages varied slightly depending on the individual year, interracial incidents were not found disproportionate to intraracial incidents. The trends in the data from 2000 to 2005 tend to follow a similar pattern to those found from 1991 through 1999. That is, incidents among different race offenders do not appear any more likely than incidents among same race offenders, all things being equal.

Table 9.4 also examines the rate of intraracial and interracial incidents per 1,000 male inmates incarcerated in TDC from 2000 through 2005. There was no clear pattern observed in terms of the rates of incidents. What the analysis does show is that the rates of intraracial and interracial "serious offender assaults" are almost identical—that desegregation appears to have led to no more violence than segregation.

Table 9.3. Desegregation in Texas Prisons, 2000–2005

Year	TDC Population	System Race Percentages			Total Double Cells	Desegregated Double Cells	Percentage of Desegregated Double Cells	Inmates in Desegregated Double Cells	Inmates in Segregated Double Cells
		Black	White	Hispanic					
2000	133,680	43	31	26	24,513	15,369	62.7%	30,738	18,288
2001	127,452	42	31	28	25,043	16,851	67.3%	33,702	16,384
2002	126,104	41	31	28	25,573	17,946	70.2%	35,892	15,254
2003	129,260	40	31	29	25,358	17,573	69.3%	35,146	15,570
2004	132,366	39	31	30	23,394	14,429	61.7%	28,858	17,930
2005	134,233	38	31	30	23,358	14,591	62.5%	29,182	17,534

Note: Population Information obtained from Texas Department of Criminal Justice-Institutional Division (TDCJ-ID) Fiscal Year Statistical Reports, 2000–2005. Data on double cells and desegregation obtained from TDCJ-ID report "Number of Integrated General Population Cells by Unit and Custody," 2000–2005. Totals are averages for the years indicated. Statistics include private prison double cells and desegregation figures for 2000–2003 only; 2004–2005 private cell information not available. Calculations by percentages may be slightly off due to rounding. Changes in the number of double cells, particularly decreases from year to year, indicate housing and/or custody changes by the TDCJ-ID.

Certain figures on racial percentages and desegregated double cells for 2000 and 2001 were not available from the TDCJ-ID. Statistics for 2000 were computed by taking the averages of 1999 and 2002. Statistics for 2001 were computed by taking the averages for 2000 and 2002.

Table 9.4. Inmate-on-Inmate Incidents in the Texas Prison System, 2000–2005

Year	TDC Male Population	Total Number of Incidents	Type of Incident		Percentage of Total Incidents		Rate of Incidents Per 1,000 Inmates	
			Intraracial	Interracial	Intraracial	Interracial	Intraracial	Interracial
2000	125,749	1,831	992	839	54%	46%	8	7
2001	120,252	1,045	508	537	49%	51%	4	4
2002	118,904	1,274	624	650	49%	51%	5	5
2003	121,998	1,436	715	721	50%	50%	6	6
2004	124,766	1,601	841	760	53%	47%	7	6
2005	126,361	1,532	780	752	51%	49%	6	6
Total		8,719	4,460	4,259	51%	49%		

Notes: Indicates the rate of intraracial and interracial incidents per 1,000 male inmates by year. Population data obtained from the Texas Department of Criminal Justice–Institutional Division (TDCJ-ID) Fiscal Year Statistical Reports, 2000–2005. Male population totals are year-end averages for the years indicated.

Limitations

There are limitations to the data analysis that would have improved our ability to more fully understand the impact of desegregation in Texas prisons. One major limitation is that we lacked data on the number and rate of incidents prior to cell desegregation in 1991. It could be the case that the rate of incidents was significantly higher in the post-desegregation period compared to the rate prior to desegregation, after accounting for population changes. This is not known. Despite this limitation, previous analyses revealed that desegregated cell partners were no more likely to engage in violence than were cell partners who remained racially segregated—at least officially documented and after accounting for the proportion of desegregated double cells. There is no evidence to suggest this trend has changed into the new millennium.

Coupled to the last point, our data analysis was limited in that we did not have access to individual data on the inmates involved in incidents. Thus we were not able to compare the general characteristics of inmates involved in interracial and intraracial incidents or to compare racially mixed cell partners to racially homogeneous cell partners.[22] Perhaps desegregated cellmates were somehow different than inmates who remained segregated by race in cells (e.g., in seriousness of current commitment, age, or previous incarcerations), and this may have impacted outcomes. While we believe the random cell-assignment process protected against such an obvious selection bias, it is always possible. Further, the lack of individual data did not allow us to fully examine the potential for chronic offenders. It is possible that a relatively small proportion of inmates committed a disproportionate amount of incidents. Based on the data retrieved by TDC, this cannot be determined.

An unavoidable but nonetheless important limitation is that our analysis was restricted to agency-collected data. The benefits and disadvantages to such data have been much discussed in the literature and so we do not repeat it here. However, there is no doubt that officially collected data is limited: for example, prison officers may not have uncovered all incidents, certain inmate populations may have been more scrutinized than others, interracial incidents may have received more official attention than intraracial incidents (or vice versa), and different staff at different prison units may have employed different procedures to resolve similar types of incidents. Whether this occurred is unknown, but it is certainly a possibility.[23] To further understand the dynamics of incident reporting, it would have been useful for us to have had a more qualitative perspective, not only on how desegregation unfolds from day to day, but how incidents are dealt with by institutional authorities. There are certainly more limitations to officially collected data, but the above are those that could have impacted the analysis and the perspective on the outcomes of desegregation in Texas prisons. Notwithstanding the limitations, the bottom line is that desegregation appears to have had a neutral effect on the level of violence among inmates in TDC as officially documented. Desegregation may not have led to a reduction in inmate-on-inmate levels of violence, but the evidence presented in this study does not suggest that it made things worse. While the color of inmates involved in incidents may have changed from the time when Texas prisons were segregated, it is also the case that no massive and persistent race war has occurred.[24] Maybe the best indicator of this finding, and of the apparent success of desegregation, is that TDC continues to desegregate inmates today on a scale not matched by any prison system in the country. Indeed, TDC desegregates more inmates within cells than most state prison systems have inmates. Six years into the millennium, TDC shows no signs of slowing its desegregation policy.

Conclusion: Desegregation as a Non-Issue in Texas Prisons

Based on an analysis of fifteen years of official data, the imposition of desegregation has never led to the dire predictions of massive interracial or racially motivated violence. Although interracial and racially motivated incidents could be prevented with complete and utter racial segregation, TDC abandoned this policy in 1965. The data also do not suggest that the motivation for incidents crossing racial boundaries is automatically or typically race-based. *Rather, the motivation for interracial incidents is likely the same as that which leads to intraracial incidents: the inconvenience of imprisonment, not racial hatred.* Although racially motivated incidents occur, the overwhelming majority of inmate-on-inmate incidents in Texas prisons cannot be characterized in this way.

The fact that the IDF was discontinued in 2000 and TDC's inmate-on-inmate incident reporting and documentation process was modified presented a methodological problem for exploring the aftermath of desegregation over the long term. However, these two changes are significant on their own. First, the IDF was discontinued and the data collection protocol was modified because the system was no longer required to make periodic court reports on the progress toward desegregation, including information on outcomes as measured by the IDF. The cessation of these requirements was in direct relation to TDC's progress with desegregation. Second, and perhaps most important, these changes were the result of a major transformation in attitude concerning desegregation. When desegregation began, the IDF was a tool for TDC to document the need for racial segregation. Even as TDC began desegregating offenders in double cells, 7,000 days after Allen Lamar filed his suit with the court, the IDF served as a valuable tool to present evidence to the court, in case the results of desegregation justified the fears of prison officials.

Since then, desegregation has become a non-issue not only for the *Lamar* court, but for TDC as well. Based on conversations with TDC officials and observations at numerous TDC units over the last several years, desegregation is an accepted fact of prison life in Texas, and color-blind cell assignments are a routine procedure, as evidenced by the high rate at which the system desegregates cells. As one high-ranking TDC official remarked in 2000, "It would be more difficult for us not to do it. . . . We are not going back to those days."[25] Despite the potential problems with official data and other limitations in our data analysis, the continuing rise in cell desegregation is perhaps the greatest indicator that the policy did not lead to massive unrest in the Texas prison system.

In February 2005, the U.S. Supreme Court ruled in *Johnson v. California* that prison officials cannot employ blanket policies of racial segregation in classifying and housing inmate populations. In effect, prison authorities cannot use race to segregate inmates unless specific and particularized circumstances deem the use of race necessary for safety and security. Even then, racial segregation should be a temporary expedient, and applied only to affected inmates.

Soon after this decision, we traveled to TDC's Diagnostic Unit in Huntsville, Texas (Byrd Unit), one of the initial intake facilities of TDC where inmates stay a short time until they are transferred to their long-term prison unit. This intake/diagnostic/transfer unit was not subject to the *Lamar* stipulations on cell desegregation, and thus inmates continued to be racially segregated well into 2005 (although inmates were desegregated in all other aspects at this unit).[26] Following the Court's decision in *Johnson*, TDC embarked on desegregating this and other similar units in late 2005. At Byrd, prison officials viewed desegregation matter-of-factly—it was just something that was going to be done. Instead of taking thousands of days, desegregation commenced at this unit within a few months and without fanfare.

Desegregation has even become a source of pride for the Texas prison system. From all available evidence, Texas prisons are the most racially desegregated institutions in the country, and California prison officials flocked to Texas in 2005 to see how TDC accomplished this massive transformation. TDC officials were clearly proud of their accomplishments and were extremely forthcoming with advice and perspective for their California counterparts. A system (and state) with one of the richest and most shameful histories of racial segregation in America was in 2005 the model for the largest state prison system in the nation.

The absence of disproportionate interracial and racially motivated violence, the discontinuation of the IDF, and sustained progress toward desegregation are perhaps the greatest indicators that desegregation has been accomplished successfully in Texas prisons over the long term. Despite the fact that inmates do not appear to like it, and notwithstanding the occasional racial disturbance or racially motivated attack, cell desegregation invokes little fanfare or sensationalism in today's Texas prison system. Although we do not have evidence that desegregation diffused racial tension or decreased racial prejudice among TDC inmates, there is no evidence to suggest that it automatically leads to disproportionate racial violence and disorder. This is an important finding, for it suggests that massive amounts of racial violence and disorder are not an inevitable result of the desegregation of prison cells, despite what inmates or others may think about this policy. In the final chapter, then, we attempt to explain the outcomes of this massive natural experiment in the Texas prison system.

PART III

A COLORLESS SOCIETY?

CHAPTER 10

The Most Unlikely Place

Between 1892 and 1954, Ellis Island was the primary immigrant processing station in the United States. Over 12 million immigrants came through here during this period, from a multitude of lands and speaking a multitude of languages. They were tested and examined for medical problems and other concerns, then let out the "back door" and dispersed throughout the country.

In one sense, America was indeed a great melting pot, where people from various countries and walks of life came together. However, complete ethnic and racial mixing never occurred. For many immigrants, Ellis Island was their only experience with intense interracial or interethnic contact. Once out the back door, most immigrants sought refuge with their fellow countrymen in the neighborhoods of great American cities.

In a sense, Texas prisons function like miniature Ellis Islands: men and women from different walks of life, experiences, races, and ethnicities are transported here, examined, and processed. Yet Texas prisons are places where the melting pot is maintained and long-term mixing is achieved. Indeed, the caged melting pot in Texas may be one of the most desegregated places in American society.

In this book we have examined how the Texas prison system accomplished desegregation and maintained this caged melting pot while situated within a state that had a long history of forced and de facto racial segregation. What remains is a discussion of why desegregation in Texas prisons unfolded without the dire consequences many had predicted. In the final chapter, we examine the factors that we believe can explain TDC's relatively successful outcomes in the aftermath of large-scale prisoner desegregation. To begin, we focus on research regarding racial and ethnic contact.

Narrowing the Racial Divide

For decades, scholars have sought to understand the determinants and consequences of contact across different racial and ethnic groups.[1] The earliest
inquiries into racial and ethnic contact were spurred by the realization that
the ideal of the great American melting pot never materialized.[2] Indeed, assimilation for the Ellis Island immigrants of the late 1800s and early 1900s did
not take place on any large scale. One unified culture was not created among
the throngs of Irish, Italians, Germans, and other Europeans; these and other
ethnic groups had in a sense become the "unmeltables."[3]

Ethnic separation was not limited to the emerging industrial areas in the
Northeast and Midwest, where many of the Ellis Island immigrants originally
settled. Racial and ethnic separation also occurred in the paternalistic South.
But it was different in the South. There, segregation occurred predominantly
along racial lines and was legally mandated. Even after the fall of forced segregation laws, de facto segregation by color persisted in all aspects of public
life—long after the most extreme ethnic divisions had abated in other parts
of the country.

Early researchers sought to understand this divide, highlighted by both
forced and self-imposed patterns of racial and ethnic segregation. Urban field
sociologists studied the larger trends. Social psychologists, in contrast, focused on the individual level and were among the first in the early twentieth
century to examine the social, physical, and psychological divisions among
different racial and ethnic groups. They were also the first to study the determinants of interracial and interethnic contact and the conditions for successful contact.[4]

We have learned much about racial and ethnic relations since these early
researchers began studying such divisions in America. At the same time,
much has changed in the social, physical, and, some would say, psychological proximity among different racial and ethnic groups.[5] Indeed, interracial
and interethnic contact is considerably more likely today than when early
researchers first sought to understand this issue. The shrinking or narrowing
of the racial and ethnic divide was most heavily influenced by public policy
through which the barriers to contact were diminished and the social distance
between different racial and ethnic groups was reduced.

Despite the efforts of social policy makers and the progress that has been
made in society, however, the wider society racial and ethnic divide has not
yet completely closed, particularly the color line. True and lasting interracial
contact remains elusive simply because individuals have the freedom to self-
segregate, regardless of widespread social policy. While it is true that blacks,

whites, Hispanics, and other racial and ethnic group members come into frequent contact with each other in schools, on airplanes, and in other public places, such contact is mostly short-term, casual, and fleeting. It cannot be described as integration in the true sense of the word, although it may qualify as one of many levels of desegregation.[6] This reality in society at large prevents an in-depth examination into the consequences of complete and compulsory interracial contact.

Unlike the persistent racial divide in the wider society, however, Texas prisons forced social and physical proximity between members of different racial groups. As a result of *Lamar*, inmates could no longer self-segregate themselves as before. Interracial contact became a certainty even for those inmates who randomly received a same-race cellmate. Desegregation of the common areas ensured inescapable, albeit short-term, racial mixing for all inmates despite the remaining potential for self-segregation and avoidance.

Lamar created a window through which to explore what happened when the racial divide was closed in what may be the most volatile place in American society: the penitentiary double cell. This natural experiment also created an opportunity—much like World War II created a unique opportunity for Samuel Stouffer and colleagues to explore race relations and a plethora of other social dynamics among American servicemen—to study the specific conditions under which Texas racially desegregated its prisoners. Desegregation was externally forced, intense, and of a magnitude and duration not matched in any other social setting. In this environment, how did Texas administrators prevent inmate-on-inmate violence and disorder that many predicted would result?[7] A useful framework with which to explore this question is the equal-status contact hypothesis.

The Situational Dynamics of Equal-Status Contact

Numerous theories exist to explain the outcomes of interracial contact. We believe that the most useful of all frameworks to understand the outcomes of desegregation in Texas prisons is the equal-status contact hypothesis, or contact hypothesis, proffered by noted psychologist Gordon Allport in 1954. At the individual unit of analysis, the contact hypothesis holds that interracial contact counters negative racial stereotypes and promotes positive racial attitudes by providing "sensitizing" information to the norms, values, experiences, and lifestyles of others. In short, familiarity erases ignorance and paves the way for positive racial interaction.[8]

The contact hypothesis as originally formulated focused on attitudinal change (including decreased prejudice) following interracial contact, although the actions of those in contact are also consistent with the principles of the contact hypothesis.[9] In our view, actions are much more consequential than attitudes following interracial contact. Indeed, what inmates think or feel about desegregation is less important than how they act when faced with it. Even Allport recognized this when he remarked that "what people actually do in relation to groups they dislike is not always directly related to what they think or feel about them."[10] In other words, positive interracial attitudes are not necessary for positive interracial contact.

Although contact is necessary, we do not believe contact alone is sufficient to explain the outcomes of Texas prisoner desegregation; the contact hypothesis suggests as much. A major assumption of the contact hypothesis is that positive contact outcomes are conditioned by several factors, including that the contact be *equal status contact* (that the individuals are of equal status when in contact), that the contact occurs under *cooperative conditions* (that the individuals are pursuing common goals in the absence of intergroup competition), and that contact occurs in the presence of *institutional support* (that contact is supported by authorities, law, or custom).[11] It is through the contact hypothesis that we frame and guide an explanation of the aftermath of prisoner desegregation in Texas.[12]

Conditions That Affected Desegregation Outcomes in Texas Prisons

Equal-Status Contact

The foundation of TDC's racial desegregation plan called for the equalization of status among all inmates housed in double cells. This is a major assumption of the contact hypothesis—the closer the individuals are to equal status, the greater likelihood of successful outcomes.

TDC approximated equal status by matching inmates on such criteria as age, height, weight, criminal sophistication, active and passive tendencies, and other institutionally relevant behavioral factors to promote prison security and inmate control. By reducing status differentials, exclusive of the racial and ethnic background of cell partners, Texas's desegregation plan was much more sophisticated than simply mixing up the races to achieve some sort of racial quota. Ironically, Texas's plan was all about desegregation, but had very little to do with race. It was simply part of an overall classification scheme that attempted to match the most appropriate inmates together, regardless of race, unless race (as a result of behavioral concerns) had to be considered to ensure the safety and security of staff, inmates, and institutions. Both theoretically and in reality, inmates were status equals on factors that mattered to institutional security during the time they were locked in their cells.[13]

The ability of prison managers to equalize status within the cells and other housing areas was conditioned by a major advance to prison operations only a few years before wholesale desegregation commenced. Prodded by *Ruiz v. Estelle* stipulations, TDC formulated and implemented a revised classification scheme. Certain stipulations of the *Lamar* decree were made expressly dependent on TDC's implementation of the *Ruiz* classification plan.

Once implemented, the classification plan, despite initial problems, enhanced the staff's ability to gather relevant and appropriate information on offenders—a crucial factor toward the goal of reducing status differentials among inmates assigned to double cells and other housing areas via the desegregation protocol. The new classification plan, along with random cell assignment, allowed prison staff to reduce status differentials among cell partners and accomplish cell desegregation simultaneously. In the worst-case scenario, the classification system and random assignment procedure made it more likely that inmates within a desegregated cell could coexist without violence.

Cooperative Conditions

Positive interracial contact is also believed to be enhanced through cooperative conditions, a concept that includes broader ideas such as the pursuit of common goals and the absence of competition. Although the concept of cooperative conditions has no universal definition and has been measured in various ways, we believe that it does relate more broadly to the concept of "favorable conditions."[14] For example, one way favorable conditions might have been obtained is if prison managers desegregated only those inmates wanting or indifferent to desegregation. Favorable or cooperative conditions might have also resulted by allowing inmates to choose cell partners of a different race. Lawyers for the prison system proposed a plan of inmate choice to the Department of Justice and the court, but this plan was severely criticized and was eventually abandoned.

The fact that desegregation was externally forced upon the prison system suggests that desegregation did not occur under the most cooperative or favorable of conditions at the individual level. This does not mean, however, that the desegregation process was unfavorable as it unfolded at the organizational level. Organizationally, Texas prison administrators were allowed to approach desegregation in an incremental fashion. The *Lamar* decree process dragged on for nearly twenty years before TDC finally implemented a cell desegregation plan. During that period, TDC was allowed, despite objections by the DOJ and the threat of sanctions from the court, the necessary time to devise, modify, and implement a cell desegregation plan that worked for them.

The incremental process, much as with the desegregation of the American military and many of the earliest and most extensive prison reform cases, refers to more than an incremental time frame. The concept of incrementalism concerning judicial involvement in prison matters also refers to a process whereby the specific mandates of a broader decree, such as desegregating living quarters, are developed and honed over time consistent with the peculiarities of a particular prison system and the larger external forces impacting its administration.[15] The fact that desegregation was allowed to unfold in an incremental fashion rather than through a coercive and abrupt remedial court order surely contributed to the long-term positive outcomes. Although desegregation was externally forced on both administrators and inmates, the condition of incrementalism meant that desegregation proceeded as favorably as possible at the organizational level despite opposition by inmates, administrators, and staff at the individual level.

Texas prison administrators also fostered cooperative desegregation conditions by placing a premium on the removal of predatory inmates from the general prison population. In the 1990s, the Texas prison system experienced the largest increase of inmates in its history. Units received more than 80,000 new felony offenders, over 30,000 in 1994 to 1995 alone, stressing an already burgeoning prison system.[16] To address the onslaught of new prisoners and remain in compliance with a *Ruiz*-influenced and a legislatively mandated prison population cap, TDC added several new prison units in the mid-1990s—a move that consequently became the largest prison facility expansion in the nation. Importantly, during this building phase TDC invested heavily in administrative segregation to house incorrigible inmates in single cells and/or to disperse them throughout the state under more restrictive custody classifications.

In no small way, such changes dampened the influence of disproportionately problematic inmates—inmates who had previously been housed in the general prisoner population—by allowing "regular" inmates to do their own time without significant tension or pressure to resist the desegregation order.[17] The prison system also implemented a proactive and preemptive plan to identify and remove confirmed gang members and members of security threat groups from the general prisoner population. Among other reasons, this was done to prevent gang-related violence, recruitment, extortion, and other activities that might inflame racial animosities.

Taken together, the larger organizational processes of system expansion and gang preemption contributed to favorable conditions by allowing the great majority of inmates, those without exceptional prejudice, to adapt to desegregation without peer pressure from intransigent inmates to "stay down" with their own race—including the pressure to perpetrate cross-racial assaults to avoid desegregation and thus curry favor with their racial or ethnic peers. Based on inmate comments, the pressure within the races during the early years of desegregation was more intense than between the races. From all indications, much of this pressure was alleviated once the prison system proactively removed the minority of troublemakers from the general population.

The preceding discussion is important because research on the contact hypothesis has consistently revealed that interracial anxiety and threats can obstruct contact and any potential positive outcomes from that contact.[18] Although contact was not necessarily obstructed because desegregation was forced, there was certainly a level of anxiety and threat within and between racial groups because of this policy. Removing the intransigent inmates alleviated some of these pressures and anxieties.

Allport also explained that equal-status contact was not likely sufficient to alleviate deep-seated prejudice and would likely work only for those individuals with an "ordinary" degree of prejudice.[19] We contend that gang members and other malcontents, those who are much smaller in number but produce a disproportionate amount of violence and disorder in prisons, are not "ordinary" in that regard and perhaps hold the strongest and most irrational objections to desegregation.[20] Removing and isolating this smaller but more problematic group of prisoners from "regular" inmates had an important impact on the aftermath of racial desegregation.

Through TDC's proactive efforts, those prisoners most likely to perpetrate a racially motivated or gang-related attack and/or to pressure other inmates to resist desegregation were effectively isolated from the general prisoner population.[21] The "unmeltables" were inmates who clung to racial identity and loyalty above all else. Removing and isolating them allowed the majority of inmates to do their time without fear of reprisal.

All this is not to suggest that some sort of replacement effect did not occur—efforts by the prison system to isolate the bad apples probably did not solve the problem of the intransigent and racially biased inmate once and for all. Rather, TDC's procedure diluted their influence and kept the problems caused by such inmates at bay and enhanced cooperative conditions within the units. This is also not to suggest that the ordinary inmates who remained in the general population housing areas preferred or advocated for desegregation. Rather, their preference for a single-race cell was not so great as to lead to violence, and the removal or dilution of outside pressures conditioned this outcome to some degree.

Institutional Support

A final condition of the equal-status contact hypothesis suggests that positive interracial outcomes are enhanced by institutional support, defined by Allport as support by law, custom, or institutional authorities. Clearly, the court and the DOJ supported desegregation. More important than their support, however, was the eventual endorsement of desegregation by the prison system. Once prison authorities accepted desegregation as inevitable, inmates may have more readily accepted it as well.

Desegregation was forced, Texas prison administrators were committed to it, and ultimately there was little that inmates could do to subvert the policy.[22] When viewed in this way, the forced nature of desegregation may have had the unintended consequence of uniting inmates. In a batch-living environment, inmates in Texas found themselves "in a common predicament," forced to make do under the circumstances and to tolerate and survive the pains of desegregation together.[23] Gresham Sykes noted years ago that inmates must cope with the pains of imprisonment together.[24] The eventual sanctioning of desegregation by the prison system allowed inmates a reason to accept desegregation without violence. It was forced upon them and there was nothing they could do about it — it was the prison system and the court who were their scapegoats. Indeed, in 1999, nearly a decade after the policy became operational, Hemmens and Marquart found that many Texas "exmates" reported that they did not strenuously object to prison desegregation.[25]

While it is debatable as to whether prison administrators were truly committed to desegregation, there is a multitude of evidence of the prison system's endorsement of desegregation on a practical basis. Perhaps no indicator of TDC's commitment is as strong as the tremendous strides made toward desegregation following implementation in August 1991. From the end of 1991 through 1992, prison managers increased the percent of desegregated double cells from 25 to 41 percent, and to over 60 percent by the end of 1999. By 2002, the system had racially mixed in upward of 70 percent of all double cells system-wide, equaling more than 17,000 double cells desegregated or 34,000 inmates. This progress has remained consistent through 2005.

The figures on desegregated cells are in addition to full desegregation in other aspects of the prison round, including but not limited to dayrooms, dining facilities, field squads, and dormitories. Despite years of active and passive resistance concerning the *Lamar* decree, progress in the racial desegregation of double cells and other areas in the prison environment is evidence that TDC supported this policy on a practical basis, despite initial misgivings.

Beyond their strides over the last fifteen years, however, TDC also has clearly demonstrated support of desegregation by ensuring that inmates who resisted the policy suffered for their behavior. Inmates who refused a desegregated cell assignment lost good time, were placed in solitary confinement, and/or received a higher custody classification, among numerous other coercive sanctions. This fact was also reported by many inmates responding to the survey we placed in the Texas prison newspaper roughly a decade after desegregation commenced. If these punishments did not work, offending inmates were placed in single cells and separated from the general population for extended periods of time. Thus Texas prisoners faced real and palpable consequences for resistance. Desegregation was inevitable, and the only real choice for most inmates was to accept it regardless of what they felt about it.

Desegregation in the Totality of Circumstances

The aftermath of Texas prisoner desegregation was no doubt conditioned by factors that went well beyond mixing individuals of different races. While a simple mixing of the races may work in some situations and with certain individuals, in prisons the situation was and is different. On the whole, prisons draw disproportionate numbers of the most violent and least stable individuals in American society.[26] Prisons are places where racial and ethnic identity has been and continues to be one of the most dominant influences of inmate behavior, and pressure to stay loyal only to one's race is extreme.[27] The fact that desegregation was accomplished to such a degree in a prison environment makes the outcomes of this study even more surprising. Yet desegregation was much more than the blind mixing of the races to meet a quota. The outcomes were undoubtedly conditioned by careful attention to the classification, matching, and housing of the right inmates. Desegregation also did not unfold in a vacuum. A number of additional factors, including many external to the prison environment, were influential as well. For example, desegregation depended in many ways on the tolerance of the *Lamar* court and the DOJ to work with TDC in an incremental fashion. Desegregation also depended on the appropriations of the Texas Legislature during the prison system expansion and, ironically, the improvements to the prison system that resulted from the fiercely resisted *Ruiz v. Estelle* mandates. At the broadest level, desegregation was influenced by the decades of progress that occurred outside Texas prison walls. Absent the above, the outcomes of racial desegregation in Texas prisons may have been very different. Overall, then, desegregation in Texas prisons resulted from the totality of the above conditions, internal and external.

No evidence is available to suggest that desegregation decreased prejudice, increased tolerance, or led to other types of positive attitudinal outcomes.[28] We simply do not know whether desegregation has led to other positive consequences previously blocked by segregation. We also do not know whether desegregation increased prejudice or led to other negative consequences. What we do know is that desegregation did not unleash the Hobbesian race war predicted by many. Perhaps this is the best that one can hope for with such a controversial change to the prison environment—a change that appears unequaled in any prison system in the nation.

The goal of desegregation by way of the *Lamar* suit was not to promote racial harmony or to make Texas prisons racial utopias. Instead, the goal was to accomplish race neutrality in inmate housing and other aspects of prison operations, with the hope of maintaining prison order and control. If in fact positive racial attitudes were a byproduct, this would be additional evidence as to the success of desegregation in Texas prisons. We do not know if that has been the case. And, while continued segregation might have prevented a nominal number of incidents motivated by race, it is perhaps equally true that continued segregation may have fomented even more racial violence—an aspect noted by the U.S. Supreme Court in *Johnson v. California* (2005). Racial desegregation may not have helped in terms of other outcomes, but it did not appear to worsen the Texas prison experience by increasing violence, and it may have actually led to less violence in the long run. In this way, the policy can be considered a success due to TDC's careful attention to promote the conditions mentioned above and the totality of all circumstances surrounding the state's prison system.

Can *Lamar* Be Replicated Elsewhere?

Elsewhere in the United States, the policy of cell desegregation varies widely. The best evidence suggests that while most prison systems have desegregated larger living and common areas of the prison environment—cell blocks, tiers, dining areas, dayrooms, work assignments—many have not desegregated double cells to any large degree.[29] In a national survey of prison wardens in 2000, Henderson and colleagues found that while "90% of inmates [share] a cell . . . only 30% of these multiple occupant cells are actually integrated by race."[30]

Although Henderson and colleagues revealed that most cells remain segregated by race in our nation's prisons, 70 percent of the wardens they surveyed believed that cell desegregation would decrease (15.7 percent) or have no effect (54.3 percent) on the level of violence within their institutions. Moreover, 90 percent of wardens believed that conflict within cells that had been desegregated in their institutions was much less (2.1 percent), less (5.3 percent), or about the same (81.1 percent) as conflict within cells that remained racially segregated.[31] These survey findings lend tacit support to the official findings on the aftermath of desegregation in Texas prisons. And despite the fact that few prison systems have much experience with the effects of large-scale cell desegregation, this may be changing.

Helter Skelter in the Joint

The low levels of cell desegregation in American prisons cannot be overemphasized in light of *Johnson v. California,* a case about the use of race in double-cell housing assignments within inmate reception centers.[32]

The history of the California prison system, much like that of others, is marked by racial segregation. Even by 2005, no official policy existed with regard to racial segregation in housing. Rather, racial segregation was a longtime practice that had existed since the beginnings of that prison system. Although by 2005 the prison system had long been desegregated in other areas of prison operation such as in cell blocks and dayrooms and yards, double-cells remained almost completely segregated by race in all prison facilities.

According to California prison officials, racially segregated double cells prevented violence among rival gang members aligned along racial and ethnic lines. In a system that has been described as "ground zero" for race-based prison gangs, officials in California treated race as synonymous with gang membership and gang membership as synonymous with prison violence.[33] Very little racial mixing occurred within cells because under this line of thinking, nearly everyone was a gang member.[34] Without the racial segregation of cells, it was believed, violence would erupt. Indeed, mixing the racial and ethnic groups would set off a "Helter Skelter"–style race war behind the walls.

In 1995, California prison inmate Garrison Johnson filed a complaint in the U.S. District Court for the Central District of California challenging the California Department of Correction's (CDC) practice of segregation. After years of traveling through the federal court system, this case reached the U.S. Supreme Court in 2005 on a writ of certiorari from the Ninth Circuit Court of Appeals—the court that had in 2003 upheld CDC's practice of racial segregation as a rational and legitimate response to the problem of violence in CDC.[35]

In *Johnson*, the Court reversed the Ninth Circuit and held that prison managers cannot use race to segregate inmates except under extraordinary and limited circumstances to ensure the safety and security of inmates, staff, and institutions. This case was only the second time the U.S. Supreme Court directly dealt with the issue of racial segregation in prisons and jails, the first being nearly four decades earlier in *Lee v. Washington*.[36] While the Court did not hold CDC's practice unconstitutional, the Court had serious misgivings that racial segregation was the only way CDC could prevent racial violence. According to the Court's majority, "by insisting that inmates be housed only with other inmates of the same race, it is possible that prison officials will breed further hostility among prisoners and reinforce racial and ethnic divisions."[37]

The Court sent *Johnson* back to the Ninth Circuit where CDC's practice of racial segregation could be reviewed under the strictest of scrutiny—a more stringent legal standard than the rational basis test previously applied by the Ninth Circuit when they upheld California's segregation policy in 2003.[38] Following the Court's reversal, and prior to a rehearing on remand, CDC settled the *Johnson* case in mediation and stipulated to develop and implement a plan of cell desegregation and cease using race as the sole determining factor in cell and other housing assignments. Not surprisingly, CDC is using Texas as a model to frame and guide their desegregation protocol.[39]

The *Johnson* case is important because the ruling ultimately holds that unless extraordinary and particular circumstances exist, prison officials are generally barred from using race in the routine sorting, classifying, and housing of prisoners. Combined with the findings of Henderson and colleagues, this decision appears to impact a number of prison systems nationwide that continue to use race as a rule rather than the exception when assigning inmates to double cells. In effect, this decision means that prison systems must cell inmates in a race-neutral way; race may only be used in limited and particular circumstances where not doing so would result in violence prevented by segregation. The ruling is clear: blanket uses of racial segregation are not legally defensible, not even in prisons.

Texas as a Model for Prisoner Desegregation?

The Texas prison system racially mixes upward of 60 percent of their 23,000 double cells today. According to official data, Texas has accomplished this level of desegregation without experiencing disproportionate interracial and racially motivated violence. From all available evidence, Texas is the most racially desegregated prison system in the country. Can the lessons learned from the Texas experience apply to other systems with a mandate to desegregate their prison cells?

We have discussed the primary factors that we believe contributed to the success of racial desegregation in Texas prisons: approximating equal-status contact in double cells through a developed classification scheme and random cell assignment plan; an incremental approach to implementation; a management plan and dedicated prison space for intransigent inmates; and support and commitment from prison authorities. These conditions were situated in the totality of circumstances surrounding the Texas prison system: judicially forced desegregation; intervention by the DOJ; massive prison expansion via legislative appropriations; and improvements and changes to the system by way of *Ruiz v. Estelle*. These factors allowed TDC to successfully desegregate its prisons.

Nevertheless, we do not offer sweeping claims as to whether desegregation can be realized in other prison systems and whether the lessons learned from Texas can apply equally outside its borders. No two prison systems are alike; population, racial composition, physical capacity, existing infrastructure, experience with institutional litigation, legislative support, political climate, regional variations, relationships between inmates and staff, state's racial history, and budgets are only a few of the innumerable ways prison systems may differ, and there are a dozen more that might preclude applying the Texas experience elsewhere. This is not to suggest, however, that desegregation cannot be accomplished successfully in other prison systems. Rather, desegregating inmates must be a system-specific process considered within the total environment in which a particular prison system is situated, both internally and externally. There is perhaps no real model or best practice when it comes to inmate desegregation.

Despite system variations, there are some general lessons that can be taken from the Texas experience. First, desegregation entails much more than mixing different races within double cells with the goal of meeting a particular racial quota. Efforts must be taken to ensure that status differentials between inmates housed in double cells are reduced. Reducing status differentials depends heavily on a valid and reliable classification system. Without such a system, status differentials between inmates may be so great that any desegregated housing plan, indeed any housing plan, might coalesce into a system of competition and ultimately violence between cell partners.

Second, desegregation or perhaps any significant prison policy is unlikely to be accomplished successfully or to its full potential if disproportionately problematic inmates are not controlled and contained. Active gang members, security threat group members, malcontents, and overt bigots must either be removed from the general prisoner population or their influence dampened so as to contain the toxic effect these individuals exert on the prison environment. Absent these or equivalent measures, racial pressure and tensions may grow within and between racial groups, and the pressure against desegregation may simply be too great for it to be successful on any large scale without jeopardizing institutional security.[40]

The removal or containment of problematic inmates should not be viewed as a wholesale endorsement of segregation units for the concentration or dispersal of the incorrigibles. This type of strategy worked in Texas. And it is true that complete and utter isolation does work to some degree—at least in terms of doing a reasonable job at controlling certain inmate populations while they are in prison. However, there are consequences to this type of strategy, both inside and outside the penitentiary walls, and prison systems need to consider all the costs and benefits to the system, inmates, staff, and the larger society in deciding whether this is the most appropriate response. At the most basic level, however, the system must have the capacity to be able to attempt such a move. With the size of prison populations across the country, this may be the greatest obstacle.

Third, desegregation in Texas prisons unfolded incrementally—one zone at a time over a long period of time. TDC did not stipulate to full-scale desegregation until the system was ready for such a policy change. The courts and the DOJ, while persistent, did not put massive amounts of pressure on TDC to desegregate without a clear and well-considered plan. This is not to suggest that it will take twenty or more years for a prison system to desegregate. That it took this long in Texas was the result of a number of different realities inside and outside the prison walls. Desegregation of an entire prison system cannot occur overnight. Any remedy must proceed deliberately, carefully, and incrementally.

Finally, desegregation in TDC must be viewed as a policy that was accomplished in the context of all circumstances surrounding the Texas prison system. Desegregation went far beyond the system-specific efforts of a random housing plan and making prison decisions on a race-neutral basis. External forces such as the court, the DOJ, and the Texas Legislature shaped and guided desegregation in Texas prisons. Even for those systems attempting desegregation outside of court intervention, forces external to the prison system must be considered.

Whether systems facing cell desegregation can ensure the above conditions and even whether the above conditions would be desirable in any particular system are questions we cannot answer. Nor do we know the relative importance of each condition, and what would have occurred if one or more had been absent. In short, we viewed all the above conditions in Texas as necessary—none were sufficient in and of themselves—but some were perhaps more important than others.[41]

The bottom line is that these were the conditions that led to the successful desegregation of the Texas prison system. They were responses of the time, specific to the Texas prison system and its environment, and very much influenced by the particular dictates of the *Lamar* court, the DOJ, the system's history and experience with institutional litigation, and other influences largely external of the system itself. It is possible that if desegregation had been attempted in today's Texas prison system, under different conditions, the responses and outcomes might have been different. And it is likely that what was needed to desegregate TDC in the 1990s may have been different from what is needed elsewhere today.

California is now preparing to use elements of the Texas model in their efforts to desegregate inmates within double cells, which presents a prime opportunity to examine the desegregation experience in that state.[42] However, the California prison system of today is different in many ways from the Texas system of the 1980s and 1990s. It is much larger at both the organizational and institutional level. It is more decentralized and dispersed. It is extremely overcrowded. Recently, it has experienced tremendous turnover in its upper administration. Operation of the prison system is politically charged and impacted heavily by the California Correctional Peace Officers Association (CCPOA)—a politically powerful officers' union that had no equivalent in the TDC of the 1980s, 1990s, or today. Also important is that the California prison system appears to have a highly entrenched gang culture aligned predominantly according to race and ethnicity. At a broader level, the history of California is much different than that of Texas. Only time will tell whether California will experience the same success as Texas over the long term and what factors will ultimately contribute to that system's outcomes with desegregation—whether it be a success or failure.

For prison systems to achieve desegregation successfully, whether voluntarily or forced, they will have to reach the point where desegregation becomes the expectation and tradition of the system. The Supreme Court has made this clear for the twenty-first-century prison. How systems get to that point is largely left to the peculiarities of individual systems and their internal and external environments. Today, inmates expect desegregation in the Texas prison system—it is largely a non-issue among both inmates and staff. This institutional acceptance was not achieved overnight and without obstacles. Cloning the Texas experience might not be possible elsewhere.

Erosion and Collapse of the Color Line: Outside to Inside

In the broader context, this was a story about racial divisions and change in American society. In a more specific context, this was a story about desegregation in one of the most unlikely places in American society. The broader story was situated in Texas, a state with a rich history of racial subjugation—slavery, plantations, lynching, social exclusion, and forced racial segregation. The more specific story concerned the link between state-level occurrences and the operation of the Texas prison system—a place with an equally rich history of racial segregation and subjugation.

Over time, the barriers that ensured the complete segregation of the races in Texas eroded. By the 1960s and 1970s, the color line that had been so rigorously defended in Texas—first through violence and later through social, educational, economic, and political exclusion—had largely collapsed. The erosion and eventual collapse of the color line in Texas was heavily influenced by federal court rulings and other social policy, just as it had been in other parts of the nation. This collapse was felt in all aspects of public life, from schools to buses to parks, albeit in varying degrees and on different timetables. The collapse of the color line did not follow as quickly, however, for the prison setting.

Well after state-sanctioned segregation had been abandoned in the wider Texas society, prisoners continued to experience racial segregation and discrimination. Into the 1960s, Texas prisons were little more than color-coded institutions. Although race-exclusive prisons were eventually abandoned by Texas prison administrators in that same decade, inmates in the 1970s remained racially segregated in all other aspects of the prison regime. This practice was primarily the result of the 1927 "color law" that specifically authorized the manager of the prison system to sort and classify inmates by race. This archaic law was amended in 1975, but complete change was a long way out.[43] Texas prisons of the late 1970s still lagged years behind free-world institutions concerning the elimination of racial and ethnic segregation and discrimination. Despite desegregation elsewhere in society by the late 1960s and early 1970s, racial segregation persisted behind the walls of Texas's penitentiaries and prison farms.

By the mid-to-late 1980s, Texas prisoners routinely found themselves in desegregated cell blocks, dining halls, and dayrooms—progress of a fashion across these institutional zones. Additionally, racial segregation in other aspects of Texas prison administration, such as in field assignments, had largely disappeared according to official accounts. Indeed, in roughly a ten-year time period and with relatively little fanfare, the Texas prison system moved from almost complete segregation to desegregation in almost all aspects of prison life. Informally, self-segregation and avoidance in this new frontier of desegregation persisted among inmates of different races. Formally, the chance that inmates of a different race were to be found in the same prison cell was next to zero—there was a limit to how far Texas administrators would budge concerning desegregation in the 1980s. The color line that had long collapsed in the wider society was still fiercely defended in Texas prisons, at least in terms of double-cell housing.

The vestiges of racial segregation in Texas prisons in the 1980s were based on the belief that the desegregation of cells would transform the prison setting into a racialized war zone. The outlook for cell desegregation was thus bleak in the minds of Texas prison administrators in the 1980s. System resistance was also influenced by prison administrators who still shunned orders and decrees from judges whom they considered ignorant to the reality of prison life and administration.

While the color line persisted in the "burnin' hell," it too had eroded over time. Broader efforts at desegregating the prison system in the 1970s and 1980s represented the widening of the cracks that had formed in the prison-based color line. These cracks were initially influenced by occurrences outside the prison walls. The collapse of the Texas prison color line followed in the 1990s—but this was accomplished only after a full assault from inmate writ-writers, a federal court, and the U.S. Department of Justice. The impetus for the collapse was a prisoner lawsuit filed some twenty years prior that charged the prison system with racial and ethnic discrimination in all aspects of prison operation. What would emerge as the most contentious aspect of this lawsuit was a challenge to the most fiercely protected form of Texas prisoner segregation—the use of race in double-cell housing assignments.

Dr. Martin Luther King Jr. had a dream of an American society where people would be judged by the content of their character and not by the color of their skin. Texas prisoner Allen L. Lamar also believed prisoners should be judged only by the content of their character and not by the color of their skin. The primary motivation for his lawsuit is not completely clear, however. By some accounts, Lamar was motivated by a sincere desire to help eliminate racial segregation and discrimination in the last segregated frontier of Texas society. Some evidence suggests that black and Hispanic prisoners were at a disadvantage in Texas prisons, and that they believed they would only be able to enjoy the benefits afforded exclusively to white inmates if segregation as a policy were eliminated. Other accounts suggest that Lamar was motivated by a desire to pile on the litigation facing the prison system, regardless of the nature of the litigation. Lamar was, after all, a member of the litigation-producing Eight Hoe Squad. Yet perhaps Lamar's motivation was simply to break down the barriers of segregation so that he could be celled with his alleged white homosexual lover. Maybe the *Lamar* suit was a product of all of these motivations, and others; we will never know for certain.

Regardless of his motivations, Lamar's lawsuit led to the desegregation of the Texas prison system—a system that would ultimately end up adopting a desegregation plan that would house prisoners based on the content of their criminal and in-prison character and not the color of their skin. But Allen Lamar was no Dr. King, Rosa Parks, or Myrtle Washington—he was no groundbreaker. Allen Lamar was a career criminal—in some ways a product of a system that was meant to fix him in the first place. His first stint of incarceration was in the Gatesville School for Boys at age sixteen. With the exception of only a few years of freedom and some brief stints in the California prison system and the Federal Bureau of Prisons, Lamar would spend almost all his remaining adult life incarcerated under the authority of TDC.

According to Texas prison administrators, Lamar was a malcontent and an agitator. In the early 1970s, during his second TDC incarceration, he was placed on the Wynne Unit's Eight Hoe Squad for associating with prisoner rights advocates and participating in writ-writing activities against the prison system—something Texas prison administrators of the time considered revolutionary and an affront to prison order. Among the numerous and usually unsuccessful lawsuits he filed against TDC during the 1970s, it was *Lamar v. Coffield* that would have the greatest impact on the prison system. His charges of racial and ethnic segregation and discrimination in numerous aspects of Texas prison life became one of only a handful of class-action lawsuits that TDC faced in the 1970s and 1980s.[44] Although the litigation of Lamar's prison colleague David Ruiz would occupy the most prominent place in TDC history, the *Lamar* consent decree is perhaps best characterized as the racial twin of *Ruiz v. Estelle*. Like *Ruiz*, the *Lamar* lawsuit and eventual consent decree process had massive system-wide impacts on the operation of the Texas prison system. None was as consequential as the challenge to the last bastion of racial segregation in Texas prisons—double cells.

The *Lamar* consent decree process was a protracted affair. From the time the lawsuit was filed to eventual stipulation and compliance by TDC, two decades had been spent. Today, thirty-seven years, or more than 13,000 days, have passed since the beginnings of this lawsuit in 1972. Since 1991, TDC has a largely unblemished record of compliance with the decree. Now, a state and prison system that might arguably have the most scandalous experience with race relations in American history boasts the most racially desegregated prison system in America. Ironically, Texas prison cell blocks and cells may be the most desegregated space in American society—inside or outside of prison walls.

Conclusion

This book began by posing a simple question: What would happen if different-race inmates were mixed in a two-person cell? We now know what happened and our findings can be summarized as follows: Prisoner desegregation did not lead to any more violence than prisoner segregation; and despite massive organizational changes, the Texas experience with cell desegregation has become a tradition.

It is worth considering whether the Texas prison system would have become the most desegregated prison system in America absent the *Lamar* lawsuit, naturally evolving as the barriers to segregation further eroded in the wider society and eventually permeated the prison walls. Would Texas prison administrators still be approached today by California officials as a model for desegregation? In short, would desegregation have happened anyway? We cannot know for sure, and predicting what would have happened is always fraught with difficulties. Perhaps another inmate would have come along and taken Lamar's place in prison history. Maybe nothing would have changed, and Texas would still be segregating inmates by race in double cells as most prison systems apparently do today. We do not know. What we do know is that Lamar's lawsuit was the burr under the saddle of the Texas prison system and led to the desegregation of inmates at a level not even remotely matched by any prison system in the country.[45]

The prison setting—the institutional environment—has a powerful influence on those who pass through it. The findings of this study go against all common sense. But when viewed in light of the evidence, the findings are not all that surprising. Well before desegregation was a threat to prison administrators, the military as a social institution had become fully desegregated. In the military—perhaps the free world institution that most resembles the penitentiary—desegregation did not lead to the massive racial problems that many expected despite the severe misgivings of many soldiers. Perhaps this precedent was overlooked because of the obvious differences: soldiers are not inmates, the military is voluntary and incarceration is not, the conditions of the military promote cooperation, and numerous other reasons.[46] But if one were to scratch a little deeper, it becomes easier to recognize the power of institutions to bend and twist human behavior in ways that defy all expectations.[47] Outside of such total institutions, one can only speculate whether the same could occur in the wider society.[48]

The issue of race as described in the pages of this book illustrates that desegregation became a non-issue in the Texas prison system.[49] But the same cannot be said in the wider society, for race and its correlates are still unresolved issues, as witnessed by numerous current examples:

- The nation has evidenced sharp divisions over O. J. Simpson's trials for murder and for armed robbery. Whites are far likelier than blacks to say that Simpson was guilty of the charges and was treated fairly.[50]
- Eighty-five percent of blacks believe they and other minorities do not get the same treatment in the criminal justice system as whites.[51]
- It was only in 2007 that students of Turner County High School in Ashburn, Georgia, attended an integrated prom for the first time.[52]
- Thousands rallied for justice for black teens in Jena, Louisiana, in 2007.[53]
- Eight separate noose sightings have occurred from July to October 2007. Experts suggest their occurrence may be tied to white resentment over protests in Jena.[54]
- A former Ku Klux Klan grand dragon operates a "Redneck Shop" in Laurens, South Carolina, in a building owned by a Baptist church. Reverend David Kennedy, black civil rights activist, has attempted to have the store closed, but the law allows the shop owner to operate his business in the building until he dies. The same town, named after an eighteenth-century slave trader, still has street addresses marked with a "C," indicating homes once reserved for "colored" families.[55]

The examples above suggest that race—the color line—continues to be a persistent issue in the wider society despite decades of change and progress. The question is whether the wider society can approach a level of race neutrality where an individual's treatment is based on the content of his character and not the color of his skin. By all accounts, this level of race neutrality has been achieved in the Texas prison system—surely the most unlikely place.

Table 10.1. Hate Crime Statistics in Five States (per 100,000 Residents)

	1996	2000	2005
California	4.04	3.64	2.53
Texas	1.26	0.91	0.72
Florida	1.09	1.00	0.93
Pennsylvania	1.09	0.95	0.58
Michigan	3.70	3.33	5.25

Source: Federal Bureau of Investigation Hate Crime Statistics, http://www.fbi.gov/ucr/hc2005/index.html

Some Closing Thoughts

Throughout the history of punishment, the prison has been at the end of the criminal justice system. Virtually every textbook on the criminal justice system has organized the themes of chapters in this order: police, courts, and corrections. Offenders are arrested, processed by the courts, and ultimately punished. Most important, policies, laws, and shifts in societal values and beliefs impact and lead to change in the prison community. In this sense, prisons are reactive institutions, and rarely if ever affect the wider society. Is it possible that a prison, beyond the issue of rehabilitation, can have a positive effect on society?

This question may be approached by analyzing hate crime data. Currently, the Federal Bureau of Investigation collects, compiles, and maintains hate crime statistics for the United States. Hate crimes are those that "manifest evidence of prejudice based on race, religion, sexual orientation, or ethnicity."[56] The FBI has been collecting hate crime data since 1990, and, as of 2005, the program has compiled data from forty-nine states and the District of Columbia. The number of agencies participating in the program represents 83 percent of the nation's population.

We examined hate crime data, focusing on racially and/or ethnically motivated crimes that were reported in the five most populous reporting states (California, Florida, Michigan, Pennsylvania, and Texas) for the years 1996, 2000, and 2005. Table 10.1 presents these data in the number of hate crimes per 100,000 residents. Rates are reported for comparison purposes.

Michigan reported an increase in hate crimes between 1996 and 2005, whereas Texas showed a decrease over the same period. Among the five states listed, Texas also had the second lowest rate of hate crimes, even though it is perhaps the most racially diverse state represented in the table.[57] To be sure, hate crimes are probably underreported and other data collection problems likely exist within the data. Yet the data are remarkable in their brutal simplicity. The data show that Texas has one of the lowest rates of hate crimes despite being perhaps the most racially and ethnically diverse state in the nation.

An explanation for this situation can be traced straight to the prison. In the first chapter, we discussed how efforts to implement racial desegregation (and effect long-term value change) began at the widest margins of our society. The conditions for prison desegregation resulted from change far beyond the walls. The process was evolutionary and took decades to transpire. Desegregating the military and public school systems, for example, set the stage for the prison. In the public school setting, court rulings were the vehicle by which change occurred—from the outside in. Desegregation of the Texas prison system occurred over decades—entire prison units were desegregated, then programmatic and work details, then larger living areas such as cell blocks and dormitories, and finally the cells.

We know that the vast majority of criminal offenders originate from the most disadvantaged sectors of American society. The vast majority of prisoners also come from the poorest areas as well—social areas where attitudes of prejudice, mistrust, and bias smoulder. Texas's policy of housing rightly classified inmates in the first available cell regardless of race or ethnicity forces individuals from disparate groups and walks of life to coexist without violence. This policy just might have a carry-over effect—a dampening effect on hate crimes in the wider society. This is far from certain. Establishing a cause-and-effect relationship would require complex national data and analyses. If such a relationship were found to exist, however, it might indicate that a prison policy can benefit the wider society.

We noted in an earlier chapter that litigation often produces unintended consequences, sometimes ironically. It would be supremely ironic indeed if Texas prisons have become a key site for the production of positive interracial relationships. In 2006, the Texas prison system released roughly 42,000 inmates, or some 3,500 per month.[58] Many of those released spent some portion of their incarceration in a cell with a member of another racial or ethnic group. All of them were desegregated to some degree in other aspects of imprisonment. Tens of thousands of released Texas prisoners are returning to their former neighborhoods and places of work. Perhaps the low rate of hate crimes in Texas, compared to other large states, can be attributed to some unknown extent to TDC's policy of first available celling. If so, then a social change has occurred from the innermost to the most distant of rings.

Notes

Chapter I

1. See http://www.nationalmuseum.af.mil, the National Museum of the Air Force, for more information on Iven Kincheloe.

2. Elvis said it himself in 1956: "The colored folks been singing it and playing it just like I'm doing now, man, for more years than I know. I got it from them. Down in Tupelo, Mississippi, I used to hear old Arthur Crudup bang his box the way I do now, and I said if I ever got to the place where I could feel all old Arthur felt, I'd be a music man like nobody ever saw." See Farley, C. J. (2004, July 6). "Elvis Rocks. But He's Not the First." *Time Magazine.*

3. See Bertrand, M. J. (2000). *Race, Rock, and Elvis.* Urbana, IL: University of Illinois Press.

4. Ladino, R. (1996). *Desegregating Texas Schools: Eisenhower, Shivers, and the Crisis at Mansfield High.* Austin: University of Texas Press: 6.

5. Ibid.

6. *Jackson v. Rawdon,* United States District Court, Northern District, Texas, August 27, 1956, Civ. No. 3152.

7. Ladino, R., *Desegregating Texas Schools,* 91–92.

8. Ibid., 138–143.

9. See Sample, A. (1984). *Racehoss: Big Emma's Boy.* New York: Ballantine Books: 178–180.

10. In the TDC of the 1950s, inmates working in the field were required to weigh their sacks of cotton to meet quotas. Inmates who did not meet their quotas at "weigh up" faced disciplinary punishments for being "lazy" or otherwise insubordinate, punishments which could have included placement in solitary confinement among other coercive disciplinary sanctions.

11. Inmate has recently been replaced with the word "offender" in today's correctional institutions. Such changes generally paralleled the name changes that have come to the old prison farms. Prisons in Texas have evolved from farms (convicts), to units (inmates), to the newly labeled correctional institutions (offenders).

12. See Park, R., Burgess, E., & McKenzie, R. (1925). *The City.* Chicago: University of Chicago Press.

13. Lilly, J., Cullen, F., & Ball, R. (2007). *Criminological Theory: Context and Consequences*. Thousand Oaks, CA: Sage.

14. Ibid.

15. *Plessy v. Ferguson*, 163 U.S. 537 (1896).

16. See Jacobs, J. B. (1983). "Macrosociology and Imprisonment." In J. Jacobs (Ed.), *New Perspectives on Prisons and Imprisonment* (pp. 17–33). Ithaca, NY: Cornell University Press.

17. The history of racial desegregation at the University of Texas at Austin (UT) parallels the Texas prison situation and lends credence to the notion of zones of desegregation. For example, in 1955 UT first admitted African American students for the fall 1956 semester. In 1964, the first African American teaching assistants and faculty members were employed. Also in 1964, the University of Texas Board of Regents voted 6–1 to desegregate the dormitories. In short, desegregation occurred first at the university level, then among employees, university facilities, and student living areas. See Durden, A. M. (1979). *Overcoming: A History of Black Integration at the University of Texas at Austin*. Office of the Dean of Students, University of Texas at Austin.

18. See Jacobs, J. B. (1977). *Stateville: The Penitentiary in Mass Society*. Chicago: University Chicago Press; Irwin, J. (1980). *Prisons in Turmoil*. Boston: Little, Brown; Crouch, B. M. & Marquart, J. W. (1989). *An Appeal to Justice: Litigated Reform of Texas Prisons*. Austin: University of Texas Press; Carroll, L. (1999). *Lawful Order: A Case Study of Correctional Crisis and Reform*. New York: Garland Publishing.

19. In the coming pages we describe the Texas prison experience with in-cell desegregation and note that the Texas prison system is the most desegregated prison setting in America. While all state prison systems (and the federal prison system) have desegregated dormitories, dayrooms, work squads, and almost all other areas in the prison environment today, it is important to note that two-person cells are not racially mixed on any large scale in most U.S. prison systems, and certainly not to the degree of the Texas prison system. Despite the fact that the U.S. Supreme Court ruled in 1968 (in *Lee v. Washington*) that prison and jail administrators are generally prohibited from segregating inmates by race, this ruling did not lead to cell desegregation in state prison systems. As we explore in Chapter 4, a major reason is that the Court provided a caveat for prison administrators: "Acting in good faith and in particularized circumstances," prison authorities have the right to take into account racial tensions in ensuring order and security in prisons and jails. This caveat allowed prison administrators across the country to avoid desegregating prisoners, especially within cells, under the good-faith belief that any measure of desegregation would lead to severe racial violence.

This caveat also meant that the responsibility of providing a road map and standard for prisoner desegregation was left to the lower federal district and circuit courts. Following the *Lee* decision, inmates in various state prison systems petitioned the lower federal courts, complaining about continued segregation by prison authorities. Not surprisingly, most of the lawsuits originated from southern prison systems. The great majority of these lawsuits complained of segregated dormitories, cellblocks, work assignments, and the like. Very few lawsuits complained about cell segregation or pressed for the elimination of cell segregation. The exceptions were the inmate lawsuits in Texas (*Lamar v. Coffield*) and Oklahoma (*Battle v. Anderson*). Cases filed by inmates in U.S. district courts in these two states eventually led to cell desegregation, in addition to desegregation in other areas of prison operation. Because most of the decisions on prisoner desegregation originated in and were finally decided by U.S. district courts, the rulings applied only within state borders. This is the reason why only Texas and Oklahoma desegregate two-person cells; other states have either not faced an individual lawsuit on the issue or were required only to desegregate other areas of the prison environment, not cells. Until 2005, the U.S. Supreme Court had not dealt with the issue of segregation in prisons since 1968. In 2005, the Court held in *Johnson v. California* that blanket policies of racial segregation are prohibited and prison administrators cannot use race to segregate inmates, even within cells, unless in individual cases racial segregation is the only way to prevent violence. Because U.S. Supreme Court rulings create a standard for the country and are not constrained to federal, district, or circuit court geographical boundaries, this ruling mandates that all state prison systems and the Federal Bureau of Prisons are prohibited from segregating inmates by race, unless it is determined following an individual assessment of each offender that some must be segregated to maintain the security of institutions and the safety of staff and inmates.

Chapter 2

1. Webb, W. P. (1931). *The Great Plains*. New York: Ginn and Company: 8.

2. See Fehrenbach, T. R. (1985). *Lone Star*. New York: Macmillan.

3. Cantrell, G. (1999). *Stephen F. Austin: Empresario of Texas*. New Haven, CT: Yale University Press: 190.

4. See Fehrenbach, T. R. *Lone Star*, 143.

5. Ibid., 165.

6. Bugbee, L. (1898). "Slavery in Early Texas." *Political Science Quarterly*, 13, 648–668: 661.

7. Historical census data and maps were generated by data from the Geospatial & Statistical Data Center, University of Virginia Library. http://Fisher.lib.virginia.edu.

8. See Campbell, R. (1989). *An Empire for Slavery: The Peculiar Institution in Texas, 1821–1865*. Baton Rouge: Louisiana State University Press.

9. See Fehrenbach, T. R. *Lone Star*, 306.

10. Sam Houston was governor at the time and he sacrificed his political career by opposing Texas joining the Confederacy. He also stated that "the first gun fired in the war will be the knell of slavery." His prophecy was correct. See Campbell, R. *An Empire for Slavery*, 230.

11. See Fehrenbach, T. R. *Lone Star*, 391.

12. Roof, M. (1863, January). "The Diary of Martin Roof, Co. A." 114th O.V.I. www.fortunecity.com/westwood/makeover/347/index.htm.

13. Dickens, C. (1859). *A Tale of Two Cities*. London: Chapman and Hall: 1.

14. See Du Bois, W. E. B. (1903). *The Souls of Black Folk*. Chicago: A. C. McClurg and Co.

15. Letters from http://freedmensbureau.com/texas/index.htm.

16. Bureau of Refugees, Freedmen and Abandoned Lands, 1865–1869. National Archives Microfilm Publication M821 Roll 32. *Miscellaneous Records Relating to Murders and Other Criminal Offenses Committed in Texas 1865–1868* (transcribed as written).

17. See http://freedmensbureau.com/texas/texasoutrages3.htm.

18. Texas was not alone in passing such legislation; other former slave-owning states did the same; see Wilson, T. (1965). *The Black Codes of the South*. Tuscaloosa: University of Alabama Press.

19. The Fifteenth Amendment reads as follows: "The right of citizens of the United States to vote shall not be denied or abridged by the United States or by any State on account of race, color, or previous condition of servitude."

20. See Smallwood, J. (1981). *Time of Hope, Time of Despair: Black Texans during Reconstruction*. Port Washington, NY: Kennikat Press.

21. See Fehrenbach, T. R. *Lone Star*, 439–442.

22. In 1923, the "white primary" became state law.

23. Prairie View A&M University is part of the Texas A&M University system. See *The Handbook of Texas Online*.

24. Mr. Plessy was, in the language of the day, an octoroon. This term was used in southern states, especially Louisiana, to denote ⅛ black ancestry and ⅞ white ancestry. Quadroons were individuals with three white grandparents and one black grandparent.

25. *Plessy v. Ferguson*, 163 U.S. 537 (1896).

26. See Fehrenbach, T. R. *Lone Star*, 337–339. The Knights of the Golden Circle was a secret society that formed prior to the Civil War whose objective was to protect and even extend slavery. During Reconstruction the Ku Klux Klan appeared in Texas along with a number of other secret white supremacist groups like the Palefaces, Knights of the White Camelia, and the Teutonic Knights. The primary objective of these terrorist groups, regardless of name, was white supremacy. These groups also advocated violence. See Smallwood, J. *Time of Hope, Time of Despair*.

27. In some instances, when provoked by police brutality, African Americans rebelled against injustice. For example, the Houston race riot of 1917 occurred when African American soldiers mutinied and killed sixteen whites, including five police officers. This episode actually contributed to the rise of the Ku Klux Klan in Texas, an organization that boasted a membership somewhere between 75,000 and 90,000 members by 1922. Local Klan chapters in Texas also included as members the social and political elites, which only legitimized the group. See Brown, N. (1984). *Hood, Bonnet, and Little Brown Jug*. College Station: Texas A&M University Press.

28. See Zangrando, R. (1980). *The NAACP Crusade against Lynching, 1909–1950*. Philadelphia: Temple University Press.

29. For an informed discussion of the southern rape complex and "need" for African American scapegoats, see Cash, W. J. (1941). *The Mind of the South*. New York: Vintage Books.

30. Retrieved from http://members.aol.com/wdwylie6/1890-1899.htm.

31. The first Texas chapter of the National Association for the Advancement of Colored People (NAACP) was organized in Houston in 1912. One of its primary goals was to end lynching in America.

32. On the back of the postcard it said: "This is the barbeque we had last night. My picture is to the left with a cross over it. Your son, Joe." The event was also photographed by Fred Gildersleeve; see Smith, J. B. (2005, March 6). "The Waco Horror: and the 'Culture of Lynching.'" *Waco Tribune-Herald*. The lynching left an imprint on Waco that is still felt today where efforts are underway to improve race relations. A "Community Race Relations Coalition" was established in 2000; one of the group's

goals is to prompt county government officials to enact a resolution apologizing for the lynching.

33. See Proctor, B. H. "World War II." *Handbook of Texas Online.* Retrieved July 25, 2006, from http://www.tsha.utexas.edu/handbook/online/articles/WW/npwnj .html.

34. Hall, J. (1979). *Revolt against Chivalry: Jessie Daniel Ames and the Women's Campaign against Lynching.* New York: Columbia University Press.

35. Du Bois, W .E. B. *The Souls of Black Folk.*

36. *Nixon v. Herndon,* 273 U.S. 536 (1927).

37. *Nixon v. Condin,* 286 U.S. 73 (1932).

38. *Grovey v. Townsend,* 295 U.S. 45 (1935).

39. *Smith v. Allwright,* 321 U.S. 649 (1944).

40. See Miguel, G. (1983). "The Struggle against Separate and Unequal Schools: Middle Class Mexican Americans and the Desegregation Campaign in Texas, 1929–1957." *History of Education Quarterly,* 23: 343–359.

41. Lord, W. (1957). *Day of Infamy.* New York: Henry Holt.

42. See Moskos, C., & Butler, J. (1996). *All That We Can Be: Black Leadership and Racial Integration the Army Way.* New York: The Twentieth Century Fund.

43. See "Strength of the Army," 1 January 1946, STM-30, p. 60.

44. The policy of racial segregation in the army was the subject of scientific scrutiny during the war. In March 1943, 13,000 black and white soldiers participated in a social survey and were asked the following question: "Do you think white and Negro soldiers should be in separate outfits or should they be together in the same outfits?" Results showed that 38 percent of the black and 88 percent of the white soldiers thought that they should be in separate outfits; 26 percent of the black and 9 percent of the white soldiers said that it made no difference or they were undecided; 36 percent of the black and 3 percent of the whites checked a preference for the same outfits. See Research Branch, Special Service Division, "Attitudes of the Negro Soldier," 28 July 1943. It was not unusual for black soldiers on military athletic teams to compete against prison athletic teams made up of black prisoners.

45. See Kluger, R. (1976). *Simple Justice: The History of Brown v. Board of Education and Black America's Struggle for Equality.* New York: Alfred A. Knopf.

46. See Proctor, B. H. "World War II." *Handbook of Texas Online.* Retrieved July 25, 2006, from http://www.tsha.utexas.edu/handbook/online/articles/WW/npwnj .html.

47. See Wiggins, D. (1997). *Glory Bound: Black Athletes in a White America.* Syracuse: Syracuse University Press.

48. See *Time* (1947, September 22).

49. It should be noted that Senator Barry Goldwater was instrumental in integrating the Arizona Air National Guard in 1946, a full two years before the historic act of President Harry S. Truman. See Goldwater, B. (1990). *The Conscience of a Conservative.* Washington, D.C.: Regnery Publishing.

50. See Moskos, C., & Butler, J. *All That We Can Be,* 29–31.

51. See Duncan, D. (1950, March 27). "Sweatt Suit Called Broad Attack on All Racial Segregation." *Austin American-Statesman.*

52. *Plessy v. Ferguson,* 163 U.S. 537 (1896).

53. *Sweatt v. Painter et al.,* 339 U.S. 629 (1950). In an interesting historical foot-

note, one of the justices on the Supreme Court was Tom Clark, a Dallas native born in 1899 and a 1922 graduate of the University of Texas Law School. Appointed by President Harry S. Truman to the Court in 1949, Clark was the first Texan to sit on the Court.

54. See "Jim Crow Test Looms in Arrest" (1953, August 1). *Austin American-Statesman.*

55. See also *Hernandez v. State of Texas*, 347 U.S. 475 (1954). This landmark case decided that Mexican Americans and all other racial groups in the United States had equal protection under the Fourteenth Amendment, and paved the way for Mexican Americans to serve on juries.

56. *Brown v. Board of Education*, 347 U.S. 483 (1954).

57. See annotated draft decree regarding *Brown v. Board of Education*, April 8, 1955, p. 2. The phrase "with all deliberate speed" was drafted by Justice Felix Frankfurter.

58. See Parks, R. (1992). *Rosa Parks, My Story.* New York: Puffin Books.

59. See "Mansfield School Desegregation Incident." *Handbook of Texas Online.*

60. See Armor, D. (1995). *Forced Justice: School Desegregation and the Law.* New York: Oxford University Press.

61. McElhaney, J., & Hazel, M. V. Dallas, Texas. *Handbook of Texas Online.* Retrieved August 6, 2006, from http://www.tsha.utexas.edu/handbook/online/articles/DD/hdd1.html. Integration of the public schools proceeded more slowly, and the school district remained under court supervision until 1994.

62. LeCompte, M. L. "Sports." *Handbook of Texas Online.* Retrieved August 6, 2006, from http://www.tsha.utexas.edu/handbook/online/articles/SS/xzs1.html.

63. Among the players for Kentucky that season was forward Pat Riley, who would later coach five championship teams for the NBA Los Angeles Lakers and Miami Heat. In subsequent years Adolph Rupp, who had previously coached black players in high school and in all-star games, was to be unfairly painted as an arch-segregationist. Kentucky had defeated a similarly all-white Duke team in the semifinals, while Texas Western had defeated an integrated Michigan squad featuring Cazzie Russell.

64. See http://www.hoophall.com/, the official web site of the Basketball Hall of Fame. At the time of the game and for years afterward, however, little comment was made about the racial significance of the lineups and the game's outcome.

65. LeCompte, M. L. "Sports." *Handbook of Texas Online.* Retrieved August 6, 2006, from http://www.tsha.utexas.edu/handbook/online/articles/SS/xzs1.html.

66. See Jordan, B., & Hearon, S. (1979). *Barbara Jordan: A Self Portrait.* Garden City, N.Y.: Doubleday.

67. Justice handed down controversial decisions that transformed the Texas adult and juvenile correctional systems in the 1970s. See Kemerer, F. R. (1991). *William Wayne Justice: A Judicial Biography.* Austin: University of Texas Press.

68. Kemerer, F. R. "United States v. Texas." *Handbook of Texas Online.* Retrieved August 6, 2006, from http://www.tsha.utexas.edu/handbook/online/articles/UU/jru2.html.

69. In 1972, LULAC became a "plaintiff-intervener" in the case that was extended to include all persons of "Mexican-American descent or nationality in the State of Texas." See *United States of America and the GI Forum and LULAC, Plaintiff intervenors, v. State of Texas*, Civil Action No: 6:71-CV-5281.

70. See Temple-Raston, D. (2003). *A Death in Texas: A Story of Race, Murder, and a Small Town's Struggle for Redemption*. New York: Owl Books.

71. See "The 2006 Houston Survey of African Americans." Retrieved August 15, 2006, from http://www.tsu.edu/media/center/SOPASURVEY_7-21-06.pdf.

Chapter 3

1. See Kluger, R. (1976). *Simple Justice: The History of Brown v. Board of Education and Black America's Struggle for Equality*. New York: Alfred A. Knopf.

2. Warren's phrase "all deliberate speed" in *Brown II* was borrowed from Justice Felix Frankfurter, who used it in two opinions in the 1940s; the phrase suggests a "progression of action" rather than immediate resolution of an issue that was impossible in state and federal government. See Kluger, R. *Simple Justice*, 742–744.

3. Nineteen members of the Senate and eighty-one members of the House of Representatives signed the document. The other Texas senator at the time, Lyndon Johnson, was among only three senators representing the states of the old Confederacy who did not sign (the others were Tennessee's Estes Kefauver and Albert Gore Sr.). See Congressional Record, 84th Congress, Second Session, Vol. 102, part 4 (1956, March 12). Washington, D.C.: Governmental Printing Office: 4459–4460.

4. The 101st Airborne Division, or "Screaming Eagles," led the way in the D-Day Invasion and helped turn the tide during the Battle of the Bulge in World War II.

5. See DeMillo, A. (2007, February 25). "Little Rock District Free of Federal Eyes." *Houston Chronicle*, p. A4. In 2007, Governor Mike Huckabee of Arkansas welcomed to the governor's mansion the nine individuals who as students had required Army escort to desegregate Central High in 1957. Huckabee noted the irony of the meeting at the very same mansion where Governor Orval Faubus had "made many of the decisions that kept them the targets of hatred from white segregationists." See "The Road to Central High." (2007, September 24). *Dallas Morning News*, p. 3A.

6. Cohodas, N. (1997). *The Band Played Dixie: Race and the Liberal Conscience at Ole Miss*. New York: Free Press.

7. See Crain, R. L. (1968). *The Politics of School Desegregation*. Chicago: Aldine Publishing Company.

8. We are not suggesting that events which unfolded in Arkansas and Mississippi are the only school desegregation cases that defined the outer limits of public reaction to desegregation. Indeed, Boston, Charlotte, and Milwaukee all qualify as intense cases in this regard. See Formisano, R. (1991). *Boston against Busing*. Chapel Hill: University of North Carolina Press; Gaillard, F. (2006). *The Dream Deferred: The Landmark Struggle for Desegregation in Charlotte, North Carolina*. Columbia: University of South Carolina Press; and Dougherty, J. (2004). *More than One Struggle: The Evolution of Black School Reform in Milwaukee*. Chapel Hill: University of North Carolina Press.

9. *Borders v. Rippy*, 250 F.2d 690 (5th Cir. 1957).

10. See *Borders v. Rippy*, 250 F.2d 690 (5th Cir. 1957). Thurgood Marshall was an attorney for the plaintiffs.

11. The School Board wanted additional time to study the issue and ordered the superintendent of the DISD to continue the policy of segregated schools in the 1956–57 school year.

12. See Read, F. "Judicial Evolution of the Law of School Integration since Brown," esp. 14.

13. School officials in Texas boasted that 52 percent of its school districts were desegregated between 1954 and 1964. See Crain, R. L. *The Politics of School Desegregation*.

14. See Linden, G. (1995). *Desegregating Schools in Dallas: Four Decades in the Federal Courts*. Dallas: Three Forks Press.

15. See "Race, Ethnicity, and Class in Dallas." (2002, January). *D Magazine*.

16. Other consequences of desegregation either directly or indirectly related to desegregation of the DISD have been considered. These include graduation rates, drop-out rates, state-mandated standardized tests and scores, parental satisfaction, and teacher perceptions, among numerous others. The point here, without further analysis, is that desegregation has been attained legally, but perhaps other unintended consequences have resulted.

17. Engel, K., & Rothman, S. (1984). "The Paradox of Prison Reform: Rehabilitation, Prisoners' Rights, and Violence." *Harvard Journal of Law and Public Policy 7*, 413.

18. MacGregor, M. J. (1985). *Integration of the Armed Forces 1940–1965*. Center of Military History, United States Army, Washington, D.C.

19. See Col. Eugene R. Householder, speech before Conference of Negro Editors and Publishers, December 8, 1941, AG 291.21(12-1-41) (1).

20. MacGregor, M. J. *Integration of the Armed Forces 1940–1965*.

21. See ibid.

22. The research team involved in the American soldier studies consisted of Samuel A. Stouffer, Edward A. Suchman, Leland Devinney, Shirley Star, Robin Williams Jr., Arthur and Marion Lumsdaine, M. Brewster Smith, Irving Janis, Leonard Cottrell, Carl Hovland, Louis Guttman, Paul Lazarsfeld, and John Clausen—a veritable "who's who" in the history of American sociology. See *Studies in Social Psychology in World War II: Volumes I–V.* (1949). Princeton, NJ: Princeton University Press. It should also be noted that 12,235 soldiers (7,442 African American soldiers and 4,793 white soldiers, in two separate data sets) completed the self-administered questionnaire. For additional information on the survey methodology and respondents, see *The American Soldier in World War II: Attitudes of Negroes and Attitudes toward Negroes.* (1943, March). The Roper Center for Public Opinion Research (USAMS 1943–SO32) at http://www.ropercenter.uconn.edu/.

23. The results of the survey, entitled "Opinions About Negro Infantry Platoons in White Companies of 7 Divisions," and numerous other documents pertaining to the desegregation of the military can be found at the Truman Library (http://www.trumanlibrary.org/index.php), an online source of important military papers, memorandums, and correspondence.

24. *Studies in Social Psychology in World War II: Volumes I–V,* 593.

25. MacGregor, M. J. *Integration of the Armed Forces 1940–1965*.

26. Moskos, C. C., & Butler, J. S. (1996). *All That We Can Be: Black Leadership and Racial Integration the Army Way*. New York: Twentieth Century Fund.

27. See Scarville, J., Burton, S., Edwards, J., Lancaster, A., & Elig, T. W. (1999). *Armed Forces Equal Opportunity Survey*. Washington, D.C.: Defense Manpower Data Center, Survey Program and Evaluation Division, U.S. Department of Defense.

28. See Moskos, C. C., & Butler, J. S. *All That We Can Be*, 3–6. See also *Gang-Related Activity in the U.S. Armed Forces Increasing*. National Gang Intelligence Center, January 12, 2007.

29. See Scarville, J., Burton, S., Edwards, J., Lancaster, A., & Elig, T. W. (1999). *Armed Forces Equal Opportunity Survey*.

30. See, for example, the research by Dornbusch, S. (1955). "The Military Academy as an Assimilating Institution." *Social Forces* 33, 317; Hansen, S. (1999). "The Racial History of the U.S. Military Academies." *Journal of Blacks in Higher Education* 26, 111–116; and Sykes, R., Larntz, K., & Fox, J. (1976). "Proximity and Similarity Effects on Frequency of Interaction in a Class of Naval Recruits." *Sociometry* 39, 263–269.

31. See note, "Lessons in Transcendence: Forced Associations and the Military." *Harvard Law Review* 117, 1981 (2004).

32. Allport, G. (1954). *The Nature of Prejudice*. Boston: Addison-Wesley.

Chapter 4

1. One of the problems when discussing racial segregation and desegregation in prisons is that there are different levels of desegregation. For example, many prisons systems were completely segregated by race from their inception through the 1960s, with separate prisons for whites, blacks, and Hispanics. Throughout the 1960s and 1970s, several prison systems allowed inmates of different races to coexist in the same facility, but segregation remained in all other aspects, including cell blocks, cell block tiers, cell assignments, and job assignments. In the 1980s and 1990s most prison systems across the country allowed inmates of different races to live in the same cell block or cell block tier and/or work in the same field squads, although few prison systems had policies requiring inmates of different races to be housed in the same cell. Thus, various levels have characterized the desegregation of prison inmates over time. Today, the last vestige of racial segregation in prisons is the absence of desegregated cell assignments on any large scale in most U.S. prison systems. Although the U.S. Supreme Court struck down racial segregation in prisons as a matter of public policy in 1968, various levels of segregation persisted in U.S. prison systems. Only in 2005 did the Supreme Court reiterate that segregation in prisons and jails was unconstitutional, save for particular circumstances that might warrant the temporary separation of the races on a narrowly tailored basis. That case concerned racially segregated cell assignments.

2. Johnston, N. (1994). *Eastern State Penitentiary: Crucible of Good Intentions*. Philadelphia: Philadelphia Museum of Art: 92.

3. Jacobs, J. (1983). *New Perspectives on Prisons and Imprisonment*. Ithaca: Cornell University Press.

4. Johnston, N. *Eastern State Penitentiary*, 90.

5. Simmons, L. (1957). *Assignment Huntsville: Memoirs of a Texas Prison Official*. Austin: University of Texas Press: 85–86.

6. Perhaps the most egregious examples come from Alabama, Arkansas, Mississippi, Georgia, Louisiana, and Texas, but most other southern states, such as Florida and Tennessee, could also be characterized by such racial segregation.

7. Jacobs, J. *New Perspectives on Prisons and Imprisonment*, 84.

8. There is some debate as to which states are in the Deep South. Most observers include Alabama, Arkansas, Mississippi, and Louisiana. Others include Florida, Georgia, South Carolina, and Tennessee.

9. Jacobs, J. *New Perspectives on Prisons and Imprisonment*, 84. This is in reference to a 1940 Alabama law that provided for the racial segregation of prisoners and was the impetus for the *Washington v. Lee* (1966) and *Lee v. Washington* cases (1968).

10. Oshinsky, D. (1996). *Worse than Slavery: Parchman Farm and the Ordeal of Jim Crow Justice.* New York: Free Press: 247. *Gates v. Collier,* 349 F. Supp. 881 (N.D. Miss. 1972).

11. A defining feature of southern prisons, not often found in the North and other regions of the country, was the presence of field camps and large dormitory or "tank"-based housing. This helped to promote the segregation of inmates by race.

12. Murton, T., & Hyams, J. (1969). *Accomplices to the Crime: The Arkansas Prison Scandal.* New York: Grove Press: 175.

13. Ibid., 176.

14. Alabama Department of Corrections History. Retrieved on November 7, 2006, from http://www.doc.state.al.us/history.asp.

15. Barnes, H., & Teeters, N. (1959). *New Horizons in Criminology.* Englewood Cliffs, NJ: Prentice Hall: 466.

16. *Brown v. Board of Education,* 347 U.S. 483 (1954).

17. There is sure to be much variation concerning the level of segregation. Despite this, the general practice favored racial segregation in southern prison systems.

18. Henderson, M., Cullen, F., Carroll, L., & Feinberg, W. (2000). "Race, Rights, and Order in Prison: A National Survey of Wardens on the Racial Integration of Prison Cells." *Prison Journal,* 80, 295–308.

19. See, for example, ibid. It should be noted that while the practice of "official" racial segregation has changed in prison systems over the last several decades, inmates still "unofficially" engage in extreme forms of self-segregation by race on the yard, in cell block dayrooms, and in other areas where they are afforded the freedom to self-segregate.

20. McCleod, R. (1978). "Racial Desegregation of Inmate Housing on the Wynne Unit, Texas Department of Corrections: Its Early Implementation." Master's Thesis. Huntsville, TX: Sam Houston State University.

21. Feeley, M., & Rubin, E. (2000). *Judicial Policy Making and the Modern State.* Cambridge: Cambridge University Press.

22. Smith, C. (2000). "The Governance of Corrections: Implications of the Changing Interface of Courts and Corrections." In C. Friel (Ed.), *Boundary Changes in Criminal Justice* (pp. 113–166). Washington, D.C.: U.S. Department of Justice.

23. *Ruffin v. Commonwealth,* 62 Va. 790 (1871).

24. Jacobs, J. *New Perspectives on Prisons and Imprisonment*, 35.

25. It must be understood that both the prisoners' rights movement and the civil rights movement were impacted by numerous factors, only one of which was intervention by the Supreme Court. Indeed, these two massive movements depended on the receptivity and efforts of the lower federal courts, civil rights lawyers willing to support the cause of marginalized prisoners, and the actions of state legislatures. See,

Jacobs, J. *New Perspectives on Prisons and Imprisonment*, 33–60, "The Prisoners' Rights Movement and Its Impacts."

26. Smith, C. "The Governance of Corrections."

27. Del Carmen, R. (2001). *Criminal Procedure: Law and Practice.* Belmont, CA: Wadsworth: 16.

28. Smith, C. "The Governance of Corrections."

29. Ibid.; *Cooper v. Pate*, 387 U.S. 546 (1964). See also Feeley, M., & Rubin, E. *Judicial Policy Making and the Modern State.*

30. Feeley, M., & Rubin, E. *Judicial Policy Making and the Modern State.* See also Jacobs, J. *New Perspectives on Prisons and Imprisonment.*

31. Jacobs, J. *New Perspectives on Prisons and Imprisonment.* Section 1983 originated as the Ku Klux Klan Act of 1871.

32. Smith, C. "The Governance of Corrections."

33. Jacobs, J. *New Perspectives on Prisons and Imprisonment*, 36.

34. The *Cooper* decision was important in three ways. First, the issue in the case surrounded religious freedom. Perhaps more than any other claim by inmates, the right to be free from religious discrimination was one of the most fundamental rights in American society—even for prisoners. Despite the fact that the discrimination claim involved inmates, it would have been constitutionally difficult to allow prison authorities such wide discretion in the wake of the civil rights movement. Second, the *Cooper* ruling gave inmates a stage in the federal court system to sue government officials under federal law. Historically, standing for prisoners would seldom be entertained by state court judges, most of whom were elected or political appointees. Siding with prisoners was not something that was favorably looked upon, especially for future reelection campaigns. Federal judges, on the other hand, are appointed for life tenure, with less pressure to conform to larger societal and political views regarding prisoners. Perhaps most important is that the *Cooper* decision came at a time when the composition of the Supreme Court was perhaps at its liberal zenith, led by Chief Justice Earl Warren. Thus, *Cooper* was important, but the receptivity of the Court to inmate claims was paramount. Although the prisoners' rights movement cannot be attributed solely to the *Cooper* decision, it was important. See Jacobs, J. *New Perspectives on Prisons and Imprisonment* for an excellent discussion on the significance of *Cooper* and other factors that spurred the prisoners' rights movement.

35. For an excellent review of federal court action and how the stage was set for prisoner litigation during this time, see Feeley, M., & Rubin, E. *Judicial Policy Making and the Modern State;* Smith, C. "The Governance of Corrections."

36. *Washington v. Lee*, 263 F. Supp. 327 (M.D. Ala., 1966).

37. See quote from the Alabama statute in Jacobs, J. *New Perspectives on Prisons and Imprisonment*, 84.

38. *Washington v. Lee*, 263 F. Supp. 327 (M.D. Ala., 1966); *Brown v. Board of Education*, 347 U.S. 483 (1954).

39. *Lee v. Washington*, 390 U.S. 333 (1968).

40. Ibid.

41. Jacobs, J. *New Perspectives on Prisons and Imprisonment.*

42. Ibid., 84.

43. But segregation also undoubtedly continued because of the steadfastness of

prison administrators (especially in the South) to buck the authority of the Court's opinions by dragging their feet. Feeley, M., & Rubin, E. *Judicial Policy Making and the Modern State.* See also Schlanger, M. (1999). "Beyond the Hero Judge: Institutional Reform Litigation as Litigation." *Michigan Law Review* 97, 1994–2036.

44. On the number of cases and states in which they were situated, see, for example, Trulson, C., & Marquart, J. (2002). "Inmate Racial Integration: Achieving Racial Integration in the Texas Prison System." *Prison Journal,* 82, 498–525.

45. It is not known whether these state prison systems were racially desegregated to a degree in order to avoid scrutiny, or whether there is another explanation for the lack of court action. From all available evidence, it is unlikely that those systems that avoided court scrutiny were racially desegregated within cells.

46. Harris, K., & Spiller, D. (1977). *After Decision Implementation of Judicial Decrees in Correctional Settings.* Washington, D.C.: U.S. Department of Justice.

47. In addition to the fear-of-violence argument, some lower federal court cases, however, did present issues that prisoners of different races were not treated equally, such that segregation led to the denial of privileges given only to white inmates. Such a claim harkens to the separate but equal arguments of desegregation cases in the wider society. In *McClelland v. Sigler,* 456 F.2d 1266 (8th Cir. 1972), federal judge Warren Urbom compared segregation in a prison to segregation in a school setting in that it could result in feelings of inferiority. Also see *Sockwell v. Phelps,* 20 F. 3d 187 (5th Cir. 1994), where inmates Sockwell, Rochon, and Crittle argued that black inmates were at a disadvantage compared to white inmates housed in a two-man cell because white prisoners received preferential treatment: white cells were called to showers and to sell plasma first, enjoyed better store and telephone privileges, and had a better view of televisions. As the Court has noted in the past, equal discrimination is still discrimination protected by the Constitution. Thus, perhaps one of the only semi-valid arguments for a segregation policy in prisons was the fear-of-violence argument. It is unlikely that any differential treatment or separate but equal argument would have withstood any chance of validating a segregation argument in prisons without the claims of fear of extreme violence.

48. Trulson, C., & Marquart, J. "Inmate racial integration."

49. For further discussion on prisoner desegregation cases in general, see also Schlanger, M. "Beyond the Hero Judge."

50. *Wilson v. Kelly,* 294 F. Supp. 1005 (N.D. Ga. 1968).

51. *Rentfrow v. Carter,* 296 F. Supp. 301 (N.D. Ga. 1968).

52. Ibid., 6.

53. *McClelland v. Sigler,* 456 F. 2d 1266 (8th Cir. 1972).

54. *United States v. Wyandotte County, Kansas,* 480 F. 2d 969 (10th Cir. 1973).

55. *Mickens v. Winston,* 462 F. Supp. 910 (E.D. Va. 1978). The argument of inadequate supervision combined with the fear of violence has been used in other cases. Specifically, see *Rentfrow v. Carter,* 296 F. Supp. 301 (N.D. Ga. 1968).

56. *Stewart v. Rhodes,* 473 F. Supp. 1185 (S.D. Ohio 1979).

57. *Blevins v. Brew,* 593 F. Supp. 245 (W.D. Wis. 1984).

58. Henderson, M., Cullen, F., Carroll, L., & Feinberg, W. "Race, Rights, and Order in Prison."

59. *White v. Morris,* 811 F. Supp. 1185 (S.D. Ohio 1992) and *White v. Morris,* 832 F. Supp. 1129 (S.D. Ohio 1993).

60. *Sockwell v. Phelps*, 20 F. 3d 187 (5th Cir. 1994).

61. *Williams v. McKeithen*, CA 71–98 (M.D. La. 1975).

62. *Sockwell v. Phelps*, 20 F. 3d 187 (5th Cir. 1994).

63. Rideau, W. & Sinclair, B. (1985). "Prisoner Litigation: How It Began in Louisiana." *Louisiana Law Review*, 45, 1061.

64. *Taylor v. Perini*, 365 F. Supp. 557 (N.D. Ohio 1972).

65. *Holt v. Sarver*, 442 F. 2d 304 (8th Cir. 1971); *Holt v. Hutto*, 363 F. Supp. 194 (E.D. Ark. 1973); *Finney v. Arkansas Board of Corrections*, 505 F. 2d 194 (8th Cir. 1974); and *Finney v. Mabry*, 546 F. Supp. 628 (E.D. Ark. 1982).

66. *Guthrie v. Evans*, 93 F.R.D. 390 (S.D. Ga. 1981).

67. Chilton, B. (1991). *Prisons under the Gavel: The Federal Court Takeover of Georgia Prisons*. Columbus: Ohio State University Press.

68. *Howard v. Collins*, U.S. App. Lexis 32235 (8th Cir. 1997), and *Jacobs v. Lockhart*, 9 F. 3d 187 (8th Cir. 1993).

69. *Thomas v. Pate*, 493 F. 2d 151 (7th Cir. 1974), and *United States v. Illinois*, Civil Action No. 76-0158 (S.D. Ill. 1976).

70. *Battle v. Anderson*, 376 F. Supp. 402 (E.D. Okla. 1974).

71. *Gates v. Collier*, 349 F. Supp. 881 (N.D. Miss. 1972).

72. For further review, see Trulson, C., & Marquart, J. "Inmate Racial Integration."

73. Numerous indicators could be considered aftermaths of desegregation. This section focuses on the aftermath criterion of inmate-on-inmate violence. This is perhaps the most consequential of all aftermath criteria.

74. For a review of these and other studies, see Trulson, C., & Marquart, J. (2002). "Racial Desegregation and Violence in the Texas Prison System." *Criminal Justice Review*, 27, 233–254.

75. Carroll, L. (1974). *Hacks, Blacks, and Cons: Race Relations in a Maximum Security Prison*. Prospect Heights, IL: Waveland.

76. Jacobs, J. (1977). *Stateville: The Penitentiary in Mass Society*. Chicago: University of Chicago Press.

77. Jacobs, J. (1982). "The Limits of Racial Integration in Prison." *Criminal Law Bulletin*, 18, 117–153: 120–121.

78. Irwin, J. (1980). *Prisons in Turmoil*. Boston: Little, Brown: 72–73.

79. Two studies have examined the issue of race relations in juvenile facilities, and desegregation somewhat indirectly: Bartollas, C., Miller, S., & Dinitz, S. (1976). *Juvenile Victimization: The Institutional Paradox*. New York: John Wiley and Sons; and Dishotsky, N., & Pfefferbaum, A. (1979). "Intolerance and Extremism in a Correctional Institution: A Perceived Ethnic Relations Approach." *American Journal of Psychiatry*, 136, 1438–1443. In addition, several studies have examined the ideas of race relations and desegregation through an examination of interracial sexual assault: Carroll, L. (1977). "Humanitarian Reform and Biracial Sexual Assault in a Maximum Security Prison." *Urban Life*, 5, 417–436; Chonco, N. (1989). "Sexual Assaults among Male Inmates." *Prison Journal*, 68, 72–82; Davis, A. (1968). "Sexual Assaults in the Philadelphia Prison System and Sheriff's Vans." *Transaction*, 6, 8–16; Lockwood, D. (1980). *Prison Sexual Violence*. New York: Elsevier; Scacco, A. (1975). *Rape in Prison*. Springfield, IL: Charles C. Thomas; Wooden, W., & Parker, J. (1982). *Men behind Bars: Sexual Exploitation in Prison*. New York: Plenum Press. See also the following

article for an excellent review of these and other studies on the subject: Man, C., & Cronan, J. (2002). "Forecasting Sexual Abuse in Prison: The Prison Subculture of Masculinity as a Backdrop for Deliberate Indifference." *Journal of Criminal Law and Criminology*, 92, 127–185.

80. See Trulson, C., & Marquart, J. "Inmate Racial Integration." See also Trulson, C., Marquart, J., Hemmens, C., & Carroll, L. (2008). "Racial Desegregation in Prisons." *Prison Journal*, 88, 270–300.

81. *Gates v. Collier*, 349 F. Supp. 881 (N.D. Miss. 1972).

82. Oshinsky, D. *Worse than Slavery*, 250.

83. Taylor, W. (1999). *Down on Parchman Farm: The Great Prison in the Mississippi Delta*. Columbus: Ohio State University Press: 8–12.

84. Chilton, B. *Prisons under the Gavel*.

85. See, for example, Henderson, M., Cullen, F., Carrolls, L., & Feinberg, W. "Race, Rights, and Order in a Prison." *White v. Morris*, 811 F. Supp. 1185 (S.D. Ohio 1992); and *White v. Morris*, 832 F. Supp. 1129 (S.D. Ohio 1993).

86. The following cases required desegregation as a component of a larger conditions of confinement case or other reasons not centrally related to the fear-of-violence argument: *Holt v. Sarver*, 442 F. 2d 304 (8th Cir. 1971); *Gates v. Collier*, 349 F. Supp. 881 (N.D. Miss. 1972); *Taylor v. Perini*, 365 F. Supp. 557 (N.D. Ohio 1972); *Holt v. Hutto*, 363 F. Supp. 194 (E.D. Ark. 1973); *Battle v. Anderson*, 376 F. Supp. 402 (E.D. Okla. 1974); *Thomas v. Pate*, 493 F. 2d 151 (7th Cir. 1974); *Finney v. Arkansas Board of Corrections*, 505 F. 2d 194 (8th Cir. 1974); *United States v. Illinois*, Civil Action No. 76-0158 (S.D. Ill. 1976); *Finney v. Mabry*, 546 F. Supp. 628 (E.D. Ark. 1982); *Jacobs v. Lockhart*, 9 F. 3d 187 (8th Cir. 1993); *Howard v. Collins*, U.S. App. Lexis 32235 (8th Cir. 1997); and *Walker v. Gomez*, 307 F. 3d 369 (9th Cir. 2004). This list is not inclusive of all lower federal court cases dealing with inmate racial segregation.

87. West's Texas Statutes and Codes (1974). *Director's Authority and Pay*. Title 108 Penitentiaries, Art. 6166j: 313–314. St. Paul, MN: West Publishing Company.

88. Crouch, B., & Marquart, J. (1989). *An Appeal to Justice: Litigated Reform of Texas Prisons*. Austin: University of Texas Press: 16, which refers to the 1921 Rules, Regulations, and Statutory Laws of the Texas Prison System.

89. Stone, W., McAdams, C., & Kollert, J. (1974). *Texas Department of Corrections: A Brief History*. Huntsville: Research and Development Division Report, Texas Department of Corrections. The "Walls" Unit during the Civil War served as a prison for Union soldiers. Details of the early population at the Walls are sketchy and fragmented. The racial composition of the system was not known at that time, but anecdotal accounts suggest most convicts were white. In the event that a black or Hispanic convict was in the prison system, they were completely separated from white convicts.

90. This is somewhat of an oversimplification of the diversity of Texas, for unlike most other southern states, Hispanics were also a relevant group concerning both social and prison life. The bottom line is that Texas was much more than black and white.

91. We refer to the "Texas prison system" even though this moniker was not officially adopted by the Texas Legislature until 1927.

92. Walker, D. (1988). *Penology for Profit: A History of the Texas Prison System, 1867–1912*. College Station: Texas A&M University Press.

93. Ibid. See also *The New Handbook of Texas* (1996). Austin: Texas State Historical Association.

94. Crouch, B., & Marquart, J. *An Appeal to Justice.* See also Walker, D. *Penology for Profit,* who explains that "first-class" convicts such as those convicted of murder, arson, rape, horse stealing, burglary, perjury, or robbery were not permitted to work outside the prison walls. All other "second-class" convicts were sent to work in the lease system. Regardless of placement, in the fields or cell blocks in Huntsville, prisoners were strictly segregated by race.

95. Walker, D. *Penology for Profit.*

96. Martin, S., & Ekland-Olson, S. (1987). *Texas Prisons: The Walls Came Tumbling Down.* Austin: Texas Monthly Press.

97. Handbook of Texas Online, Prison System. Retrieved on May 30, 2006, from www.tsha.utexas.edu/handbook/online/articles/PP/jjp3.html. Also see Walker, D. *Penology for Profit.*

98. See http://www.lrl.state.tx.us/research/interim/reportDisplay.cfm?subjectID =4976&subject=Prison+labor for some of these early legislative investigations and inquiries into the lease and convict lease systems.

99. Handbook of Texas Online, Prison System. Retrieved on May 30, 2006, from www.tsha.utexas.edu/handbook/online/articles/PP/jjp3.html.

100. See, for example, Crouch, B., & Marquart, J. (1989). *An Appeal to Justice.*

101. George, A. (1895). *Texas Convict.* Bowie, TX: City Job Office: 7.

102. Walker, D. *Penology for Profit.*

103. The convict lease period continued up until roughly 1910. A letter written on June 15, 1907, by J.W. Reed Cedar Company shows a request for a convict lease. The text reads in its original uncorrected form as follows:

> Dear Sir: I notice an article in yesterdays Statesman, stating that your board would shortly receive bids for the least of a limited number of State Convicts, and as we are in need of men to Chop Cedar Timber, we would be glad to have you write us more fully in regard to leasing the convicts. What would be the minimum number of men you would lease us, and the minimum length of time, we could get them for? Also state who would be expected to pay the expense of guarding and maintaining the Convicts, and any other information you may be able to give us on the subject. Thanking you for an early reply, we beg to remain, Yours very truly, J.W. Reed Cedar Company.
> About what would the men cost us per month?

View the original scanned letter at http://www.tsl.state.tx.us/governors/rising/campbell-prisons.html.

104. Dates that prison farms came online are listed according to information provided on unit profiles at www.tdcj.state.tx.us. According to the published literature found online, there is some disagreement as to when the land was purchased. Official data collected by the Texas Department of Criminal Justice are used.

105. By the 1920s, the Texas prison system owned more than 81,000 acres of land across the eastern portion of Texas, much of it in the Sugar Land area on the Imperial Farm sugar plantation and what became the 1909 site for the Central Prison Farm.

106. Walker, D. *Penology for Profit,* 100–101.

107. In the 2002 movie *Sweet Home Alabama*, one character noted: "A plantation by any other name is just a farm. But it does roll off the tongue a little sweeter, doesn't it?"

108. It should also be noted that the punishments on the early prison farms were somewhat typical of a slave plantation. Most infamous was the bat, a long leather strap used to whip misbehaving inmates.

109. Walker, D. *Penology for Profit*, 126.

110. This reference refers to a quote in Oshinsky, D. *Worse than Slavery*, 55.

111. See ibid. for a similar discussion of life on prison farms in Mississippi.

112. See, for example, Tomlin, H. (1909). *The Man Who Fought the Brutality and Oppression of the Ring in the State of Texas for Eighteen Years and Won*. N.p.: 21.

113. Simmons, L. (1957). *Assignment Huntsville: Memoirs of a Texas Prison Official*. Austin: University of Texas Press. See this source generally for aspects of the 1930s Texas prison system.

114. This change was somewhat informal. Indeed, laws of the State of Texas governing penitentiaries still referred to penitentiaries as "farms" well into the 1970s and beyond.

115. The prison farms of the late 1800s and early 1900s generally featured dormitory style housing and had few cells. By the 1960s, however, Texas had opened several new prison facilities: Byrd (1964); Coffield (1965); Ellis (1965); and Ferguson (1967). As opposed to the prison farms, these new "units" had cell blocks and cells, along with dormitory housing areas. These living areas were completely segregated prior to 1965. Although the farms were still referred to as such informally, as a matter of formality, all Texas prisons were called units by the mid-1960s.

116. Hammett, A. B. J. (1963). *Miracle within the Walls*. Corpus Christi: South Texas Publishing: 90–93. This book was in large part a dedication to the service of O. B. Ellis, director of the Texas prison system, after his death at a 1961 Texas prison system board meeting.

117. See, for example, Sample, A. (1984). *Racehoss: Big Emma's Boy*. New York: Ballantine Books. Observations by those in or around Texas prisons at the time demonstrate the degree of racial segregation practiced in the system well into the 1960s. Albert "Race" Sample, a former Texas convict, wrote about his experience as a Texas prisoner in the late 1950s and 1960s and remarked: "Retrieve, formerly an all-white prison unit, had been repopulated a few years previously with the worst, most incorrigible black cons that were in the prison system." Despite the periodic shifting of races from one prison farm to the next, the rule remained in Texas prisons that races were to be kept separate in all aspects of prison administration.

118. See films made at the Ellis Unit in the 1960s by Jackson and his colleagues at http://www.folkstreams.net/film,122. Also see Jackson, B. (1972). *Wake up Dead Man: Afro-American Worksongs of Texas Prisons*. Cambridge, MA: Harvard University Press.

119. Ibid.

120. See, for example, ibid. This compilation of worksongs focused on the experience of black convicts working on racially segregated field force lines. Jackson did his work primarily at Ramsey I and II, Ellis (opened 1965), and Wynne.

121. Horton, D., & Nielsen, G. (2005). *Walking George: The Life of George John Beto and the Rise of the Modern Texas Prison System*. Denton: University of North Texas Press: 228.

122. Crouch, B., & Marquart, J. *An Appeal to Justice*, 246.

123. West's Texas Statutes and Codes (1975). Director's authority. Title 108 Penitentiaries, Art. 6166j: 1167. St. Paul, MN: West Publishing Company. It is unknown as to whether the change in the 1927 law allowing prisoner separation by "color" had anything to do with the 1972 filing of *Lamar v. Coffield* by inmate Allen Lamar (Lamar alleged discrimination against black inmates in the Texas prison system). In all likelihood, this change was significantly related to the Joint Committee on Prison Reform's recommendation to the Texas Legislature in 1974. Certainly, however, the *Lamar* suit was not far from the minds of the legislature.

124. Martin, S., & Ekland-Olson, S. *Texas prisons: The Walls Came Tumbling Down.* Freund, C. (1974, n.d.). "Reform Issue Heated in Huntsville Prison." *Dallas Morning News:* n.p.

125. Freund, C. (1974, n.d.). "Reform Issue Heated in Huntsville Prison." *Dallas Morning News:* n.p.

126. Texas Legislature. (1974). "Final Report of the Joint Committee on Prison Reform of the Texas Legislature." Retrieved July 6, 2006, from Legislative Reference Library from http://www.lrl.state.tx.us/research/interim/reportDisplay.cfm?subject ID=4976&subject=Prison+labor. This quote is in reference to pages 43–45 of the final report.

127. This mention of pending litigation was in reference to *Lamar v. Coffield*, 72-H-1393 (1972), a case from the U.S. District Court for the Southern District of Texas, filed by black inmate Allen L. Lamar and other inmates of the Texas prison system.

128. There were six recommendations concerning treatment by race; only the first three dealt specifically with racial and ethnic discrimination faced by inmates. The other recommendations dealt with discrimination against employees in hiring, training employees in human relations, and providing bilingual rules and regulations and programs to inmates.

129. Texas Legislature. "Final Report of the Joint Committee on Prison Reform of the Texas Legislature."

130. Ibid. Cover letter to members of the Sixty-fourth Legislature.

131. Crouch, B., & Marquart, J. *An Appeal to Justice*, 119.

132. Ibid.

133. Despite the fact that some progress was made, such as the broad desegregation of dormitories and wings in the summer of 1979, along with certain field forces, it would remain the official policy and practice of the Texas prison system to keep the races separate in all other areas of prison housing, namely cell block tiers and double cells, until the early 1990s.

Chapter 5

1. H. H. "Pete" Coffield, in his capacity as chairman of the Texas Board of Corrections, and each member of the Texas Board of Corrections (Walter L. Pfluger, James M. Windham, Lester Boyd, Walter M. Mischer, David D. Allen, W. Ervin James, Fred W. Shield, and L. H. True), were named as defendants in the lawsuit. W. J. Estelle, only one month on the job as the new director of TDC, succeeding George J. Beto, was also named as a defendant, as was Beto himself, who had resigned as director of TDC on September 1, 1972.

2. The eight inmates were Ernesto R. Montana, David R. Ruiz, Raul A. Rodriquez, Isaias Lara, Salvador Gonzales, Daniel Villalpando, Eduardo Salazar Mauricio, and David Robles. *Ruiz v. Estelle*, 503 F. Supp. 1265 (1980).

3. It should come as no surprise that many of these intervening inmates were members of the Eight Hoe Squad (discussed later in this chapter). In future intervention, several other Eight Hoe Squad members either were allowed or attempted to intervene in the case. For an excellent discussion of the dynamics of the Eight Hoe Squad, see Martin, S., & Ekland-Olson, S. (1987). *Texas Prisons: The Walls Came Tumbling Down*. Austin: Texas Monthly Press.

4. The four black defendant-intervenors were Eugene Alvarez, Nathan Cook, Robert Davis, and Willie Sewell. The two Mexican-American inmates were Reynaldo de la Cruz and Richard B. Martinez.

5. Between the October 1972 filing of the case and 1977, two cases with similar types of issues pertaining to racial and ethnic discrimination were consolidated with *Lamar v. Coffield*, Civil Action No. 72-H-1393 (1977): *Enriquez, et al. v. Estelle*, Civil Action No. 73-H-1374, and *Lamar v. Coffield, et al.*, Civil Action No. 72-H-1478. Civil Action No. 72-H-1478 was a civil rights lawsuit filed by Lamar that alleged TDC defendants (Coffield, Beto, McAdams, Shannon, and Pack) maintained racial discrimination and prosecution of black prisoners. In this suit, Lamar claimed that a manuscript that he had written which outlined his thoughts on economic, social, and political aspirations of blacks was confiscated by prison officials for racial reasons.

6. Lorenzo Davis was also a party to the original claims made by Lamar despite the case being styled with Lamar as the lead plaintiff.

7. *Lamar v. Coffield*, Consent Decree, Civil Action No. 72-H-1393 (1977). 2–3. This is the actual wording used by the court when referring to racial and ethnic groups of inmates.

8. Ibid.

9. Ibid.

10. It is actually unclear whether Lamar was born on this date in 1935, 1936, or 1937. Official Texas prison system records note 1935, Texas Youth Commission documents both 1935 and 1936, Lamar's mother 1936, and Federal Bureau of Prisons records 1937. Any inconsistency in ages and dates is a result of this discrepancy. We utilize 1936 for consistency.

11. Major portions of these sections on Lamar's childhood, including his delinquent and criminal history, were constructed from official documents maintained by the Texas Department of Corrections (TDC). All records were supplied to the author by TDC in February 2007. These records consist of Lamar's three incarcerations in TDC under inmate numbers (166341, 195139, and 391546, including federal register number for interstate transfers 11839-077). Portions of this record contained information about Lamar's stay in the Gatesville State School for Boys, including information on official arrests outside of the State of Texas.

12. Texas Department of Corrections, Admission Summary, Allen L. Lamar, #166341. Correspondence and official records to TDC from Superintendent of State Training School for Boys, Gatesville, Texas, April 17, 1962.

13. Correspondence and official records to TDC from Superintendent of State Training School for Boys, Gatesville, Texas, April 17, 1962.

14. Correspondence from TDC to Ms. Beulah Wilkins (Allen Lamar's mother)

on April 17, 1962, requesting that Mrs. Wilkins provide social history information about Allen Lamar.

15. Ibid.

16. Correspondence and official records to TDC from Superintendent of State Training School for Boys, Gatesville, Texas, April 17, 1962.

17. Ibid. Included in the information from the Superintendent of the Gatesville State School for Boys was the original court officer report on Lamar's delinquent and social history at his adjudication and eventual commitment to the State School for Boys. The quote in this section was taken directly from that report.

18. Ibid.

19. It was not until 1918 in Texas that the state raised the age of adult criminal responsibility to a minimum of seventeen. Prior to this time, the age of adult criminal responsibility was age nine, meaning those nine and older would be treated with adult justice and could be sent to work under the lease and contract systems or to Texas prison farms, which were adopted in the late 1800s and early 1900s. Prior to 1836, the age of adult criminal responsibility was age eight in Texas. Only in 1943 did the state adopt civil based procedures for juveniles.

20. Handbook of Texas Online, Gatesville State School for Boys. Retrieved on February 24, 2006, from www.tsha.utexas.edu/handbook/online/articles/GG/jjg2 .html.

21. Ibid.

22. Ibid.

23. Correspondence and official records to TDC from Superintendent of State Training School for Boys, Gatesville, Texas, April 17, 1962.

24. Lamar's self-report of these offenses to Texas prison officers indicate that disciplinary actions taken at the Gatesville State School for boys were for three escapes, for "talking back," and for sniffing gas. Texas Department of Corrections, Admission Summary, Allen L. Lamar, #166341.

25. Correspondence and official records to TDC from Superintendent of State Training School for Boys, Gatesville, Texas, April 17, 1962.

26. Texas Department of Corrections, Admission Summary, Allen L. Lamar, #166341. Files of the Identification and Criminal Records Division, State of Texas Department of Public Safety. FBI #654715B.

27. Texas Department of Corrections, Admission Summary, Allen L. Lamar, #166341. Files of the Identification and Criminal Records Division, State of Texas Department of Public Safety. FBI #654715B.

28. In official documents of this offense, there are numerous references to the fact that Lamar stole the purse from a "white woman."

29. Texas Department of Corrections, Admission Summary, Allen L. Lamar, #166341. Files of the Identification and Criminal Records Division, State of Texas Department of Public Safety. FBI #654715B.

30. Lamar received roughly one month of credit on his prison terms for the time he spent in the county jail prior to his pleas of guilty in Smith and Tarrant Counties.

31. It is unknown why this request was made and whether Lamar had anything to do with it. While only speculation, it is perhaps the case that Lamar found his time in the Bureau of Prisons more comfortable than what he had already experienced in TDC. Mr. Hyder's letter was sent to TDC on April 24, 1962, roughly fourteen days

into Allen's sentence. Also of interest is that Allen's mother wrote L. W. Hughes, the director of the Bureau of Classification and Records for TDC, on April 21, 1962, and relayed similar sentiments. This letter, uncorrected, reads:

> I, Mrs. Beulah Wilkins, the mother of Allen Lamar, am writing this letter concerning Allen's problems. Allen was given narcotics at the age of 13. Due to this fact he has spent most of this life in various correction institutions. Since his habit has cause him to be involved with the state and Federal Law. I have ask for their help, and they have informed me that they would co-operate together and try to get him in a Federal Narcotics Hospital. Since Allen has asked the Judge in Tyler, Texas for help, the State has consent to work out solution with the Federal—I am quite sure that you will receive a detail letter explaining the matter from them as soon as possible. Besides the narcotic problem Allen also has a serious illness. He received an operation in a Federal Institution. This operation was for a Throat desease but it has not heal yet. Allen has in his possession a statement from Dr. Snyder the physician I had him taking treatments from when he was home.

32. Texas Department of Corrections, Admission Summary, Allen L. Lamar, #166341. Elton M. Hyder (personal communication to Mr. Leon W. Hughes, Director of Bureau of Classification and Records, Texas Department of Corrections), April 24, 1962.

33. Texas Department of Corrections, Admission Summary, Allen L. Lamar, #166341.

34. Allen L. Lamar (personal communication to Richard C. Jones, Texas Department of Corrections), May 27, 1962.

35. Allen L. Lamar (personal communication to George J. Beto, Texas Department of Corrections), June 6, 1962.

36. George J. Beto (personal communication to inmate Allen L. Lamar, Texas Department of Corrections), June 14, 1962.

37. It was not uncommon for Beto to meet with several inmates a week at various prison units. Beto was known as "Walking George" by TDC wardens and officers, a moniker that reflected his hands-on administrative style and his frequent and unannounced visits to Texas prison units. Beto also believed that speaking personally with inmates was a valuable source of intelligence that could be used to preempt administrative and legal problems. See, for example, Dilulio, J. (1987). *Governing Prisons: A Comparative Study of Correctional Management.* New York: Free Press.

38. This was contrary to Lamar's claim that he was a Methodist at his prison admission and his mother's claim that he was raised Methodist. Lamar likely converted to Islam in TDC.

39. Beto was a Lutheran minister, as was his father. It is not known if this had anything to do with his specific tracking of Muslim prisoners. His concern and management style with Muslim prisoners probably relates to his experience on the Illinois Parole Board and his close friendship with former Stateville prison warden Joseph Ragan. Ragan, too, had issues with Muslim prisoners. See Crouch, B., & Marquart, J. (1989). *An Appeal to Justice: Litigated Reform of Texas Prisons.* Austin: University of Texas Press: 38–43.

40. George J. Beto (personal communication to L. W. Hughes, Texas Department of Corrections), July 2, 1962.

41. A hoe squad refers to a TDC job reference. Prisoners on the hoe squad were assigned to "stoop labor" in the fields, some of the toughest prisoner jobs in TDC at the time. Normally, most prisoners would begin their sentence on the hoe squad and then over time be rewarded with less laborious jobs, provided their attitude and conduct warranted such assignment.

42. The Point Incentive Program (PIP) was a method used by TDC in terms of evaluating inmates' progress and for awarding or taking away good-time credits. Inmates were rated as follows: unsatisfactory, below average, average, good, and outstanding on various indicators such as work, conduct, attitude, educational participation, recreational participation, religious participation, personal development, Alcoholics Anonymous, vocational training, and other special types of assignments.

43. Texas Department of Corrections Disciplinary Report, Inmate Allen Lamar #166341, September 20, 1963.

44. L. W. Hughes (personal communication to Warden McAdams, Texas Department of Corrections), September 20, 1963.

45. Jackson, B. (1972). *Wake Up Dead Man: Afro-American Worksongs of Texas Prisons*. Cambridge, MA: Harvard University Press. This excellent work focuses on black inmates working on the racially segregated hoe squads of the 1960s Ellis Unit.

46. Texas Department of Corrections Disciplinary Report, Inmate Allen Lamar #166341, October 11, 1964.

47. Warden C. L. McAdams (personal communication to Inmate Allen Lamar #166341, Texas Department of Corrections), April 19, 1965.

48. Texas Department of Corrections, Admission Summary, Allen L. Lamar, #166341.

49. The following is a description of events in this crime as taken from Lamar's appeal of his criminal conviction. The robbery was shown to have occurred about 9:00 A.M. The arresting officer testified that shortly thereafter he received a description of the automobile and its occupants over a police radio message, and while in search for the robber's automobile, he received another report. That report came from another officer in the chase and provided more complete information, including the license number of the automobile, which they were able to secure during their unsuccessful efforts to stop the same. The arresting officer further testified that he gave chase when he observed a 1958 Ford occupied by two "colored fellows" as it was being driven eighty or eighty-five miles per hour. While the officer was pursuing the automobile, he observed the driver steering the car with one hand as he leaned over and stuck something under the seat. The arrest was affected at 10:15 A.M. on the same morning, and the two men were carried to Slanton, Texas, where they were identified by the victim as the men who had robbed him. He also identified the automobile in custody of the police as being the identical vehicle that was at his gasoline pump at the time of the robbery.

50. See Martin, S., & Ekland-Olson, S. *Texas Prisons: The Walls Came Tumbling Down*, which details the background of Frances Jalet and how she became involved in Texas prisoner litigation.

51. Center for American History, Frances Jalet-Cruz Papers. University of Texas at Austin.

52. Martin, S., & Ekland-Olson, S. *Texas Prisons: The Walls Came Tumbling Down*.

53. Frances Jalet-Cruz (personal communication to Edward Mallet, Center for American History). Frances Jalet-Cruz Papers. University of Texas at Austin.

54. Allen L. Lamar (personal communication to Frances Jalet, Center for American History). Frances Jalet-Cruz Papers. University of Texas at Austin, January 9, 1974.

55. Martin, S., & Ekland-Olson, S. *Texas Prisons: The Walls Came Tumbling Down*. For an extended discussion of the Eight Hoe Squad and its history, see this excellent source.

56. Ibid., 53. This text is perhaps the single greatest source on the emergence of reform litigation in the Texas prison system and explains in abundant detail the circumstances surrounding Frances Jalet's efforts to assist TDC prisoners.

57. Ibid.

58. Extensive efforts were made to locate and retrieve Lamar's depositions in the District Court for the Southern District of Texas and Lamar's prison file during the time he filed the original suit. The District Court, after repeated requests, could not locate the file, which over the span of this lawsuit included hundreds of boxes. The file was located at the court's location in Houston, but from there could not be found. Texas prison administrators did uncover two of Lamar's three prison files, his first incarceration and his third incarceration in TDC, to which we were given full access. After significant efforts, the file for Lamar's second incarceration could not be located. Perhaps more of Lamar's motivation could have been found in these documents.

59. Crouch, B., & Marquart, J. *An Appeal to Justice: Litigated Reform of Texas Prisons*, 51.

60. Ibid., 52.

61. Document retrieved from the Center for American History. Frances Jalet-Cruz papers. University of Texas at Austin. This document, titled "Imperialism Means Imprisonment," was written by Lamar. This manifesto was allegedly confiscated by TDC officials for what Lamar claimed were "racial reasons." This confiscation led Lamar to file Civil Action 72-H-1478, *Allen Lamar v. Coffield, Beto, McAdams, Shannon, and Pack*, in which he claimed that TDC officials maintained racial discrimination and prosecution of black prisoners and that TDC officers denied him freedom of expression and free speech. Civil Action 72-H-1478 was eventually consolidated with *Lamar et al. v. Coffield et al.*, Civil Action 72-H-1393, the key racial discrimination and segregation case in this book.

62. Martin, S., & Ekland-Olson, S. *Texas Prisons: The Walls Came Tumbling Down*, 53.

63. Ibid.

64. In fact, Lamar did have a history of challenging racial segregation and discrimination prior to this lawsuit. From the moment of his criminal conviction that led to his second TDC incarceration, Lamar had challenged racial discrimination in jury selection. He had also filed suit against the Harris County Jail System concerning racial discrimination.

65. Martin, S., & Ekland-Olson, S. *Texas Prisons: The Walls Came Tumbling Down*, 53.

66. Inmate L. D. (personal communication, December 13, 2000). Letter in possession of the authors.

67. Several prisoners wrote to one of the present authors in 2000–2001 stating that they had known Lamar and reiterating the claim of the inmate quoted in the preceding letter.

Chapter 6

1. It should be noted that representing attorneys for the Texas attorney general's office and the U.S. Department of Justice changed several times during the course of this lawsuit. However, counsel for TDC inmates did not change.

2. Gerald Birnberg (personal communication, May 23, 2006).

3. Ibid.

4. Schlanger, M. (1999). "The Courts: Beyond the Hero Judge: Institutional Reform Litigation as Litigation." *Michigan Law Review,* 74, 1994–2036.

5. Discussions with a former counselor in the *Lamar* suit who believed that the Department of Justice took such an active role in this case because they were interested in being viewed as supporting civil rights. This individual also noted that they chose to focus on the civil rights of prisoners because they were relatively harmless politically.

6. TDC interoffice communication (communication to wardens and answers in response to DOJ interrogatories, September 27, 1974). This question posed to wardens was actually question number 2 of the DOJ interrogatories.

7. TDC interoffice communication (communication to wardens and answers in response to DOJ interrogatories, September 27, 1974). This question posed to wardens was actually question number 22 of the DOJ interrogatories.

8. TDC interoffice communication (communication to wardens and answers in response to DOJ interrogatories, September 27, 1974). This question posed to wardens was a part of question number 22 of the interrogatories.

9. Gerald Birnberg (personal communication, May 23, 2006).

10. TDC interoffice communication (communication to wardens and answers in response to DOJ interrogatories, September 27, 1974).

11. According to Gerald Birnberg, attorney for the black plaintiff class and Allen Lamar, negotiations continued until the day before trial. By the time of trial, all parties agreed to consent decree stipulations. According to a reputable source who wishes to remain anonymous, one reason the DOJ and individual plaintiff class lawyers agreed to a consent decree was that TDC and their lawyers arrived at the Federal Courthouse in Houston with a truckload of documents that would be used at trial. This strategy, if true, was perhaps an attempt to overwhelm and shock the opposing parties into a settlement absent litigation. This could not be verified.

12. Gerald Birnberg (personal communication, May 23, 2006).

13. *Lamar v. Coffield,* Consent Decree, Civil Action No. 72-H-1393 (1977): 4.

14. Ibid., 4–9. Minor portions of wording were taken out of the provisions of the consent decree.

15. At the time of the *Lamar* consent decree, TDC had experienced litigation. However, none had attacked wholesale the operation of the entire Texas prison system with the breadth and depth of *Lamar.* Despite the fact that *Lamar* never went to trial, unlike the better known *Ruiz* litigation, it stimulated massive operational changes in TDC, changes on par with those stimulated by *Ruiz.*

16. Texas Department of Corrections, Affirmative Action Plan, November 14, 1977: Preface.

17. Ibid., 4.

18. United States Comments on Defendants' Affirmative Action Plan, *Lamar v. Coffield*, Consent Decree, Civil Action No. 72-H-1393 (1977): 2.

19. Ed Idar, Special Assistant Attorney General (personal communication to the Honorable Robert O'Conor, Jr., January 25, 1978).

20. Frances Jalet (personal communication to W. J. Estelle, December 27, 1973). Center for American History, University of Texas at Austin.

21. W. J. Estelle (personal communication to Frances Jalet, January 18, 1974). Center for American History, University of Texas at Austin.

22. Allen L. Lamar (personal communication to Frances Jalet, April 24, 1974). Center for American History, University of Texas at Austin.

23. *Lamar v. Steele*, 693 F. 2d 559 (5th Cir. 1982): 559–562.

24. Ibid. On appeal to the Fifth Circuit, Lamar was awarded attorney's fees from Officer Steele individually. The issue of damages was remanded back to the original trial court for reconsideration.

25. TDC consultant Dr. Sherman Day (personal communication to TDC Director J. W. Estelle, April 19, 1979).

26. Defendants' Twenty-Two Month Progress Report. February 14, 1980.

27. Texas Department of Corrections Treatment Directorate (April 30, 1980). Lamar action plan questionnaire review, Research, Planning and Development Division, 20.

28. The significance of this cannot be overemphasized. At the Southern District, Judge William Wayne Justice and Judge Robert O'Conor and later Judge Lynn Hughes likely had frequent contact about these cases. Indeed, certain aspects of *Lamar* were expressly dependent upon *Ruiz* compliance.

29. Crouch, B., & Marquart, J. (1989). *An Appeal to Justice: Litigated Reform of Texas Prisons.* Austin: University of Texas Press: 126–127. Certain aspects of Judge Justice's ruling were eventually overturned by the Fifth Circuit Court of Appeals. However, this case had massive impacts on TDC operation.

30. Stipulation and Order Modifying Court's Order of March 5, 1984.

31. United States' Objections to Defendants' Plan for Assignment of Inmates to Two-Person Cells. September 6, 1985.

32. Ibid.

33. Defendants' Response to the United States' Petition for Imposition of Sanctions; Motion to Reconsider; Motion to Modify; and Motion to Transfer (March 25, 1991).

Chapter 7

1. Texas Department of Corrections, Admission Summary and Prison Files, Allen L. Lamar, #391546. Information on Lamar's progress in the Federal Bureau of Prisons was contained in yearly evaluations sent to TDC by the Federal Bureau of Prisons. Information in this section draws on those yearly evaluations of Lamar.

2. Allen Lamar, Federal Register Number, 11839-077. The exact date of Lamar's death is not known.

3. Crouch, B., & Marquart, J. (1989). *An Appeal to Justice: Litigated Reform of Texas Prisons*. Austin: University of Texas Press: 191–193.

4. Ibid.

5. Ibid.

6. Dilulio, J. (1987). *Governing Prisons: A Comparative Study of Correctional Management*. New York: Free Press.

7. The major class-action suits included *Guajardo v. Estelle*, which dealt with inmate correspondence to lawyers and the media and possession of law books within cells; *Lamar v. Coffield*, which dealt with racial segregation and discrimination in TDC operation; *Corpus and Sellars v. Estelle*, which dealt with the use of "jailhouse lawyers" in the assistance of other TDC prisoners; and *Ruiz v. Estelle*, which addressed numerous areas of TDC operation including the use of Building Tenders and overcrowding.

8. Gerald Birnberg (personal communication, May 23, 2006).

9. Status Conference, Judge Lynn N. Hughes, May 5, 1986. Order, Lynn N. Hughes, May 8, 1986.

10. Ekland-Olson, S. (1986). "Survey: Eligibility for Racially Integrated Cell Housing." Unpublished.

11. Texas Department of Corrections (1986). "Fact sheet: Nonfatal Stabbings by Race."

12. Kiely, K., & Freelander, D. (1986, October 8). "TDC is accused of not complying with court order, desegregation at issue." *Houston Post*, pp. A5–A8.

13. Ibid.

14. Ibid.

15. Stipulation and Order, Lynn N. Hughes, November 20, 1986.

16. Stipulation and Order Regarding Implementation of Rational Objective Criteria for Assignment of Inmate Housing and Jobs and For Monitoring Thereof, December 21, 1987, Ordered, December 29, 1987.

17. Defendants' Response to the United States' Petition for Imposition of Sanctions; Motion to Reconsider; Motion to Modify; and Motion to Transfer, March 25, 1991, pp. 14–15.

18. Jeremy Schwartz, Attorney for DOJ Special Litigation Section (personal communication to Michael Hodge, Texas Assistant Attorney General representing TDC, July 27, 1989).

19. Michael Hodge, Texas Assistant Attorney General representing TDC (personal communication to Jeremy Schwartz, Attorney for DOJ Special Litigation Section, August 3, 1989).

20. Nancy K. Juren, Assistant Attorney General representing TDC (personal communication to Jeremy Schwartz, Attorney for DOJ Special Litigation Section, October 26, 1989).

21. Texas Department of Criminal Justice, Institutional Division (Internal communication: Preliminary analysis of interracial incidents between two or more inmates which resulted in major punishments, October 1, 1988–June 30, 1989, Classification and treatment directorate, October 12, 1989).

22. Defendants' Response to the United States' Petition for Imposition of Sanc-

tions; Motion to Reconsider; Motion to Modify; and Motion to Transfer, March 25, 1991.

23. John R. Dunne, Assistant Attorney General DOJ (personal communication to Nancy K. Juren, Assistant Attorney General representing TDC, July 13, 1990).

24. John R. Dunne, Assistant Attorney General DOJ (personal communication to Nancy K. Juren, Assistant Attorney General representing TDC, May 14, 1990).

25. Defendants' Response to the United States' Petition for Imposition of Sanctions; Motion to Reconsider; Motion to Modify; and Motion to Transfer, March 25, 1991: 20.

26. Texas Department of Criminal Justice—Institutional Division (1990, June). In-Cell integration committee: Inter-Office Communications.

27. Zook, J. (1991, February 7). "Fines Sought against State in Prison Case." *Houston Chronicle*, pp. 13A.

28. Ibid.

29. Ibid.

30. Defendants' Response to the United States' Petition for Imposition of Sanctions; Motion to Reconsider; Motion to Modify; and Motion to Transfer, March 25, 1991: 21.

31. Like *Ruiz* (the most contested lawsuit ever faced by TDC), beginning compliance with *Lamar* stipulations took decades. After decades, however, TDC stipulated to the dictates of William Wayne Justice, and did so virtually overnight as in *Lamar*. Despite the fact *Lamar* and *Ruiz* were filed in the same year (1972), stipulation to the cell desegregation issue in *Lamar* occurred nearly five years after major compliance with *Ruiz*. By this time, and heavily influenced by the experience with *Ruiz* (including the massive rise in inmate homicides in 1984–1985), TDC was experiencing massive changes that can help explain the system's move toward compliance with *Lamar*.

32. TDC began implementing training on racial desegregation while the plan was under review by the DOJ. The plan had also not been accepted and ordered by the court at this time.

33. Texas Department of Criminal Justice—Institutional Division. (1991, August). Status report on implementation of the March 1991 plan for in-cell integration: Appendix H.

34. It should be noted that not all general population inmates are held in cells. The great majority are housed in dormitory housing, which had long been desegregated by TDC. The plan applied only to those in the general population custodies of minimum, medium, and close who were to receive cell housing assignments. However, all inmates would be evaluated as to their desegregation eligibility in the event that they required cell placement in the future.

35. The random cell assignment process and selection of the first available cell was not purely random with regard to all factors, but only with regard to race. Prison officials did not blindly house the inmate in the first available cell if it would result in a security risk by placing a passive inmate in the first available cell that contained an aggressive convict. It was the first available cell consistent with an inmate's security and health needs, regardless of race. Race was only considered in the selection of the cell if, for example, housing a member of one race with a member from a different race would be a security risk.

36. TDC continued to racially segregate cells in receptions centers through 2005. Following the U.S. Supreme Court decision in *Johnson v. California* (2005), TDC set out to racially desegregate cells in reception centers. By this time, racial desegregation was an accepted and routine policy in TDC. A visit to one reception center in Texas (Byrd Unit, Huntsville, Texas) in late 2005 suggested that prison officers viewed the desegregation of this facility with little concern.

37. Texas Department of Criminal Justice — Institutional Division. (1991, August). Status report on implementation of the March 1991 plan for in-cell integration.

38. Ibid.

39. By this time, TDC had long desegregated other living and common areas, most notably, dormitory housing arrangements.

40. For example, Zook, J. "Fines Sought against State in Prison case," pp. 13A.

41. Fair, K. (1991 June 22). "Racial Tension Expected as Prisons Integrate Cells." *Houston Chronicle*, pp. 1A; 18A.

42. Ibid.

43. For example, Mitchell, M. (1991, July 23). "Integration was Reason for Escape." *Palestine Herald Press*, pp. A1; A10.

44. Ibid.; Mitchell, M. (1991, July 23). "TDCJ Officials Set to Integrate Prisoners' Cells." *Palestine Herald Press*, pp. A1; A10.

45. Mitchell, M. "Integration was Reason for Escape," pp. A1; A10.

46. Ibid.

47. Ibid.

48. Texas Department of Criminal Justice. (1992, July). Procedures for the management of inmates who refuse integrated cell assignments.

49. Ibid. Theoretically, an inmate could incur multiple refusals during a single attempt to house them. Since an inmate remained eligible for desegregation even after a refusal, a situation could occur in which all "next available cells" would result in a racially desegregated cell assignment, and hence multiple refusals during one attempt to house the inmate. Provided the inmate was disciplined on each count, this means that in one attempt to house the inmate, a refusing inmate could potentially lose all good time, drop several time-earning classes, be restricted to a cell with loss of all privileges, be moved to close custody, and/or be placed in solitary confinement. This was a high price to pay for cell refusals. Several inmates who responded to a racial desegregation survey placed in the prison newspaper remarked of how they had lost years of good time and suffered other consequences because they refused to accept a desegregated cell assignment. Clearly, TDC followed through with real sanctions for those who refused a cell assignment.

50. Texas Department of Criminal Justice. (1991, October). Monitoring survey No. 1: In-Cell integration plan. Inmates who have refused integrated cell assignments.

51. Susan Bowers, Senior Trial Attorney DOJ (personal communication to Nancy K. Juren, Assistant Attorney General, Texas Attorney General's Office, June 4, 1992).

52. Consult court docket for specific references to such requests by inmates.

53. *Lamar v. Coffield*, 951 F. Supp. 629 (S.D. Tex. 1996).

Chapter 8

1. Texas Department of Criminal Justice—Institutional Division. (1990, June). In-Cell integration committee. Inter-Office Communications.

2. TDC had also stipulated to and were in compliance with other *Lamar* issues pertaining to the removal of racial and ethnic discrimination in such areas as job assignments, non-cell housing such as in dormitories, inmate publications, punishments, the use of racial and ethnic epithets, and additional areas in the original *Lamar* decree and agreed judgment. The remaining and contentious issue of cell desegregation was the last component of the *Lamar* decree.

3. *Ruiz v. Estelle*, 503 F. Supp. 1265 (1980).

4. McLeod, R. (1978). *Racial Desegregation of Inmate Housing on the Wynne Unit, Texas Department of Corrections: Its Early Implementation.* Unpublished master's thesis. Sam Houston State University, Huntsville, TX.

5. During the June 1991 training, a total of 1,627 staff members—from all levels of TDC operation, from regional directors to correctional officers—were trained on all aspects of *Lamar* and in-cell desegregation, including the use of the IDF. Information obtained from "Rank/Title and Number of Staff Trained on Implementation of In-Cell Integration Plan."

6. Despite the fact that the IDF did not become officially adopted until late 1991, it was already being used prior to this time and there was a full year of data for 1991. It should also be noted again that the IDF did not track all offender incidents in TDC, only those involving two or more known inmates where a disciplinary report was filed on at least one inmate. Thus, it probably captured more serious inmate-on-inmate incidents, those of most concern to prison administrators. Like any official data collection, the IDF probably suffered from limitations of incident discovery and documentation on the part of officers. The extent of this is unknown, but it is likely that the IDF in some way underestimated the entire number of incidents in TDC. The assumption is that whatever was captured by the IDF was consistently done throughout the years regardless of the racial makeup of inmates involved in the incident. The trends in the data seem to support this conclusion, but it cannot be known for certain.

7. The entering of IDF data was done through a simple interface that required only that staff members check a box on the interface, the exception being the narrative of the incident which had to be typed. This interface would flag potential errors in data entry that made errors in IDF data entry minimal.

8. Fields on the IDF were used to determine whether an incident involved inmates of the same race (intraracial) or a different race (interracial), whether the incident was racially motivated, whether the incident was gang-related, and whether the incident occurred among cell partners. The IDF also included fields for a brief narrative of the incident, whether the incident involved weapons, the location of the incident, including the injury level sustained by inmate(s), and whether the offender was a victim or assailant among other areas of information.

9. In reality, TDC had been using the IDF since 1988, but it was not a formal part of monitoring desegregation outcomes. Prior to 1991, the IDF form was used in pilot data collection and it primarily served as a tool to argue that desegregation, particularly among medium- and close-custody inmates, would not be desirable because

of higher levels of violence. We had access to a partial year of IDF form data from 1990, but because TDC did not collect systematic data on double cells, this data was not used. Lagging a year also allowed time for any problems with the IDF to be overcome. We begin the data analysis in 1991, when double-cell data were systematically collected and maintained and the point when double cells began being desegregated on a large-scale basis.

10. The only changes to the IDF came in the form of minor changes in TDC, for example, changing the name of a particular custody or the adding of a different classification. There were no substantive changes to the actual form, the types of incidents qualifying for IDF completion, or the procedure by which they were to be completed. Thus, the IDF remained relatively unchanged during the 1990s until it was discontinued in 2000.

11. TDCJ Executive Services (personal communication, August 8, 2006).

12. We realize there are numerous issues to officially collected data. One major concern is that prison officers may handle similar incidents differently and this would impact the level and type of incidents documented within or between different prison units. Regardless of these and other concerns with official data, the IDF data collection is the "official" record on the aftermath of cell desegregation.

13. It should be noted that the main TDC housing area, dormitories, was fully desegregated in that black and white and Hispanic inmates lived in the same dormitory, and sometimes in the same "cubicle" area of the dormitory. Thus, the actual number of inmates desegregated was far more than the number housed exclusively within double cells.

14. Trulson, C., &. Marquart, J. (2002). "Inmate Racial Integration: Achieving Racial Integration in the Texas Prison System." *Prison Journal*, 82, 498–525.

15. Texas Department of Criminal Justice-Institutional Division. (2005). Offenders restricted from in-cell integration, percent of double cells desegregated, 1991–2005.

16. Because of missing data in 1997 due to TDC software changes in this year, the figures for 1997 are a product of averages from the years 1996 and 1998.

17. This category was not broken down into fist/feet/hands or verbal altercation.

18. Texas Department of Criminal Justice-Institutional Division. (1991, August). Status report on implementation of the March 1991 plan for in-cell integration: Appendix D.

19. Despite the best efforts by prison officers, it was perhaps difficult to untangle the true motivations behind interracial assaults. The concept of racial motivations is a fleeting concept: there may be numerous motives to engage in an interracial assault, some of which may be at least tacitly related to race.

20. Data were not sufficiently detailed to make a determination of "repeat offender" incidents. Thus, it could have been the case that many incidents, even racially motivated incidents, were the result of repeat performances by a few inmates.

21. Using all male inmate-on-inmate incidents in TDC (35,995) as a baseline, and including unclear determinations with incidents confirmed racially motivated, the percent of racially motivated incidents was roughly 28 percent of all incidents. Using only interracial incidents as a baseline number reveals that confirmed and unclear determinations for racial motivation rise to roughly 63 percent of all interracial incidents. It is faulty, however, to assume that all unclear determinations were racially

motivated, although some may make that argument. Concluding that one half of the unclear racial motivations were actually motivated by race, and using all interracial incidents as a baseline number, reveals roughly 35 percent of interracial incidents as racially motivated. Regardless of interpretation, one must remember that these incidents were spread across numerous TDC units, thousands of inmates, and over nearly a decade.

22. For example, the intraracial rate of incidents in 1991 is 48 per 1,000 inmates and was calculated by dividing the number of intraracial incidents in 1991 by the TDC male population in 1991 (as found in Table 8.2), and multiplied by 1,000 (2,269 divided by 47,262 multiplied by 1,000 = 48).

23. It is worth noting that correctional officers among the various units probably were not able to detect all inmate-on-inmate incidents, and it is equally likely that not all inmate-on-inmate incidents were reported whether they were interracial or intraracial. This is simply a disadvantage of official data, whether involving prison incidents or arrests for crimes in the larger society.

Chapter 9

1. All else being equal usually never works out that way. Procedurally, TDC's random assignment plan to the first available cell should have guaranteed that the only difference between the segregated and desegregated double cell populations was just that. In both populations, TDC officers attempted to ensure equal status in cells based on factors critical to institutional security. In reality, we will never know if the segregated and desegregated cell populations were truly equals.

2. The random nature of TDC's cell desegregation policy is important when comparing both raw numbers and rates of violence in the desegregated and segregated cell populations. The assumption is that the inmates in the desegregated and segregated cell populations are equal on the factors that might make a difference when engaging in an inmate-on-inmate incident.

3. One plausible explanation for the slightly disproportionate (high) level of interracial cell partner incidents relative to the proportion of desegregated double cells in 1991 and 1992 may relate to the newness of this policy in TDC. Particularly in 1991, desegregated inmates may have in fact perpetrated a disproportionate number of interracial cell partner assaults, due in some way to race, because of this major policy change. In short, they had not been conditioned to this change yet. Another possibility may be that officers paid more attention to documenting interracial cell partner incidents than intraracial cell partner incidents, especially in 1991, when the newness of this policy and disproportionality were greatest. These are only speculations but they are plausible. Even noting these possibilities, the discrepancy between the proportion of double cells desegregated and the proportion of interracial cell partner violence was still quite small.

4. The random celling process occurred after TDC made race-neutral determinations such as custody level. For example, cell-eligible inmates would not be placed in the first available and appropriate cell anywhere in a particular prison unit. Their custody level would first be determined; once at that custody's cell block, they would be randomly housed.

5. A case could also be made that the lower level of interracial violence relative to the proportion of desegregated cells resulted from removing the boundaries to segregation. In short, segregation actually produced more tension and violence, and when those boundaries were removed via cell desegregation, tensions and violence decreased. There may or may not be some truth to this argument, but we do not believe it explains the slight differences between the proportion of desegregated cells and the proportion of interracial cell partner incidents, just as we do not believe this difference can be explained by a selection bias.

6. Racial restrictions occur for a defined set of reasons, including occurrences in the free world and in prison. Some potential justifications for racial restrictions include confirmed membership in a group or gang that espouses racial superiority, a history of interracial incidents as victim or perpetrator in prison over a short period of time (e.g., three or more interracial incidents in two years), or free world interracial victimization (including family members) by another race. This list is not exhaustive. In reality, racial restrictions occurred on a case-by-case basis and can be supported by a number of other valid situations related to maintaining prison security and order. Yet they are few and far between.

7. In any given year, TDC racially restricts less than 1 percent of all inmates who are eligible for double cells. The percent of restricted double cell eligible inmates hovers around .20–.35 percent for any given year, as reported in the TDCJ-ID report "Offenders Restricted from In-Cell Integration, 1991-2005." Thus, desegregation in TDC cannot be characterized as focusing only on the best risks. Only those with documented and valid reasons are racially restricted. Even then, racial restrictions are periodically reevaluated such that a restricted inmate could become eligible for desegregation.

8. We did not have access to individual data concerning the types of inmates segregated and desegregated within cells over time. We can only assume that TDC's cell-assignment process was random—that each inmate had an equal chance at receiving a segregated or desegregated cell assignment provided they were not racially restricted—and that the segregated and desegregated cell populations were not somehow different. It was also noted that racial restrictions were extremely rare.

9. Although these incidents would have been prevented and not been considered racially motivated cell partner incidents without in-cell desegregation, it is certainly possible these individuals could have been involved in a racially motivated incident without necessarily being cell partners. Assuming cell partnership would have been the only instance in which the individuals involved would have had the opportunity to be involved in a racially motivated incident, this then is the true impact of in-cell desegregation in the Texas prison system.

10. Instead of second-guessing TDC procedure and accuracy in determining racial motivations, we chose to adhere to their determinations of an incident as racially motivated or not. Assuming officers made mistakes in these determinations, however, one might reasonably assume that one-half of the unclear determinations might have actually been racially motivated. Even doing so reveals that roughly two-thirds of all interracial cell partner incidents were not racially motivated—a virtual handful of incidents among the expansive TDC of the 1990s.

11. Despite the extremely low number of racially motivated cell partner incidents, such incidents did occur at a slightly higher level than would be expected based on the

population of inmates desegregated within double cells. This is with the exception of 1991, 1993, and 1994. In other years, racially motivated cell partner incidents were disproportionate to racially motivated incidents overall. For example, in 1995, 33 percent of all racially motivated incidents were among desegregated cell partners, although desegregated cell partners accounted for roughly 26 percent of the TDC population. Despite some evidence of disproportionality in certain years, the raw numbers of differences are extremely small, in addition to the extremely small number of racially motivated incidents. Based on the entire decade, however, the 329 racially motivated cell partner incidents accounted for 24 percent of all racially motivated incidents, whereas racially desegregated cell partners accounted for 23 percent of all TDC male inmates, on average. In an overall view, there was little evidence of racially motivated cell partner incidents occurring disproportionate to racially motivated incidents among non-celled desegregated inmates.

12. For interpretation, the rate of 15 per 1,000 intraracial incidents in 1991 is obtained by taking the raw number of intraracial cell partner incidents in 1991 (275), divided by the number of inmates segregated within cells in 1991 (18,212), multiplied by 1,000. The rate of 22 per 1,000 interracial incidents in 1991 is obtained by taking the number of interracial cell partner incidents in 1991 (136), divided by the number of inmates desegregated within cells in 1991 (6,134), multiplied by 1,000.

13. We realize that with complete racial segregation, such as separate prisons for white, black, and Hispanic inmates, all interracial and racially motivated incidents would be prevented.

14. However, it is still possible that the cell partners in this study who engaged in racially motivated violence would have had at least some opportunity to do so while not desegregated cell partners. We do not know if all these incidents would have been avoided with continued cell segregation, or whether all would have still occurred. It can even be argued that cell desegregation prevented the more general racially motivated violence and thus, without desegregation, there would have been more violence. The U.S. Supreme Court in *Johnson v. California* (2005) even noted the possibility that segregation may exacerbate the racial tensions in prisons. Of course, it can be argued the other way as well.

15. Many changes have come to the organization of the *Echo* since 2000. Much of this was in response to the escape of seven TDC inmates from the John Connally prison unit in December 2000.

16. Renaud, J. (2002). *Behind the Walls: A Guide for Families and Friends of Texas Prisons*. Denton: University of North Texas Press.

17. Ibid.

18. Responses were kept in their original form, including misspellings and other grammatical errors.

19. It should be noted that racial proportions in TDC were quite balanced over the decade of the 1990s, and even more so after 2000. While black inmates were the most prevalent racial group, the population was well represented by white and Hispanic inmates. It was not the case that a huge majority were one race versus the other, which might then contribute to a higher rate of intraracial incidents, by proportion.

20. The abandonment of the IDF led to severe restrictions on the breadth of data obtained by TDC as related to examining the impact of desegregation beyond 1999. While TDC continued to collect data on inmate-on-inmate incidents, such data did not have numerous important data fields as on the IDF.

21. Of the inmate-on-inmate incidents documented by TDC from 2000 to 2005, not shown in tabular form is that roughly 66 percent were characterized as an offender assault (50 percent) or an offender assault with a weapon (16 percent). Six percent of incidents were characterized as a "disturbance" by TDC, 1 percent were characterized as a "racial disturbance," and just over 26 percent were characterized as an attempted sexual assault. TDC experienced twenty-four homicides during this time, which accounted for less than one-half of one percent of all inmate-on-inmate incidents.

22. We realize our use of aggregate statistics to explain the individual behavior of inmates can be considered an ecological fallacy of sorts. Since we did not have access to forms of individual data, we do not specifically assume that our aggregate data and assumptions would apply to all individual cases.

23. We received one letter from an inmate that gave interesting qualitative detail as to the potential of the mentioned factors. This well-educated and long-time prison inmate explained that intraracial incidents among Hispanics tend to receive much attention by prison officials because of underlying gang issues. This inmate also explained that interracial violence, particularly that perpetrated on white inmates, was underreported. White inmates are turned into "cash cows," according to this inmate, and incidents against them take place "away from prying eyes. Cells are invaded. Guards are occupied while beatings are administered in shower stalls. Not only does this happen frequently, but there also exists a belief among many Anglo officers that an Anglo convict who reports violence, who complains of beatings, is weak and therefore not worthy of attention." This is not to suggest that TDC has not experienced its share of racial disturbance or riots. These do happen but not at a consistent pace, nor are they attributed to cell desegregation.

24. What we are suggesting here is that with complete and utter racial segregation, TDC would have likely experienced the same frequency of incidents than before desegregation. With desegregation, only the color of inmates involved in incidents changed, and the motivation of such cross racial incidents was rarely due to race. We cannot confirm for certain this would have happened.

25. Sherman Bell, TDC official (personal communication, March 19, 2000).

26. Such units were not subject to *Lamar* stipulations because TDC argued that they needed time to observe and evaluate inmates so as to better house them in the first available and appropriate cell once they arrived at their long-term prison unit— something that could not be done without a period of observation and evaluation of new prison commitments. Interestingly, this is the same argument used by the California Department of Corrections in defending their segregation practice in reception centers in 2005.

Chapter 10

1. Surprisingly, however, very little systematic attention has focused on racial and ethnic contact and outcomes in the prison environment—despite a plethora of anecdotal accounts of periodic race riots and racial strife.

2. Gordon, M. (1964). *Assimilation in American Life*. New York: Oxford University Press. This is not to say that racial and ethnic relations were not studied to some extent prior to this time. Rather, it is to suggest that the more systematic inquiry did not develop until the very early 1900s.

3. Dinitz, S. (1978). "Nothing Fails Like a Little Success." *Criminology*, 16, 225–238.

4. Schaefer, R. (2008). *Racial and Ethnic Groups*, 8th ed. Upper Saddle River, NJ: Prentice-Hall.

5. The concept of psychological proximity is perhaps best embodied in the concept of integration. Whereas desegregation concerns the removal of the barriers to interracial and interethnic contact, integration is much different. Integration is more about a state of mind that cannot be forced or achieved by the removal of barriers.

6. Even in places where there is high interracial contact, such as in schools and in the workplace, individuals are relatively free to self-segregate and avoid each other to a great degree. This is not integration; rather, it remains a form of desegregation. Indeed, desegregation can be viewed on a scale of intensity. Interracial contact with the opportunity to self-segregate and avoid is less intense than desegregation where one is forced into interracial contact with little to no opportunity for self-segregation or avoidance. Thus, desegregation in public schools, police agencies, and the workplace, for example, is much different than desegregation in Texas prisons or the military where members of different racial groups are in situations of close and inescapable proximity. This is true even for those not sharing a cell with a member of another race. There is perhaps no social setting that can approximate the intensity, duration, and magnitude of interracial contact that is found in the prison setting. And still, desegregation in the Texas prison system cannot be accurately described as integration in the true sense of the word.

7. Robertson, J. (2006). "Separate but Equal in Prison: *Johnson v. California* and Common Sense Racism." *Journal of Criminal Law & Criminology*, 16, 795–848.

8. Allport, G. (1954). *The Nature of Prejudice*. Boston: Addison-Wesley. See also, Ellison, C., & Powers, D. (1994). "The Contact Hypothesis and Racial Attitudes among Black Americans." *Social Science Quarterly*, 75, 385–400. It should be noted that the contact hypothesis was a framework about intergroup relations in general, whether they be racial, religious, ethnic, or otherwise.

9. See, for example, a study that examined outcomes. Sherif, M., Harvey, O. J., White, B., Hood, W. R., & Sherif, C. W. (1961). *Intergroup Conflict and Cooperation: The Robbers Cave Experiment*. Norman: Oklahoma University Book Exchange.

10. Allport, G. *The Nature of Prejudice*. See also Ellison, C., & Powers, D. "The Contact Hypothesis and Racial Attitudes among Black Americans."

11. Ibid. Although the tenets of the contact hypothesis are predicated primarily at the individual or social-psychological level, the contact hypothesis does implicate that structural conditions operate as well to condition interracial contact. See also Pettigrew, T. (1998). "Intergroup Contact Theory." *Annual Review of Psychology*, 49, 65–85.

12. There are some limitations as to the application of the contact hypothesis. For example, the relative importance of each condition is not known, nor whether all conditions must be present for positive contact outcomes. The contact hypothesis also made little mention of the determinants of contact in the first place or the relative importance of the intensity of contact and the level of exposure to members of different racial groups. Also neglected was a discussion of whether the group or venue in which contact occurs makes a difference, for example, among prison inmates in a penitentiary or among members of an athletic team at a university. The concepts of the contact

hypothesis are also somewhat unclear theoretically and methodologically, and have been operationalized in numerous ways in the literature. Regardless of these and other recognized limitations, the basic premise of the contact hypothesis has much relevance to understanding the outcomes of the desegregation of Texas prison inmates. This premise is that positive outcomes following interracial contact are most likely found in the presence of conditioning factors—contact alone is not sufficient. This perspective seems especially applicable to desegregation in the prison environment. Moreover, a reading of literature on the contact hypothesis leaves one with the impression that certain conditions, when present, serve to enhance interracial contact outcomes or facilitate positive interracial outcomes. This is not to suggest that all conditions must be present. The major problem with the contact hypothesis, however, is that the conditions offered by Allport are so wide-ranging that they are amendable to numerous proxies and definitions. Research has also revealed that the contact hypothesis can generalize to various locales. For a good review, see Pettigrew, T. "Intergroup Contact Theory." For a discussion of some of the various operationalizations, and a critique of previous research on the equal status contact hypothesis, see Trulson, C., & Marquart, J. (2002). "The Caged Melting Pot: Toward an Understanding of the Consequences of Desegregation in Prisons." *Law & Society Review,* 36, 743–781. See also Pettigrew, T. "Intergroup Contact Theory."

13. The concept of "equal status" is a fleeting concept. There is perhaps no social setting where two individuals can truly be considered status equals. This is especially the case if one considers both expected and perceived ideas of equal status. However, TDC's random-celling plan attempted to match the most compatible offenders within cells on factors that would normally produce important status differentials *in the prison setting.* For example, by placing two "passive" inmates together, the status differential of "strong" versus "weak" or "active" versus "passive" is lessened or avoided. There may have been numerous other status differentials that TDC was unable to account for when it attempted to match inmates to the closest extent possible. Yet the factors the system used were closely linked to behavioral outcomes in prison.

14. See generally Trulson, C., & Marquart, J. (2002). "The Caged Melting Pot."

15. Feeley, M., & Rubin, E. (2000). *Judicial Policy Making and the Modern State.* New York: Cambridge University Press. The "larger realities of prison administration" refer to the idea that prison administration does not exist within a vacuum. Although at one time prison systems were largely autonomous organizations, the reality of prison administration post-1970s was the heavy reliance on outside entities, such as the state legislature, in their operation. The importance of incrementalism is that oftentimes prison administrators were unable to implement the mandates of decisions and decrees without the financial backing of the legislature. Prison administrators could only move toward full compliance once support by legislatures or other entities was secured.

16. Fabelo, T. (1999). *Sourcebook of Texas Adult Justice Population Statistics, 1988–1998.* Austin: Criminal Justice Policy Council.

17. This is not to say that there were not other inmates to fill the place of those removed from the general population ranks. We have no evidence to suggest there was or was not a replacement effect. However, we know that the lack of appropriate space for such offenders in the late 1980s led to these inmates being housed in the general prisoner population—a factor that TDC administrators conceded would have made desegregation impossible and very dangerous at that time.

18. Pettigrew, T. "Intergroup Contact Theory."

19. Allport, G. *The Nature of Prejudice*, 281. See also Ellison, C., & Powers, D. "The Contact Hypothesis and Racial Attitudes among Black Americans."

20. Gaes, G., Wallace, S., Gilman, E., Klein-Saffran, J., & Suppa, S. (2002). "The Influence of Prison Gang Affiliation on Violence and Other Prison Misconduct." *Prison Journal*, 82, 359–385.

21. Some may consider this a selection bias, for example, that Texas single-celled gang members and others, thus precluding the desegregation of the worst risks. Two facts need to be noted with such a claim. First, gang members and other intransigent inmates constituted an extremely small proportion of inmates in the Texas prison system during the timeframe of this study—roughly 5 percent systemwide. The second is that prison administrators cannot operate the prison setting as a controlled experiment on race relations. Security criteria dictated that these individuals be removed from the general population for prisoner and staff safety and institutional security. Thus, while some of the worst risk inmates were weeded out and not able to have a chance at desegregation, such would have occurred without the desegregation mandate. And, some of the worst risk inmates were not predators, but potential prey that needed protection. The other 90–95 percent of general prisoner population inmates were eligible for desegregation. And it is not the case that such inmates, from all accounts, actually preferred to be mixed with another race.

22. This argument might also hold true for those at the unit level who were steadfastly opposed to desegregation in the late 1980s and early 1990s when desegregation was about to become a reality.

23. Sherif, M. (1966). *In a Common Predicament.* Boston: Houghton-Mifflin.

24. Sykes, G. (1958). *The Society of Captives.* Princeton: Princeton University Press.

25. Hemmens C., & Marquart, J. (1999). "The Impact of Inmate Characteristics on Perceptions of Race Relations in Prisons." *International Journal of Offender Therapy and Comparative Criminology*, 43, 230–247. An alternative unintended consequence, however, is that inmates may react to racial desegregation with an "us against them" mentality, thus displacing violence from each other onto staff members. On that same note, offenders may also recognize that officers have little say concerning desegregation.

26. Jacobs, J. (1982). "The Limits of Racial Integration in Prison." *Criminal Law Bulletin*, 18, 117–153: 120–121.

27. Irwin, J. (2005). *The Warehouse Prison: Disposal of the New Dangerous Class.* Los Angeles: Roxbury Publishing Company.

28. See, however, Hemmens C., & Marquart, J. "The Impact of Inmate Characteristics on Perceptions of Race Relations in Prisons." *International Journal of Offender Therapy and Comparative Criminology*, 43, 230–247.

29. Henderson, M., Cullen, F., Carroll, L., & Feinberg, W. (2000). "Race, Rights, and Order in Prison: A National Survey of Wardens on the Racial Integration of Prison Cells." *Prison Journal*, 80, 295–308.

30. Ibid.

31. Ibid.

32. *Johnson v. California*, 543 U.S. 499 (2005).

33. Oral arguments in *Johnson v. California*. November 2, 2004, p. 26. Oral argu-

ments can be retrieved at http://www.supremecourtus.gov/oral_arguments/argument _transcripts/03-636.pdf.

34. *Johnson v. California*, 543 U.S. 499 (2005).

35. *Garrison Johnson v. State of California*, 321 F.3d 791 (9th Cir. 2003).

36. *Lee v. Washington*, 390 U.S. 333 (1968).

37. *Johnson v. California*, 543 U.S. 499 (2005).

38. The Ninth Circuit originally held the CDC's practice constitutional under the rational basis test. This test is normally used in prisoner rights cases. Under this test, rules, regulations, and practices that impinge on inmates' constitutional rights are considered inherently valid as long as the rule, regulation, or practice is related to a legitimate penological interest such as to maintain security, control, and rehabilitation. The U.S. Supreme Court held that the rational basis test was inappropriate in this instance. Because race is considered a suspect classification, any differential treatment or classification by race is considered inherently suspect, and must be subject to the legal standard of strict scrutiny. For the CDC to prevail in the Ninth Circuit on a reverse and remand, they would have to prove that their blanket policy of racial segregation is the only way to prevent violence among inmates. Such arguments almost always fail, particularly when race is the classification of scrutiny. See Trulson, C., Marquart, J., & Mullings, J. (2007). "A Failure to Integrate: Equal Protection and Race in American Prisons." In Craig Hemmens (Ed.), *Current Legal Issues in Criminal Justice* (pp. 177–194). Los Angeles: Roxbury.

39. Jordan, M. (2006, March 21). "California Prisons Uneasily Prepare to Desegregate Cells." *Wall Street Journal*, p. B1. Available online at http://online.wsj.com/public/ article/SB114290971697503763-c_Bc66XQDv_Y3oGhmny49FBuPHc_20070321. html?mod=blogs.

40. For further discussion, see Trulson, C., Marquart, J., Hemmens, C., & Carroll, L. (2008). "Racial Desegregation in Prisons." *Prison Journal*, 88, 270–300.

41. Hindsight is always 20/20, but this is not simply retrospection after the fact. The factors mentioned were critical to TDC's success.

42. As of July 2008, California is currently implementing a cell desegregation program at two prison institutions and will roll out desegregation to institutions across the state in the coming months.

43. This 1975 amendment included a clause that forbade discriminating against inmates on the basis of race, creed, color, or national origin.

44. Although TDC faced numerous individual inmate lawsuits during this timeframe, the *Lamar* suit was one of four class-action suits faced by TDC.

45. Recognizing the problems with speculation, however, our guess is that desegregation would have been unlikely to be accomplished to the degree found in today's Texas prison system in the absence of institutional litigation. The best evidence to support this speculation is that the great majority of prison systems around the country still routinely segregate inmates by race in double cells, and perhaps also segregate within other aspects of prison administration. Unless forced or prodded to do so, it is unlikely that these systems will change significantly in the near future. Whether or not the Court's ruling in *Johnson* will impact this prediction remains to be seen. Although California is embarking on racial desegregation as this is written, they also face an individual lawsuit.

46. It is true, however, that a claim could be made that the military was not that

much different from prisons in terms of clientele and reasons for joining when the military was desegregated by President Truman in 1948.

47. Haney, C., & Zimbardo, P. (1998). "The Past and Future of U.S. Prison Policy." *American Psychologist*, 53, 709–727. The momentum that can be generated within institutions is a powerful force. The "Stanford Prison Experiment" is a prime example of such institutional momentum. Another excellent frame of reference on the power of institutions and institutional momentum is the well-known obedience experiments conducted by Stanley Milgram. In his studies, Milgram noted that those subjects willing to go the distance and administer what they perceived as high voltage shocks to a learner were far from sadistic human beings. As Milgram stated, the situation that they were faced with carried such a high level of momentum with it that some simply could not stop. This is also a particularly useful way to view desegregation in Texas prisons. The institutional momentum against desegregation was significant. However, once this momentum was reversed, desegregation proceeded and has now become an accepted fact of prison life in Texas, among both administrators and inmates. It is a tradition now, a tradition that brings a level of predictability and routine, much like racial segregation provided prior to 1991.

48. We encourage the reader to consult the classic work on total institutions by Irving Goffman for a more complete treatment of the power of institutions to strip and deprogram institutional wards. Goffman, I. (1961). *Asylums*. New York: Anchor Books. If one stepped into a Texas prison unit today, perhaps the first thing that one would notice is a sea of white. It would not be white faces, but rather white uniforms. All inmates in Texas prisons wear prison-issued white uniforms. Like other aspects of the prison ceremony in Texas, such as short hair cuts and prison numbers, the garb worn by TDC inmates is a symbol of the Texas prison process, which attempts to wash away all the imported baggage of inmates. Importantly, these symbols may also serve to wash away or diminish racial identity such that in the batch living environment of the prison, status as an inmate supersedes other imported identities. This important part of the power of institutions may be related to the outcomes experienced in the aftermath of desegregation in Texas prisons.

49. This is not to suggest the Texas prison system is free of all racial strife or conflict at the inmate level. Organizationally, desegregation is an accepted fact of prison administration.

50. Fram, A. (2007, September). "Poll: Simpson Divides Whites, Blacks." Accessed on September 27, 2007, from http://news.aol.com/story/_a/poll-simpson-divides-whites-blacks/n20070927174909990014?ecid=RSS0001.

51. Ibid.

52. Keck, K. (2007, September). "Students Attend School's First Integrated Prom." Accessed on September 27, 2007, from http://www.cnn.com/2007/US/04/23/turner.prom/index.html.

53. Farwell, S. (2007, September 21). "Texans Join Thousands Rallying for Justice for Black Teens." *Dallas Morning News*, pp. 1A; 13A. See also Farwell, S. (2007, September 20). "Marching Behind Six Young Men: Concern for Black Defendants in Louisiana Fills Texas Buses." *Dallas Morning News*, pp. 1A; 9A.

54. Mike Nizza. (2007, October 11). "Did Jena 6 Outcry Bring Back the Noose?" *Dallas Morning News*, p. 2A.

55. Katrina Goggins. (2008, March 11). "Redneck Shop vs. the Reverend." *Dallas Morning News*, p. 8A.

56. See http://www.fbi.gov/ucr/hc2005/index.html for information regarding hate crime statistics and reporting by agencies.

57. Based on 2005 census data, Texas's population comprised 49 percent whites, 35 percent Hispanics, and 12 percent African Americans. The same figures for California were, respectively, 44, 35, and 7 percent; Florida, 62, 20, and 16 percent; Michigan, 78, 4, and 14; and Pennsylvania, 83, 11, and 4 percent. See the United States Census Bureau, State and County Quickfacts, at http://www.census.gov/.

58. Statistical Report, Fiscal Year 2006. Texas Department of Criminal Justice.

Select Bibliography

Allport, G. (1954). *The Nature of Prejudice*. Boston: Addison-Wesley.

Brown, N. (1984). *Hood, Bonnet, and Little Brown Jug*. College Station: Texas A&M University Press.

Campbell, R. (1989). *An Empire for Slavery: The Peculiar Institution in Texas, 1821–1865*. Baton Rouge: Louisiana State University Press.

Carroll, L. (1974). *Hacks, Blacks, and Cons: Race Relations in a Maximum Security Prison*. Prospect Heights, IL: Waveland.

Carroll, L. (1999). *Lawful Order: A Case Study of Correctional Crisis and Reform*. New York: Garland.

Crouch, B., & Marquart, J. (1989). *An Appeal to Justice: Litigated Reform of Texas Prisons*. Austin: University of Texas Press.

Dilulio, J. (1987). *Governing Prisons: A Comparative Study of Correctional Management*. New York: Free Press.

Durden, A. M. (1979). *Overcoming: A History of Black Integration at the University of Texas at Austin*. Office of the Dean of Students, University of Texas at Austin.

Feeley, M., & Rubin, E. (2000). *Judicial Policy Making and the Modern State*. Cambridge: Cambridge University Press.

Fehrenbach, T. R. (1985). *Lone Star: A History of Texas and the Texans*. New York: Macmillan.

Goffman, I. (1961). *Asylums*. New York: Anchor Books.

Harris, K., & Spiller, D. (1977). *After Decision: Implementation of Judicial Decrees in Correctional Settings*. Washington, D.C.: U.S. Department of Justice.

Horton, D., & Nielsen, G. (2005). *Walking George: The Life of George John Beto and the Rise of the Modern Texas Prison System*. Denton: University of North Texas Press.

Irwin, J. (1980). *Prisons in Turmoil*. Boston: Little, Brown.

Jackson, B. (1972). *Wake Up Dead Man: Afro-American Worksongs of Texas Prisons*. Cambridge, MA: Harvard University Press.

Jacobs, J. (1983). *New Perspectives on Prisons and Imprisonment*. Ithaca, NY: Cornell University Press.

Kluger, R. (1976). *Simple Justice: The History of Brown v. Board of Education and Black America's Struggle for Equality*. New York: Alfred A. Knopf.

Ladino, R. (1996). *Desegregating Texas Schools: Eisenhower, Shivers, and the Crisis at Mansfield High.* Austin: University of Texas Press.

Martin, S., & Ekland-Olson, S. (1987). *Texas Prisons: The Walls Came Tumbling Down.* Austin: Texas Monthly Press.

McLeod, R. (1978). "Racial Desegregation of Inmate Housing on the Wynne Unit, Texas Department of Corrections: Its Early Implementation." Master's thesis, Sam Houston State University, Huntsville, TX.

Moskos, C., & Butler, J. (1996). *All That We Can Be: Black Leadership and Racial Integration the Army Way.* New York: Twentieth Century Fund.

Oshinsky, D. (1996). *Worse than Slavery: Parchman Farm and the Ordeal of Jim Crow Justice.* New York: Free Press.

Park, R., Burgess, E., & McKenzie, R. (1925). *The City.* Chicago: University of Chicago Press.

Renaud, J. (2002). *Behind the Walls: A Guide for Families and Friends of Texas Prisons.* Denton: University of North Texas Press.

Sample, A. (1984). *Racehoss: Big Emma's Boy.* New York: Ballantine Books.

Smallwood, J. (1981). *Time of Hope, Time of Despair: Black Texans during Reconstruction.* Port Washington, NY: Kennikat Press.

Sherif, M. (1966). *In a Common Predicament.* Boston: Houghton Mifflin.

Sherif, M., Harvey, O. J., White, B., Hood, W. R., & Sherif, C. W. (1961). *Intergroup Conflict and Cooperation: The Robbers Cave Experiment.* Norman: Oklahoma University Book Exchange.

Simmons, L. (1957). *Assignment Huntsville: Memoirs of a Texas Prison Official.* Austin: University of Texas Press.

Studies in Social Psychology in World War II: Volumes I–V (1949). Princeton: Princeton University Press.

Sykes, G. (1958). *The Society of Captives.* Princeton: Princeton University Press.

Taylor, W. (1999). *Down on Parchman Farm: The Great Prison in the Mississippi Delta.* Columbus: Ohio State University Press.

Walker, D. (1988). *Penology for Profit: A History of the Texas Prison System, 1867–1912.* College Station: Texas A&M University Press.

Webb, W. P. (1931). *The Great Plains.* New York: Ginn and Company.

Select Court Cases

Battle v. Anderson, 376 F. Supp. 402 (E.D. Okla. 1974).

Blevins v. Brew, 593 F. Supp. 245 (W.D. Wis. 1984).

Borders v. Rippy, 250 F.2d 690 (5th Cir. 1957).

Brown v. Board of Education, 347 U.S. 483 (1954).

Brown v. Board of Education, 349 U.S. 294 (1955).

Garrison Johnson v. State of California, 321 F.3d 791 (9th Cir. 2003).

Gates v. Collier, 349 F. Supp. 881 (N.D. Miss. 1972).

Johnson v. California, 543 U.S. 499 (2005).

Lamar v. Coffield, Consent Decree, Civil Action No. 72-H-1393 (S.D. Tex. 1977).

Lamar v. Coffield, 951 F. Supp. 629 (S.D. Tex. 1996).

Lamar v. Steele, 693 F. 2d 559 (5th Cir. 1982).

Lee v. Washington, 390 U.S. 333 (1968).

McClelland v. Sigler, 456 F.2d 1266 (8th Cir. 1972).

Mickens v. Winston, 462 F. Supp. 910 (E.D. Va. 1978).

Plessy v. Ferguson, 163 U.S. 537 (1896).

Rentfrow v. Carter, 296 F. Supp. 301 (N.D. Ga. 1968).

Ruiz v. Estelle, 503 F. Supp. 1265 (1980).

Sockwell v. Phelps, 20 F. 3d 187 (5th Cir. 1994).

Stewart v. Rhodes, 473 F. Supp. 1185 (S.D. Ohio 1979).

Sweatt v. Painter, et al., 339 U.S. 629 (1950).

Taylor v. Perini, 365 F. Supp. 557 (N.D. Ohio 1972).

United States v. Illinois, Civil Action No. 76-0158 (S.D. Ill. 1976).

United States v. Wyandotte County, Kansas, 480 F. 2d 969 (10th Cir. 1973).

Washington v. Lee, 263 F. Supp. 327 (M.D. Ala., 1966).

Williams v. McKeithen, CA 71-98 (M.D. La. 1975).

Wilson v. Kelly, 294 F. Supp. 1005 (N.D. Ga. 1968).

Index